Black Men in Chains

Narratives by Escaped Slaves

EDITED BY

Charles H. Nichols

Brown University
Providence, R.I.

Lawrence Hill & Co.

New York • Westport

Copyright © 1972 Lawrence Hill & Co. Publishers, Inc.
All rights reserved
ISBN clothbound edition: 0-88208-003-2
ISBN paperback edition: 0-88208-004-0
Library of Congress catalogue card number: 72-78320

FIRST EDITION SEPTEMBER 1972

Design by Andrea Marquez

Manufactured in the United States of America

1 2 3 4 5 6 7 8 9 10 11 12

For SAUNDERS REDDING
with deep affection and high esteem

CONTENTS

(Narratives here anthologized are arranged chronologically by
date of publication.)

PREFACE

Slave narratives—the biographies and autobiographies of ex-slaves—first appeared in eighteenth century America. Such works include, for example, *A Narrative of the Uncommon Sufferings and Surprising Deliverance of Briton Hammon, a Negro Man* (Boston, 1760) and *A Narrative of the Lord's Wonderful Dealings with John Marrant, a Black* (London, 1785). After 1831, when the antislavery effort expanded, thousands of slave autobiographies appeared. Some were dictated to or ghosted by abolitionists and contain sentimental and moral judgments added by white writers. A large number of others, however, were written by the ex-slaves themselves. Some of the fugitives used fictitious names and places because they feared recapture. But there is no doubt of the essential genuineness of the greater part of this literature. The slave's amanuenses, like Lydia Maria Child, John G. Whittier, Edmund Quincy, and Samuel Eliot, were persons of proved integrity. They were well aware that their propaganda effort against slavery could not be advanced by fraud. They reprint documents which establish their trustworthiness. For example, letters secured from his former owners are printed in the preface to Henry Bibb's narrative together with the report of a committee which substantiates the truth of his experiences. The editors were at great pains to state the extent of their tampering. Moses Roper, William Grimes, William Hayden, John Thompson, Frederick Douglass, William Wells Brown, James Pennington, Austin Steward, Henry Bibb and others wrote their own accounts of their lives.

Ulrich Phillips insisted that the authenticity of the slave narratives was doubtful. In view of his own proslavery sentiment this is not surprising. But the accounts of travelers in the old South, and documents like those collected by Phillips himself, Elizabeth Donnan, Helen T. Catterall, John Spencer Bassett, and others confirm many aspects of slavery which we find in the narratives. Another common objection to the narratives is the claim that the writers were not representative of the masses of the slaves. An examination of these works shows a wide range of experiences, personality types, and reactions to bondage. In describing their living conditions, work loads, punishments, and the organization of the plantation routine, however, the accounts show a surprising similarity. Although they are now largely out of print, the slave narratives were widely read in the nineteenth century. So widespread was the circulation of these autobiographies that Frederick Law Olmsted insisted that northern views of slavery were largely taken from the narratives of fugitive slaves.*

* For a complete study of the slave narrative see: Charles H. Nichols, *Many Thousand Gone: The Ex-Slaves Account of their Bondage and Freedom*. Leiden, Holland: Brill Publishers, 1963.

Among the earliest writings by black people in America are accounts of their own lives. Those who experienced slavery have left us intimate views of the domestic slave trade, of life and work on plantations, and of their anguished reactions to their slave status.

Most of these biographies and autobiographies appeared between 1820 and 1860 when the abolitionist crusade was at its height. But some, especially those of ex-slaves who had been brought from Africa—like Gustavus Vassa and Venture—appeared in the eighteenth century. Venture, bought on the Guinea coast in exchange for four gallons of rum, was taken to Rhode Island. Gustavus Vassa was first sold to an English sea captain in Benin and was enslaved in Barbados and in Georgia. These two men experienced the bitter hazards of the Middle Passage. For slave ships were crowded with Negroes who were chained, whipped and susceptible to disease on the long voyage across the Atlantic. Some captives hurled themselves into the sea to escape; others died under these miserable conditions before they reached the New World. It has been estimated that 900,000 Negroes were transported from Africa in the sixteenth century, 2,750,000 in the seventeenth, 7,000,000 in the eighteenth, and 4,000,000 in the nineteenth century.

When slavery as an institution became firmly established in the United States, every southern city had its slave market. Slaves were confined in pens or fenced-in yards or in jails while awaiting sale. Auctions were held regularly and a great deal of the wealth of the Old South was in Negroes who were usually sold by traders in Maryland and Virginia to planters and traders in the deep South. Richmond, Washington, D. C., Charleston, and New Orleans were great centers of the domestic slave trade. William Wells Brown and Solomon Northup describe slave auctions vividly. Dressed to their best advantage, washed and greased, the slaves stood in lines for the examination of the buyers. They were carefully examined and handled by prospective buyers, and asked about their age and physical condition. A slave showing marks of the lash was considered a bad risk. The merchandise was divided into those with skills (carpenters, coopers, coachmen, etc.), field hands, "breeding females," concubines, and children.

Planters were frequently in debt. Their slaves would be sold, often with the children separated from their parents. When slaves were taken from place to place they were chained in coffles. These chain gangs, marching on foot and guarded by armed traders on horseback, created a grim picture of the injustice of slavery. In Tennessee field hands who sold for $600 in 1835 brought $1200 by 1860. Speculation in slaves—the buying, breeding, and rearing of them for market—was a profitable enterprise.

Every black man in the South was presumed to be a slave unless he could prove himself free. Vagrants and convicts might be sold for the benefit of the state. Moreover, the kidnapping or luring away of Negroes who were then sold into slavery was not unknown. The first man arrested in New York after the passage of the Fugitive Slave Act of 1850 (and sent South as a fugitive slave) was, in fact, a free citizen. Solomon Northup, another citizen of New York, was kidnapped in 1841 in Washington, D. C. and sold to the slave trading firm of Birch and Company. After twelve years of bondage on a Louisiana plantation he succeeded in proving that he was entitled to his freedom.

Slavery came into being because planters needed cheap labor as Americans strove to exploit rich southern lands. By 1850 there were nearly two million Negroes working on cotton, tobacco, rice, and sugar plantations. After the invention of the cotton gin and the growth of the cotton market, the planters fiercely defended what they called "the peculiar institution." The field hands, therefore, were expected to help their owners wrest a living from the soil. The plantation was managed by an overseer who appointed a driver to keep the labor force producing. When cotton was to be picked the fastest workers were placed at the head of the rows and the others forced to keep up. Northup tells us that each slave was presented with a sack strapped around his neck. The picker moved down each row picking the bolls of cotton, leaving the unopened bolls, and being careful not to break off the branches. Each slave's load was weighed, and if it fell short of the expected weight, the slave was whipped. Women and children worked alongside the men in the fields. Roused at dawn, the field hands were expected to work until after dark. Other chores were demanded of them as well, such as caring for livestock, and the slaves usually prepared their own evening meals of corn pone or "hoe cake." Women with infants worked with their children strapped on their backs. Hence long, unremitting toil was the lot of field hands while house servants, carpenters, blacksmiths, and artisans may have had a somewhat easier life. They had an opportunity to learn from their masters, and no doubt some owners had genuine affection for them.

Travelers in the *ante bellum* South have reported that the homes of typical cotton farmers were crude indeed. Built of rough boards or logs, without floors, beds, or other furniture, the slave cabins were little better than the shelter provided for cattle and pigs. As for food, each slave was allowed a peck of corn or meal a week. To this were added salt and a few herrings. The slaves sometimes supplemented their meager fare by hunting 'possum, by fishing, and by growing a few vegetables. Nearly all the slave narrators complain that especially as children they were often hungry. The clothing provided for slaves was minimal: shirts, pants and dresses of coarse cotton cloth, a blanket and only rarely, hats and shoes. Insufficient diet, hard work, and physical punishment made the slaves' health precarious, and, as medical help was scarce and primitive, the slaves suffered deficiency diseases such as dysentery, ague, fever and consumption. Infant mortality was high, and their life expectancy appallingly short.

John Hope Franklin estimates that in 1860 there were only 384,884 owners of slaves among a white population of eight million. Most of these were small farmers: 200,000 had fewer than five, and 338,000 fewer than twenty slaves. Harriet Jacobs and William Wells Brown were house servants; Josiah Henson and Solomon Northup were overseers and drivers. Frederick Douglass and James W. C. Pennington were skilled workmen. The other ex-slaves whose experiences we have reproduced in this book were, for the most part, field hands. Few of them had well-to-do masters. On the contrary, they dwell upon the financial hardships of their owners, most of whom were small farmers ever fearing foreclosure. These planters lived in crude, frontier-like surroundings with few comforts. Isolated from cities, schools, and the opportunity for culture, they were usually rough and violent men for whom drinking, horse racing, gambling, and cockfighting were the common amusements. Henson writes that "quarrels and brawls of the most violent description" erupted at gatherings of the slaveholders at the local tavern. The cohabitation of masters with their slave women was so common that Harriet Martineau insisted that their wives were "the chief slaves of the harem." Many mistresses were apparently embittered by this concubinage and vented their spleen on the slaves.

Nor did the Old South offer its inhabitants much opportunity for education. Illiteracy was high among the white population and almost universal among the blacks, for there were very few schools, colleges, libraries, and newspapers in the slave states. Southern politicians discouraged the spread of printed matter and of foreigners in their states, fearful as they were of abolitionist propaganda. They passed strict laws forbidding anyone to teach slaves to read and write. Even well-to-do Southerners had very limited vocational choices: farming, soldiering, politics, or law. While the North and the West were developing new industry, expanding trade, building railroads and canals, schools and colleges, and diversifying farming, the South stagnated. Slavery blighted its progress. The slaves, therefore, learned little from the

master class. Some learned semi-skilled trades and the care of a
household. Many got some religious instruction—usually to incul-
cate obedience and patience. Men like Douglass and others heard
white people loudly proclaiming democratic ideas. Milton
Clarke, a fugitive, writes: "I listened with great wonder to the
Texas orators, as they talked about liberty. I thought it might be
as good for me as for others."

The slaveholders tried by gifts, occasional holidays, religious
training, and strict control to maintain a contented, hard working
group of slaves. But ultimately all depended on force: the whip,
chains, overseers, patrols, and the law. The flogging of both men
and women slaves was practically universal. Nor was this punishment comparable to the gentle chastisement that earlier generations gave schoolboys. The instrument used in flogging, "the bull
whip" was six feet long, its butt end loaded with lead and its supple end made of plaited, toughened leather. One of the narrators,
John Brown of Georgia, says: "I have seen a board a quarter of an
inch thick cut through with it, at one blow . . . It is also employed to whip down savage bulls or unruly cattle. I have seen
many a horse cut with it right through the hollow of the flank,
and the animal brought quivering to the ground." Slaves were
not usually disabled by the whip but were scarred for life. Many
displayed their welted and striped backs before outraged audiences at abolitionist meetings. Twenty-five lashes was considered
mild correction. A serious infraction of the code of the plantation—stealing, running away, talking back to a white man—
might sentence the offender to as many as three hundred lashes.
Other slaves were compelled to witness these scenes so that all
would be properly intimidated. On these remote farms the owner
or overseer was judge, jury, prosecutor, and executioner, and
there is plenty of evidence that he grievously abused his power.
Since no slave could testify against any white person in court,
criminal acts of overseers could only be redressed if they were
witnessed by a concerned white citizen. The patrols were small
groups of armed white men whose job it was to prevent slaves
from escaping, to forestall rebellion and to ensure the security of

the slave system. They controlled Negroes unaccompanied by whites, demanded passes or free papers of them, and jailed those who had none.

Slavery was maintained by an elaborate system of laws, the slave codes,° on the local, state and national level. These became especially restrictive after the uprisings of Denmark Vesey (1822) and Nat Turner (1831). Negroes had, of course, virtually no political or civil rights. A slave could not testify in court except against another slave, nor could he own property, enter into any contract (including marriage), or assemble with other Negroes where no white person was present. It was forbidden to teach him to read and write. "The slave lives for his master's service," read the law. "His time, his labor, his comforts are all at his master's disposal." (*Industrial Resources* II, p. 278) The plainest expression of the prevailing attitude toward the blacks was the pronouncement of Chief Justice Roger Taney of the Supreme Court in the Dred Scott case: the Negro "had no rights which the white man was bound to respect."

The tyranny imposed on the slave greatly limited the freedom of white people as well. Whites were expected to do patrol duty, and their freedom of speech was greatly limited by the fear of antislavery propaganda. Indeed, southern politicians succeeded in forcing on the Congress of the United States the "gag rule," which forbid the discussion of the slavery question in the House for several years.

It is obvious that the slave system was based on the idea that Africans were heathens—an inferior and different order of men. Europeans justified slavery by projecting their fears on the Africans whom they considered "barbarous, wild, savage natives." †
Every form of discrimination was insisted upon which would make the black man feel inferior. He was expected to bow and snatch off his hat in the presence of white people. He dare not talk back unless questioned. His demeanor must be ever humble

---

° See Winthrop Jordan, *White Over Black*, pp. 108–109.
† Ibid., p. 109.

and respectful. Slavery in the New World was very different, therefore, from slavery in Africa. African slavery was a kind of banishment from one's own tribe. But the slave was regarded as a somewhat-less-privileged member of his new family. He could marry and enjoy other rights. He might attain a high position in his master's household. He could even depend on his owner to protect him from insult and danger. This benign relationship bears no resemblance to the relationships and requirements of the plantation system in the United States.

What did it mean to be another man's property? How did the slaves feel about their situation? What emotions stirred these brutalized men? What was the nature of their "adjustment" to slavery? What did bondage do to their personalities? There were essentially three reactions of the slaves to their status: cooperation, covert aggression, and rebellion. The cooperative slave was faithful and obedient, tended to identify with his master, and sought to please him. Most of the slaves, whose lot was very hard, felt hostile and bitter and, while they feared the consequences of open rebellion, showed their anger and aggression in passive or roundabout ways. The third group includes slaves who refused to allow themselves to be used. They fought the system by sabotage, self-mutilation, flight or revolt. Clearly the conditions of a man's life determines his behavior. Most of the faithful slaves had relatively kind masters and a better-than-usual childhood. The angry and uncooperative ones suffered a more difficult life. A slave who had been cooperative, like Josiah Henson, could, when threatened with sale, turn against his master and even plan to murder him.

The behavior of the narrators was the result, then, of their childhood experiences, their relation to their masters, and their expectations in life. Few slave children ever knew their fathers or enjoyed the love and care of both parents. The fact that their mothers labored long hours meant that they were, at best, neglected. They were often hungry and forced to work at an early age. The fear and anxiety caused in the child by witnessing so much physical punishment, so many separations, and the helplessness of his parents can only be imagined. The black child could not fail to see the enormous difference between the treatment he got and the fate of a white child. He was daily surrounded by people who were enjoying life in a way he could only dream of. Yet he was compelled to live in both worlds. He had to "adjust" to the expectations of his black fellow workers as well as to those of the master.

Some of the slave narrators—like Lunsford Lane, William Hayden, Josiah Henson and Elizabeth Keckley—were very loyal for most of the time they were enslaved. Let us examine the experiences of Josiah Henson and William Hayden more closely. Josiah Henson was the first Negro child born on his master's plantation. He was, therefore, his master's "especial pet." Although his father was sold when he was very young he led a fairly secure life with his mother and a kind master. These advantages helped him to grow robust and strong. Later in his life, even under a cruel and difficult owner, he was still ambitious, hard working, and kindly disposed toward others. Henson was clever enough to survive by stealing and deceit. He informed against a dishonest overseer and was himself made superintendent of the farm. As a personal body servant, he looked after his master's needs and managed his affairs. This sense of responsibility enlarged Henson's self-respect and made him identify closely with his master's interests. He became a Christian and convinced himself that obedience was his duty. To save his master from bankruptcy he took a group of slaves through free territory to Kentucky where they were sold and returned to his master. But when his master decided to sell *him*, Henson first planned to murder his owner's son who was taking him to the New Orleans market. Later he escaped with his family to Canada. He became one of the leaders of the Dawn Community, a settlement of fugitive slaves, where he was accused of embezzling funds. He succeeded, however, in finding influential friends, traveled to the World Exhibition in London and was presented to Queen Victoria and the Archbishop of Canterbury. After reading his life story, Harriet Beecher Stowe claimed that Henson was her model for Uncle

Tom. Intelligence and physical vigor made possible Henson's remarkable survival in a world that had made him a chattel. He
knew how to roll with the punches. Years of slavery did not make
of him the fearful, aggressive, and unstable person that it made of
many others.

William Hayden was born in Stafford County, Virginia in
1785. He was sold from his mother when he was about five years
old and had many different masters during his lifetime. Constant
danger and insecurity forced him to be guarded, crafty, and superstitious. He clung to his masters and curried their favor. Hired
out to a ropemaker in Georgetown, Kentucky, he became the favorite of his employer whose children taught him to read. He
earned money and hoped for freedom. He informed against a
group of slaves who were planning an uprising—a service which
further endeared him to the slaveholder. Men like Henson and
Hayden were singled out by their owners for preferential treatment, and they responded with unusual loyalty. Without hope of
a secure future, without the opportunities for which most men
live, subject to the whims of an unjust system and cruel owners,
they clung to the most powerful persons in their lives. Henson
writes of his experiences with a certain bravado. But Hayden re-
veals more plainly the many inner conflicts, the fear and degradation which his experiences cost him.

Most of the slaves reacted to their status with deep hostility
and resistance. Their laziness, pretended illness and stupidity,
lying and deceit, stealing and half-hearted effort were, at bottom,
forms of protest. In some of them this behavior may have been
scarcely conscious. For to be a slave was to be in a constant state
of fear and anxiety. A slave child almost invariably felt abandoned by his parents. He was always suffering arbitrary and unjust punishment. He had nothing to look forward to and no incentive to strive to better his lot. A word from the tyrant who owned
him could mean pain, sale, or even death. Hence fear and hatred
hounded their every waking moment. Accounts of travelers and
owners are full of evidence that the slaves' laziness and inefficiency galled their owners. Planters complained that the Ne-

groes broke tools, mistreated the horses, and spoiled the live-stock. At the same time, an owner was surprised to see how rapidly the promise of wages or freedom transformed an "onery" servant into a productive worker. No doubt the resistance of the slaves provoked some of the outrageous cruelties committed against them.

So great was the fear and repressed rage of the slaves that their personalities were permanently affected by it. Their aggression broke out in frequent fighting among themselves and in the harsh treatment of animals. Older and stronger slaves forced the younger and weaker to respect and obey them. William Grimes, for example, fought with another slave and bit off his nose. When an overseer sought to whip a slave it was necessary to get other slaves to help him, and this hardly endeared them to one another. Masters often encouraged boxing bouts among the slaves for the owners' amusement. Indeed the entire slave system was maintained by force and violence, and the Negroes could hardly escape the influence of the masters' rude and violent behavior.

Even in their religion the Negroes expressed their resistance to bondage and their aggression toward their oppressors. They compared themselves to the children of Israel in the Bible, enslaved by the wicked Egyptians. The cornerstone of their faith was the hope that in the day of judgment the tyrants who ruled over them would get their just deserts. The high and mighty whites were to them, like the doomed people of Sodom and Gomorrah, sure to perish at last. When the roof of a barn fell in and killed John Thompson's harsh owner, Thompson felt that "God had overruled." During an epidemic of cholera in Richmond a Negro preacher saw in this plague the judgment of God against the Virginians because "they would not let my people go." In work songs and spirituals the slaves expressed their protest against slavery and their hope of freedom—both in their words as well as their wailing, plaintive tones. As Frederick Douglass wrote of such songs: "They were tones . . . breathing the prayer and complaint of souls boiling over with the bitterest anguish.

Every tone was a testimony against slavery, and a prayer to God for deliverance from chains." Harriet Tubman used the language of the spirituals to alert slaves of her approach so that she could guide them in their flight. Her "Good Ship Zion" and "Swing Low, Sweet Chariot" were code words the fugitives understood. Many work songs were direct attacks on the shareholder.

Frederick Douglass records the following song:

> We raise de wheat
> Dey gib us the corn;
> We bake de bread,
> Dey gib us de cruss;
> We sif' de meal,
> Dey gib us de huss;
> We peel de meat,
> Dey gib us de skin,
> And dat's de way
> Dey take us in.
> We skim the pot,
> Dey gib us de liquor,
> And say dat's good enough for de nigger.

In the novel of William Wells Brown, the writer includes a similar slave song:

> The big bee flies high
> The little bee makes the honey.
> The black folks make the cotton
> And the white folks get the money.

To be sure, songs are a feeble kind of protest. Some slaves presented their grievances to their masters and ran off to the woods and swamps on strike until their demands were met. A few even attempted to get justice in the courts. Moses Grandy and Solomon Bayley (like Dred Scott) sued for their freedom in the courts. There is some evidence that slave rebels resorted to sabotage, poisoning, and arson directed against their owners. Self-mutilation and suicide were not unknown. In all these kinds of protest the slaves were a kind of fifth column in the master's camp. Their laziness, malingering, arson, and sabotage made the system unprofitable, and kept alive the planters' fear of rebellion. But many chattels, in desperation, turned against their oppressors and attacked them violently. John Thompson and Solomon Northup beat their owners; Frederick Douglass subdued the "Negro-breaker," Covey. Groups of slaves plotted and rebelled against the shareholder. The slave uprisings led by such men as Gabriel Prosser, Denmark Vesey, and Nat Turner are well known. There is evidence of many, many others. But the most widespread form of protest by slaves was running away. The fugitives literally walked the enormous distances to free territory in the northern states, Canada, Mexico, or Spanish Florida—or to the fastnesses of swamps or joined Indian tribes. There were groups of fugitive slaves in the Great Dismal Swamp of Virginia and North Carolina—bands of guerrillas—who protected themselves from recapture for many years. William and Ellen Craft and Henry "Box" Brown became famous for their clever means of escape. William Craft disguised his nearly-white wife as an invalid "gentleman" and accompanied her as a body servant. They traveled from Macon, Georgia by coach, train, and boat, stopped at hotels, and eventually arrived in Philadelphia. Henry Brown was shipped in a box by freight from Richmond to Philadelphia where the box was received by the Philadelphia Vigilance Committee, an abolitionist group. Frederick Douglass borrowed a sailor's uniform and free papers and took the train from Baltimore to Philadelphia.

These rebellious slaves defied society's attempt to keep them in bondage and condemn them as outlaws. Frederick Douglass spoke for them all when he insisted that "Slaveholders have made it almost impossible for a slave to commit any crime. . . . If he steals, he takes his own; if he kills his master, he imitates only the heroes of the revolution." These valiant black men were conscious, if poorly informed, revolutionaries. The slaveholding South was therefore an armed camp, a tangle of hatred, oppression, and violence where the Negro's resistance combined with the frustration and guilt of the owners to produce a society in constant crisis. The energies of southerners were consumed in the effort to hold this explosive and unprofitable system together.

Slavery, with its single crop agriculture and resistance to new ideas, blighted the hopes of white and black.

How did slavery affect the slave's personality? There is no doubt that the slaveholder succeeded in disorganizing and unsettling the slave's personality. Slavery created a dependent, fearful person, oppressed not only by physical limitations and punishment but by a sense of his own worthlessness and inferiority. The lack of close family ties, of schooling, of hope, caused extreme anxiety. The misery and helplessness of blacks were deepened by the feeling of the apparently unlimited power of the white masters. Such a situation resulted in a deep sense of self-hatred, apathy, and fear. At the same time the standards, attitudes, and ideals of the society were set by the master class which punished severely every attempt of the slave to adopt the behavior and attitudes reserved for white people. The Negro observed his master's freedom of movement, the security of his family relations, his refusal to permit personal insult, but was himself sternly denied the chance to conduct his life in the same way. Indeed slaveholders tried to stamp out the black child's curiosity, boldness, and love of adventure. They denied him the chance to learn. And then they ridiculed him for being cowardly and stupid, for lacking incentive, for inefficiency and laziness. The conflicts of personality induced by this treatment were painful in the extreme. Fear, rage, aggression, and guilt followed each other in a compulsive cycle. The shaky ego sought to survive by deceit, pretense, and flamboyant overcompensation. Some sought release and comfort in religion, others in superstitious cults and visions of hope. Still others plotted revenge. A human being denied everything that free men around him valued and strove for could hardly have behaved otherwise. The miracle is that so many of them, when they had achieved their liberty, could lead useful lives.

The life of a slave like William Grimes illustrates well the effect of oppression on the personality. Born in 1784 in King George County, Virginia, he was the son of a wealthy planter. His father died when William was a child, and he became the property of other masters. When he was old enough to work, he was cruelly driven by black and white overseers. He attempted to run away several times but was repeatedly recaptured and brutally beaten. On one occasion he was compelled to beat out hominy after his day's work was done. Having stayed up most of the night doing his task, he was severely flogged for not doing enough. "It seems as though I should not forget this flogging when I die," he wrote. "It grieved my soul beyond the power of time to cure." At this time in his life he fancied that he was attacked by spirits who would, he wrote, "trample on me, press me to the floor, and squeeze me almost to death." He consulted fortune tellers in whose powers he fervently believed. He was terrified by a skeleton which his master's son, a medical student, kept in a garret. He frequently had hallucinations. Such superstitious illusions grew out of his terror, guilt and anxiety. He was horrified by whipping. Of one stubborn slave he wrote: "This poor man's back was cut up with the lash until I could compare it to nothing but a field lately ploughed." In desperation, Grimes at various times went on hunger strikes, tried to make himself useless to his master by breaking his own leg and attempted to run away. He drank heavily whenever he could get whisky. He consistently showed marked aggression. He fought with other slaves and bit off the nose of one of them. His resistance incensed his owner who beat him to a bloody pulp and sent him to a filthy jail. At last he managed to escape slavery by stowing away on a ship bound for Boston. Years later he was recognized by one of his master's friends and retaken. He then used all his meager savings to buy his freedom. A restless, guilty, and fearful man all his life, he had difficulty holding a job and was engaged in several law suits. The North with its prejudice and segregation treated him little better than the South.

Slavery made William Grimes a pathetic and unstable person. But many of the ex-slaves made amazing adjustments to freedom. Some, like Solomon Bayley, Peter Still, Lunsford Lane and Moses Grandy, bought their freedom, found jobs and remained in the slave states for varying lengths of time after they were free. But life in the South was difficult even for free Negroes, and they all eventually went North. Fugitives, like Douglass, William Wells Brown, William Parker, and Harriet Tubman, not only helped others escape from slavery and recapture, but actively joined the abolitionist movement. Josiah Henson and Austin Steward helped to establish and maintain new settlements of fugitive slaves in Canada, such as the Dawn Settlement and the Wilberforce Colony.

The most exciting chapter in the lives of the fugitives was their courageous struggle to protect others from recapture and their unflagging zeal in the campaign against slavery and discrimination. They joined in forming Vigilance Committees to protect black people from kidnapping by slave hunters, especially after the passage of the Fugitive Slave Act of 1850. The ex-slaves defied this law repeatedly. When the Boston police attempted to seize the runaway, Thomas Sims, in 1851, the local citizens (most of them Negroes) put up such strong resistance that two hundred policemen sneaked him away in the dead of night. So great was the force assembled by black and white abolitionists to prevent the return of Anthony Burns, that the federal government had to send troops and a warship to Boston harbor to carry Burns back to slavery. In 1851, William Parker and a group of blacks shot Edward Gorsuch, a Maryland slaveowner, in Christiana, Pennsylvania, while he and a United States marshal were trying to seize a fugitive slave. Parker and his friends fled to Canada. Shortly afterward, the runaway, Jerry, was rescued with the stalwart help of such black abolitionists as Samuel Ringgold Ward. In 1860 Harriet Tubman snatched another fugitive, Charles Nalle, from officers of the law in Troy, New York. He sped on horseback to Schenectady and freedom.

Most of the narrators began their careers as abolitionists by simply telling their experiences to antislavery audiences. Men like Samuel Ringgold Ward, William Wells Brown, James W. C. Pennington and Frederick Douglass, however, soon became as effective in denouncing slavery as Garrison, Weld, or Wendell Phillips. Surely Douglass, who later developed his own propaganda effort independently of Garrison, was widely known both in Europe and in America. Indeed it was the black population that supported the abolitionist effort most consistently. Samuel Ringgold Ward insisted that by 1855 the "antislavery advocacy, for all effective purposes, [had] passed into their hands."

The slave narrators have left us their account of what slavery meant to them. Its cruel inhumanity emerges on all their pages. Yet it is an heroic page of the history of black people who resisted tyranny and combined in the struggle to bring the South's oppressive institution down. The shadow of slavery still darkens American life. In the continuing struggle to fulfill the democratic promises of our country, the example of men like Frederick Douglass, Nat Turner, and William Wells Brown will lighten our way.

Gustavus Vassa

Gustavus Vassa was born Olaudah Equiano in Essaka, Guinea, in 1745. He and his sister were kidnapped by another African tribe and sold to European slavetraders who brought him to the West Indies and to Georgia. The account of his life is valuable for its description of African life and customs and for the African's first impressions of slavery and the customs of the New World. Sold many times, Olaudah Equiano furnishes valuable historical data on slavery in Barbados, the United States, and in Africa. He was eventually sold to a British sea captain, embraced the Christian faith, and engaged in many expeditions of the British in distant places. Eventually, having bought his freedom, and respected as a British citizen, he was associated with prominent humanitarians in their attempt to abolish slavery. Gustavus Vassa joined Granville Sharpe and others in petitioning the British parliament for an end to the slave trade. Later he returned to Africa as a missionary. *The Interesting Narrative of The Life of Olaudah Equiano or Gustavus Vassa* was first published in London in 1789. The edition used here appeared in Halifax in 1814.

Africa and the Middle Passage

That part of Africa known by the name of Guinea, to which the trade for slaves is carried on, extends along the coast above 3400 miles from Senegal to Angola and includes a variety of kingdoms. Of these the most considerable is the kingdom of Benin, both as to extent and wealth, the richness and cultivation of the soil, the power of its king, and the number and warlike disposition of the inhabitants. It is situated nearly under the line and extends along the coast about 170 miles, but runs back into the interior part of Africa to a distance hitherto I believe unexplored by any traveler and seems only terminated at length by the empire of Abyssinia—near 1500 miles from its beginning. This kingdom is divided into many provinces or districts, in one of the most remote and fertile of which I was born, in the year 1745, situated in a charming fruitful vale named Essaka. The distance of this province from the capital of Benin and the sea coast must be very considerable, for I had never heard of white men or Europeans, nor of the sea; and our subjection to the king of Benin was little more than nominal, for every transaction of the government, as far as my slender observation extended, was conducted by the chiefs or elders of the place. The manners and government of a people who have little commerce with other countries are generally very simple, and the history of what passes in one family or village may serve as a specimen of the whole nation. My father was one of these elders or chiefs I have spoken of, and was styled Embrenché—a term, as I remember, importing the highest distinction and signifying in our language a mark of grandeur. This mark was conferred on the person entitled to it by cutting his skin across at the top of the forehead and drawing it down to the eye-brows, while it is in this situation applying a warm hand and rubbing it until it shrinks up into a thick weal across the lower part of the forehead. Most of the judges and senators were thus marked; my father had long borne it. I had seen it conferred on one of my brothers, and I also was destined to receive it by my parents. Those Embrenché, or chief men, decided disputes and punished crimes, for which purpose they always assembled together. The proceedings were generally short and in most cases the law of retaliation prevailed. I remember a man was brought before my father and the other judges for kidnapping a boy, and, although he was the son of a chief or senator, he was condemned to make recompense by a man or woman slave. Adultery, however, was sometimes punished with slavery or death, a punishment which I believe is inflicted on it throughout most of the nations of Africa, so sacred among them is the honor of the marriage bed, and so jealous are they of the fidelity of their wives. Of this I recollect an instance: A woman was convicted before the judges of adultery and delivered over, as the custom was, to her husband to be punished. Accordingly he determined to put her to death, but it being found, just before her execution, that she had an infant at her breast, and no woman being prevailed on to perform the part of a nurse, she was spared on account of the child. The men, however, do not preserve the same constancy to their wives which they expect from them, for they indulge in a plurality, though seldom in more than two. Their mode of marriage is thus: Both parties are usually betrothed when young by their parents (though I have known the males to betroth themselves). On this occasion a feast is prepared, and the bride and bridegroom stand up in the midst of all their friends, who are assembled for the purpose, while he declares she is thenceforth to be looked upon as his wife and that no other person is to pay any addresses to her. This is also immediately proclaimed in the vicinity, on which the bride retires from the assembly. Some time after she is brought home to her husband, and then another feast is made to which the relations of both parties are invited. Her parents then deliver her to the bridegroom, accompanied with a number of blessings, and at the same time they tie round her waist a cotton string of the thickness of a goose-quill, which none but married women are permitted to wear. She is now considered as completely his wife, and at this time the dowry is given to the new married pair, which generally consists of portions of land, slaves, cattle, household goods, and implements of husbandry. These are offered by the friends of both parties. Besides which, the parents of the bridegroom present gifts to those of the bride, whose property she is looked upon before marriage; but after it she is esteemed the sole property of her husband. The ceremony being now ended the festival begins, which is celebrated with bonfires and loud acclamations of joy, accompanied with music and dancing.

We are almost a nation of dancers, musicians, and poets. Thus every great event, such as a triumphant return from battle or other cause of public rejoicing, is celebrated in public dances which are accompanied with songs and music suited to the occasion. The assembly is separated into four divisions that dance either apart or in succession, each with a character peculiar to itself. The first division contains the married men, who in their dances frequently exhibit feats of arms and the representation of a battle. To these succeed the married women, who dance in the second division. The young men occupy the third, and the maidens the fourth. Each represents some interesting scene of real life—such as a great achievement, domestic employment, a pathetic story, or some rural sport; and, as the subject is generally founded on some recent event, it is therefore ever new. This gives our dances a spirit and variety which I have scarcely seen elsewhere.° We have many musical instruments, particularly drums of different kinds, a piece of music which resembles a guitar, and another much like a stickado. These last are chiefly used by betrothed virgins, who play on them on all grand festivals.

As our manners are simple, our luxuries are few. The dress of both sexes is nearly the same. It generally consists of a long piece of calico, or muslin, wrapped loosely round the body, somewhat in the form of a highland plaid. This is usually dyed blue, which is our favorite color. It is extracted from a berry, and is brighter and richer than any I have seen in Europe. Besides this, our women of distinction wear golden ornaments, which they dispose with some profusion on their arms and legs. When our women are not employed with the men in tillage, their usual occupation is spinning and weaving cotton, which they afterwards dye and make into garments. They also manufacture earthen vessels of which we have many kinds. Among the rest are tobacco pipes,† made

° When I was in Smyrna I frequently saw the Greeks dance after this manner.
† The bowl is earthen, curiously figured, to which a long reed is fixed as a tube. This tube

after the same fashion, and used in the same manner, as those in Turkey.

Our manner of living is entirely plain; for as yet the natives are unacquainted with those refinements in cookery which debauch the taste. Bullocks, goats, and poultry supply the greatest part of their food. These constitute likewise the principal wealth of the country and the chief articles of its commerce. The flesh is usually stewed in a pan. To make it savory we sometimes use also pepper and other spices, and we have salt made of wood ashes. Our vegetables are mostly plantains, eadas, yams, beans, and Indian corn. The head of the family usually eats alone; his wives and slaves have also their separate tables. Before we taste food we always wash our hands. Indeed, our cleanliness on all occasions is extreme, but on this it is an indispensable ceremony. After washing, libation is made by pouring out a small portion of the drink on the floor and tossing a small quantity of the food in a certain place for the spirits of departed relations, which the natives suppose to preside over their conduct and guard them from evil. They are totally unacquainted with strong or spirituous liquors and their principal beverage is palm wine. This is got from a tree of that name by tapping it at the top and fastening a long gourd to it. Sometimes one tree will yield three or four gallons in a night. When just drawn it is of a most delicious sweetness; but in a few days it acquires a tartish and more spirituous flavour, though I never saw any one intoxicated by it. The same tree also produces nuts and oil. Our principal luxury is in perfumes. One sort of these is an odoriferous wood of delicious fragrance, the other a kind of earth, a small portion of which thrown into the fire diffuses a most powerful odor.° We beat this wood into powder and mix it with palm oil, with which both men and women perfume themselves.

In our buildings we study convenience rather than ornament. Each master of a family has a large square piece of ground surrounded with a moat or fence or enclosed with a wall made of tempered red earth, which, when dry, is as hard as brick. Within this are his houses to accommodate his family and slaves, which, if numerous, frequently present the appearance of a village. In the middle stands the principal

---

is sometimes so long as to be borne by one—and frequently, out of grandeur—by two boys.
° When I was in Smyrna I saw the same kind of earth and brought some of it with me to England; it resembles musk in strength, but is more delicious in scent and is not unlike the smell of a rose.

building, appropriated to the sole use of the master, consisting of two apartments, in one of which he sits in the day with his family; the other is left apart for the reception of his friends. He has besides these a distinct apartment in which he sleeps, together with his male children. On each side are the apartments of his wives, who have also their separate day and night houses. The habitations of the slaves and their families are distributed throughout the rest of the enclosure. These houses never exceed one story in height. They are always built of wood—or stakes driven into the ground, crossed with wattles, and neatly plastered within and without. The roof is thatched with reeds. Our day-houses are left open at the sides; but those in which we sleep are always covered and plastered in the inside with a composition mixed with cow-dung to keep off the different insects, which annoy us during the night. The walls and floors also of these are generally covered with mats. Our beds consist of a platform, raised three or four feet from the ground, on which are laid skins and different parts of a spongy tree called plantain. Our covering is calico or muslin, the same as our dress. The usual seats are a few logs of wood; but we have benches, which are generally perfumed, to accommodate strangers. These compose the greater part of our household furniture. Houses so constructed and furnished require but little skill to erect them. Every man is a sufficient architect for the purpose. The whole neighborhood afford their unanimous assistance in building them, and in return receive, and expect, no other recompense than a feast.

As we live in a country where nature is prodigal of her favors, our wants are few and easily supplied. Of course we have few manufactures. They consist for the most part of calicoes, earthenware, ornaments, and instruments of war and husbandry. But these make no part of our commerce, the principal articles of which, as I have observed, are provisions. In such a state, money is of little use; however, we have some small pieces of coin, if I may call them such. They are made something like an anchor; but I do not remember either their value or denomination. We have also markets, at which I have been frequently with my mother. These are sometimes visited by stout mahogany-colored men from the southwest of us. We call them *Oye-Eboe*, which term signifies red men living at a distance. They generally bring us firearms, gunpowder, hats, beads, and dried fish. The last we esteemed a great rarity, as our waters were only brooks and springs. These articles they barter with us for odoriferous woods and earth, and our salt of wood ashes. They always carry slaves through our land, but the strictest account is exacted of their manner of procuring them before they are suffered to pass. Sometimes indeed we sold slaves to them, but they were only prisoners of war or such among us as had been convicted of kidnapping, or adultery, and some other crimes that we esteemed heinous. This practice of kidnapping induces me to think that, notwithstanding all our strictness, their principal business among us was to trepan our people. I remember too they carried great sacks along with them, which not long after I had an opportunity of seeing fatally applied to that infamous purpose.

Our land is uncommonly rich and fruitful and produces all kinds of vegetables in great abundance. We have plenty of Indian corn and vast quantities of cotton and tobacco. Our pine apples grow without culture; they are about the size of the largest sugarloaf and finely flavored. We have also spices of different kinds, particularly pepper, and a variety of delicious fruits that I have never seen in Europe—together with gums of various kinds and honey in abundance. All our industry is exerted to improve those blessings of nature. Agriculture is our chief employment and every one, even the children and women, is engaged in it. Thus we were all habituated to labor from our earliest years. Every one contributes something to the common stock; and, as we are unacquainted with idleness, we have no beggars. The benefits of such a mode of living are obvious. The West India planters prefer the slaves of Benin or Eboe, to those of any other part of Guinea, for their hardiness, intelligence, integrity, and zeal. Those benefits are felt by us in the general healthiness of the people and in their vigor and activity. I might have added too in their comeliness. Deformity is indeed unknown amongst us; I mean that of shape. Numbers of the natives of Eboe now in London might be brought in support of this assertion for, in regard to complexion, ideas of beauty are wholly relative. I remember while in Africa to have seen three Negro children who were tawny and another quite white, who were universally regarded by myself and the natives in general, as far as related to their complexions, as deformed. Our women too were in my eyes at least uncommonly graceful, alert, and modest to a degree of bashfulness. Nor do I remember to have ever heard of an instance of incontinence amongst them before marriage. They are also remarkably cheerful. Indeed cheerfulness and affability are two of the leading characteristics of our nation.

Our tillage is exercised in a large plain or common some hours walk from our dwellings; and all the neighbours resort thither in a body. They use no beasts of husbandry, and their only instruments are hoes, axes, shovels, and beaks, or pointed iron to dig with. Sometimes we are visited by locusts, which come in large clouds, so as to darken the air, and destroy our harvest. This however happens rarely, but when it does, a famine is produced by it. I remember an instance or two wherein this happened.

This common is often the theater of war. Therefore, when our people go out to till their land, they not only go in a body but generally take their arms with them for fear of a surprise. And when they apprehend an invasion, they guard the avenues to their dwellings by driving sticks into the ground that are so sharp at one end as to pierce the foot and are generally dipped in poison. From what I can recollect of these battles, they appear to have been eruptions of one little state or district on the other to obtain prisoners or booty. Perhaps they were incited to this by those traders who brought the European goods I mentioned amongst us. Such a mode of obtaining slaves in Africa is common, and I believe more are procured this way and by kidnapping than any other. When a trader wants slaves, he applies to a chief for them and tempts him with his wares. It is not extraordinary if on this occasion he yields to the temptation with as little firmness and accepts the price of his fellow creatures liberty with as little reluctance as the enlightened merchant. Accordingly he falls on his neighbors and a desperate battle ensues. If he prevails and takes prisoners, he gratifies his avarice by selling them; but if his party be vanquished, and he falls into the hands of the enemy, he is put to death. For, as he has been known to foment their quarrels, it is thought dangerous to let him survive. And no ransom can save him, though all other prisoners may be redeemed.

We have firearms, bows and arrows, broad two-edged swords and javelins. We have shields, also, which cover a man from head to foot. All are taught the use of these weapons; even our women are warriors, and march boldly out to fight along with the men. Our whole district is a kind of militia. On a certain signal given, such as the firing of a gun at night, they all rise in arms and rush upon their enemy. It is perhaps something remarkable that when our people march to the field a red flag or banner is borne before them. I was once a witness to a battle in our common. We had been all at work in it one day as usual, when our people were suddenly attacked. I climbed a tree at some distance, from which I beheld the fight. There were many women as well as men on both sides; among others my mother was there, armed with a broad sword. After fighting for a considerable time with great fury and many had been killed, our people obtained the victory and took their enemy's Chief prisoner. He was carried off in great triumph, and, though he offered a large ransom for his life, he was put to death. A virgin of note among our enemies had been slain in the battle, and her arm was exposed in our market-place, where our trophies were always exhibited.

The spoils were divided according to the merit of the warriors. Those prisoners which were not sold or redeemed we kept as slaves. But how different was their condition from that of the slaves in the West Indies! With us they do no more work than other members of the community—even their master. Their food, clothing, and lodging were nearly the same as theirs (except that they were not permitted to eat with those who were free-born); and there was scarce any other difference between them than a superior degree of importance which the head of a family possesses in our state, and that authority which, as such, he exercises over every part of his household. Some of these slaves have even slaves under them as their own property and for their own use.

As to religion, the natives believe that there is one Creator of all things, and that he lives in the sun and is girted round with a belt that he may never eat or drink; but, according to some, he smokes a pipe, which is our own favorite luxury. They believe he governs events, especially our deaths or captivity, but as for the doctrine of eternity, I do not remember to have ever heard of it. Some, however, believe in the transmigration of souls in a certain degree. Those spirits that are not transmigrated, such as their dear friends or relations, they believe always attend them and guard them from the bad spirits or their foes. For this reason they always before eating, as I have observed, put some small portion of the meat and pour some of their drink on the ground for them; and they often make oblations of the blood of beasts or fowls at their graves. I was very fond of my mother and almost constantly with her. When she went to make these oblations at her mother's tomb, which was a kind of small solitary thatched house, I sometimes attended her. There she made her libations and spent most of the night in cries and lamentations. I have been often extremely terrified on these occasions. The loneliness of the place, the darkness of the night, and the ceremony of libation, naturally awful and gloomy, were heightened by my mother's lamentations; and these concurring with the doleful cries of birds, by which these places were frequented, gave an inexpressible terror to the scene.

We compute the year from the day on which the sun crosses the line. And on its setting that evening, there is a general shout throughout the land; at least I can speak from my own knowledge—throughout our vicinity. The people at the same time make a great noise with rattles, not unlike the basket rattles used by children here, though much larger, and hold up their hands to heaven for a blessing. It is then the greatest offerings are made; and those children whom our wise men foretell will be fortunate are then presented to different people. I remember many used to come to see me, and I was carried about to others for that purpose. They have many offerings, particularly at full moons: generally two at harvest before the fruits are taken out of the ground; and, when any young animals are killed, sometimes they offer up part of them as a sacrifice. These offerings, when made by one of the heads of a family, serve for the whole. I remember we often had them at my father's and my uncle's, and their families have been present. Some of our offerings are eaten with bitter herbs. We had a saying among us to any one of a cross temper, that if they were to be eaten, they "should be eaten with bitter herbs."

We practiced circumcision like the Jews and made offerings and feasts on that occasion in the same manner as they did. Like them also, our children were named from some event, some circumstance, or fancied forebodings at the time of their birth. I was named "Olaudah," which, in our language, signifies vicissitude or fortunate—also, one favored and having a loud voice and well spoken. I remember we never polluted the name of the object of our adoration; on the contrary, it was always mentioned with the greatest reverence; and we were totally unacquainted with swearing and all those terms of abuse and reproach which find their way so readily and copiously into the language of more civilized people. The only expressions of that kind I remember were: "May you rot," or "May you swell," or "May a beast take you."

I have before remarked that the natives of this part of Africa are extremely cleanly. This necessary habit of decency was with us a part of religion, and therefore we had many purifications and washings. Indeed, almost as many and used on the same occasions, if my recollection does not fail me, as the Jews. Those that touched the dead at any time were obliged to wash and purify themselves before they could enter a dwelling-house. Every woman, too, at certain times was forbidden to come into a dwelling-house or touch any person or any thing we eat. I was so fond of my mother I could not keep from her or avoid touching her at some of those periods. In consequence of which, I was obliged to be kept out with her, in a little house made for that purpose, till offering was made, and then we were purified.

Though we had no places of public worship, we had priests and magicians, or wise men. I do not remember whether they had different offices, or whether they were united in the same persons, but they were held in great reverence by the people. They calculated our time and foretold events, as their name imported; for we called them Ah-affoe-way-cah, which signifies calculators or yearly men, our year being called Ah-affoe. They wore their beards, and when they died they were succeeded by their sons. Most of their implements and things of value were interred along with them. Pipes and tobacco were also put into the grave with the corpse, which was always perfumed and ornamented, and animals were offered in sacrifice to them. None accompanied their funerals but those of the same profession or tribe. These buried them after sunset, and always returned from the grave by a different way from that which they went.

These magicians were also our doctors or physicians. They practiced bleeding by cupping, and were very successful in healing wounds and expelling poisons. They had likewise some extraordinary method of discovering jealousy, theft, and poisoning—the success of which no doubt they derived from the unbounded influence over the credulity and superstition of the people. I do not remember what those methods were, except that as to poisoning I recollect an instance or two, which I hope it will not be deemed impertinent here to insert, as it may serve as a kind of specimen of the rest and is still used by the Negroes in the West Indies. A young woman had been poisoned, but it was not known by whom. The doctors ordered the corpse to be taken up by some persons, and carried to the grave. As soon as the bearers had raised it on their shoulders, they seemed seized with some sudden impulse and ran to and fro unable to stop themselves. At last, after having passed through a number of thorns and prickly bushes unhurt, the corpse fell from them close to a house and defaced it in the fall. The owner being taken up, he immediately confessed the poisoning.°

° An instance of this kind happened at Montserrat in the West Indies in the year 1763. I then belonged to the Charming Sally (Captain Doran). The chief mate, Mr. Mansfield,

The natives are extremely cautious about poison. When they buy any eatable the seller kisses it all round before the buyer, to show him it is not poisoned, and the same is done when any meat or drink is presented, particularly to a stranger. We have serpents of different kinds, some of which are esteemed ominous when they appear in our houses, and these we never molest. I remember two of those ominous snakes, each of which was as thick as the calf of a man's leg and in color resembling a dolphin in the water, crept at different times into my mother's nighthouse, where I always lay with her, and coiled themselves into folds, and each time they crowed like a cock. I was desired by some of our wise men to touch these—that I might be interested in the good omens—which I did, for they were quite harmless and would tamely suffer themselves to be handled. Then they were put into a large open earthen pan and set on one side of the highway. Some of our snakes, however, were poisonous. One of them crossed the road one day as I was standing on it and passed between my feet without offering to touch me, to the great surprise of many who saw it. These incidents were accounted by the wise men, and likewise by my mother and the rest of the people, as remarkable omens in my favour.

Such is the imperfect sketch my memory has furnished me with of the manners and customs of a people among whom I first drew my breath. And here I cannot forbear suggesting what has long struck me very forcibly: namely, the strong analogy which even by this sketch, imperfect as it is, appears to prevail in the manners and customs of my countrymen and those of the Jews before they reached the Land of Promise and, particularly, the patriarchs while they were yet in that pastoral state which is described in Genesis—an analogy that alone would induce me to think that the one people had sprung from the other. Indeed this is the opinion of Dr. Gill, who, in his commentary on Genesis, very ably deduces the pedigree of the Africans from Afer and

---

and some of the crew being one day on shore were present at the burying of a poisoned Negro girl. Though they had often heard of the circumstance of the running in such cases and had even seen it, they imagined it to be a trick of the corpse bearers. The mate therefore desired two of the sailors to take up the coffin and carry it to the grave. The sailors, who were all of the same opinion, readily obeyed; but they had scarcely raised it to their shoulders before they began to run furiously about, quite unable to direct themselves, till, at last, without intention, they came to the hut of him who had poisoned the girl. The coffin then immediately fell from their shoulders against the hut and damaged part of the wall. The owner of the hut was taken into custody on this and confessed the poisoning. I give this story as it was related by the mate and crew on their return to the ship. The credit which is due to it I leave with the reader.

Afra, the descendants of Abraham by Keturah his wife and concubine (for both these titles are applied to her). It is also conformable to the sentiments of Dr. John Clarke, formerly Dean of Sarum, in his Truth of the Christian Religion. Both these authors concur in ascribing to us this origin. The reasonings of those gentlemen are still further confirmed by the scripture chronology; and if any further corroboration were required, this resemblance in so many respects is a strong evidence in support of the opinion. Like the Israelites in their primitive state, our government was conducted by our chiefs or judges, our wise men and elders; and the head of a family with us enjoyed a similar authority over his household with that which is ascribed to Abraham and the other patriarchs. The law of retaliation obtained almost universally with us as with them. Even their religion appeared to have shed upon us a ray of its glory, though broken and spent in its passage or eclipsed by the cloud with which time, tradition, and ignorance might have enveloped it. For we had our circumcision (a rule I believe peculiar to that people); we had also our sacrifices and burnt offerings, our washings and purifications, on the same occasions as they had.

As to the difference of color between the Eboan Africans and the modern Jews, I shall not presume to account for it. It is a subject which has engaged the pens of men of both genius and learning and is far above my strength. The most able and Rev. Mr. T. Clarkson, however, in his much admired "Essay on the Slavery and Commerce of the Human Species" has ascertained the cause in a manner that at once solves every objection on that account, and, on my mind at least, has produced the fullest conviction. I shall therefore refer to that performance for the theory, contenting myself with extracting a fact as related by Dr. Mitchel. "The Spaniards, who have inhabited America, under the torrid zone, for any time, are become as dark colored as our native Indians of Virginia; of which *I myself have been a witness.*" There is also another instance of a Portuguese settlement at Mitomba, a river in Sierra Leone, where the inhabitants are bred from a mixture of the first Portuguese discoverers with the natives and are now become in their complexion and in the woolly quality of their hair *perfect Negroes*, retaining, however, a smattering of the Portuguese language.

These instances and a great many more which might be adduced, while they show how the complexions of the same persons vary in different climates, it is hoped may tend also to remove the prejudice that some conceive against the natives of Africa on account of their color. Surely the minds of the Spaniards did not change with the complexions! Are there not causes enough to which the apparent inferiority of an African may be ascribed, without limiting the goodness of God and supposing he forbore to stamp understanding on certainly his own image because "carved in ebony." Might it not naturally be ascribed to their situation? When they come among Europeans, they are ignorant of their language, religion, manners, and customs. Are any pains taken to teach them these? Are they treated as men? Does not slavery itself depress the mind and extinguish all its fire and every noble sentiment? But, above all, what advantages do not a refined people possess over those who are rude and uncultivated. Let the polished and haughty European recollect that *his* ancestors were once, like the Africans, uncivilized and even barbarous. Did Nature make *them* inferior to their sons? and should *they too* have been made slaves? Every rational mind answers: No. Let such reflections as these melt the pride of their superiority into sympathy for the wants and miseries of their sable brethren and compel them to acknowledge, that understanding is not confined to feature or color. If, when they look round the world, they feel exultation, let it be tempered with benevolence to others, and gratitude to God, "who hath made of one blood all nations of men for to dwell on all the face of the earth . . . and whose wisdom is not our wisdom, neither are our ways his ways."

I have already acquainted the reader with the time and place of my birth. My father, besides many slaves, had a numerous family, of which seven lived to grow up, including myself and a sister, who was the only daughter. As I was the youngest of the sons, I became, of course, the greatest favorite with my mother and was always with her; and she used to take particular pains to form my mind. I was trained from my earliest years in the art of war. My daily exercise was shooting and throwing javelins, and my mother adorned me with emblems, after the manner of our greatest warriors. In this way I grew up till I was turned the age of eleven, when an end was put to my happiness in the following manner: Generally, when the grown people in the neighborhood were gone far in the fields to labor, the children assembled together in some of the neighbors' premises to play, and commonly some of us used to get up a tree to look out for any assailant, or kidnapper, that might come upon us; for they sometimes took those opportunities of our parents' absence to attack and carry off as many as they could seize. One day, as I was watching at the top of a tree in our yard, I saw one of those people come into the yard of our next neighbor but one, to kidnap, there being many stout young people in it. Immediately on this, I gave the alarm of the rogue, and he was surrounded by the stoutest of them, who entangled him with cords, so that he could not escape till some of the grown people came and secured him. But alas! ere long it was my fate to be thus attacked and to be carried off, when none of the grown people were nigh. One day, when all our people were gone out to their works as usual, and only I and my dear sister were left to mind the house, two men and a woman got over our walls and in a moment seized us both, and, without giving us time to cry out or make resistance, they stopped our mouths and ran off with us into the nearest wood. Here they tied our hands and continued to carry us as far as they could till night came on, when we reached a small house, where the robbers halted for refreshment and spent the night. We were then unbound but were unable to take any food, and, being quite overpowered by fatigue and grief, our only relief was some sleep, which allayed our misfortune for a short time. The next morning we left the house and continued traveling all the day. For a long time we had kept the woods, but at last we came into a road which I believed I knew. I had now some hopes of being delivered, for we had advanced but a little way before I discovered some people at a distance, on which I began to cry out for their assistance. But my cries had no other effect than to make them tie me faster and stop my mouth, and then they put me into a large sack. They also stopped my sister's mouth and tied her hands, and in this manner we proceeded till we were out of the sight of these people. When we went to rest the following night they offered us some victuals; but we refused it, and the only comfort we had was in being in one another's arms all that night and bathing each other with our tears. But alas! we were soon deprived of even the small comfort of weeping together. The next day proved a day of greater sorrow than I had yet experienced, for my sister and I were then separated, while we lay clasped in each other's arms. It was in vain that we besought them not to part us; she was torn from me and immediately carried away, while I was left in a state of distraction not to be described. I cried and grieved continually, and for several days did not eat anything but what they forced into my mouth.

At length, after many days traveling, during which I had often changed masters, I got into the hands of a chieftain, in a very pleasant country. This man had two wives and some children, and they all used me extremely well and did all they could to comfort me, particularly the first wife, who was something like my mother. Although I was a great many days journey from my father's house, these people spoke exactly the same language with us. This first master of mine, as I may call him, was a smith, and my principal employment was working his bellows, which were the same kind as I had seen in my vicinity. They were in some respects not unlike the stoves here in gentlemen's kitchens, and were covered over with leather. In the middle of that leather a stick was fixed, and a person stood up and worked it in the same manner as is done to pump water out of a cask with a hand pump. I believe it was gold he worked, for it was of a lovely bright yellow color and was worn by the women on their wrists and ankles. I was there I suppose about a month, and they at last used to trust me some little distance from the house. This liberty I used in embracing every opportunity to inquire the way to my own home; and I also sometimes, for the same purpose, went with the maidens, in the cool of the evenings, to bring pitchers of water from the springs for the use of the house. I had also remarked where the sun rose in the morning and set in the evening as I had traveled along, and I had observed that my father's house was towards the rising of the sun. I therefore determined to seize the first opportunity of making my escape and to shape my course for that quarter, for I was quite oppressed and weighed down by grief after my mother and friends; and my love of liberty, ever great, was strengthened by the mortifying circumstance of not daring to eat with the freeborn children, although I was mostly their companion.

While I was projecting my escape, one day an unlucky event happened, which quite disconcerted my plan and put an end to my hopes. I used to be sometimes employed in assisting an elderly woman slave to cook and take care of the poultry, and one morning, while I was feeding some chickens, I happened to toss a small pebble at one of them, which hit it on the middle and directly killed it. The old slave, having soon after missed the chicken, inquired after it, and on my relating the accident (for I told her the truth, because my mother would never suffer me to tell a lie) she flew into a violent passion and threatened that I should suffer for it. My master being out, she immediately went and told her mistress what I had done. This alarmed me very much, and I expected an instant flogging, which to me was uncommonly dreadful, for I had seldom been beaten at home. I therefore resolved to fly, and I accordingly ran into a thicket that was hard by and hid myself in the bushes. Soon afterwards, my mistress and the slave returned, and, not seeing me, they searched all the house. But not finding me, and I not making answer when they called to me, they thought I had run away, and the whole neighborhood was raised in the pursuit of me. In that part of the country (as in ours) the houses and villages were skirted with woods (or shrubberies), and the bushes were so thick that a man could readily conceal himself in them so as to elude the strictest search. The neighbors continued the whole day looking for me, and several times many of them came within a few yards of the place where I lay hid. I expected every moment, when I heard a rustling among the trees, to be found out and punished by my master. But they never discovered me, though they were often so near that I even heard their conjectures as they were looking about for me. And I now learned from them that any attempt to return home would be hopeless. Most of them supposed I had fled towards home, but the distance was so great, and the way so intricate, that they thought I could never reach it, and that I should be lost in the woods. When I heard this I was seized with a violent panic and abandoned myself to despair. Night too began to approach and aggravated all my fears. I had before entertained hopes of getting home and had determined when it should be dark to make the attempt; but I was now convinced it was fruitless, and began to consider that if possibly I could escape all other animals I could not those of the human kind, and that, not knowing the way, I must perish in the woods. Thus was I like the hunted deer:

—Ev'ry leaf and ev'ry whisp'ring breath
Convey'd a foe, and ev'ry foe a death.

I heard frequent rustlings among the leaves; and being pretty sure they were snakes, I expected every instant to be stung by them. This increased my anguish, and the horror of my situation became now quite insupportable. I at length quitted the thicket, very faint and hungry, for I had not eaten or drank anything all the day, and crept to my master's kitchen, from whence I set out at first, and which was an open shed, and laid myself down in the ashes with an anxious wish for death to relieve me from all my pains. I was scarcely awake in the morning, when the old woman slave, who was the first up, came to light the fire and saw me in the fireplace. She was very much surprised to see me and could scarcely believe her own eyes. She now promised to intercede for me and went for her master, who soon after came, and, having slightly reprimanded me, ordered me to be taken care of and not ill treated.

Soon after this my master's only daughter, and child by his first wife, sickened and died, which affected him so much that for some time he was almost frantic, and really would have killed himself, had he not been watched and prevented. However, in a small time afterwards he recovered, and I was again sold. I was now carried to the left of the sun's rising, through many dreary wastes and dismal woods, amidst the hideous roarings of wild beasts. The people I was sold to used to carry me very often when I was tired—either on their shoulders or on their backs. I saw many convenient well built sheds along the road, at proper distances, to accommodate the merchants and travelers who lay in those buildings along with their wives, who often accompany them. They always go well armed.

From the time I left my own nation I always found somebody that understood me till I came to the sea coast. The languages of different nations did not totally differ, nor were they so copious as those of the Europeans, particularly the English. They were therefore easily learned; and, while I was journeying thus through Africa, I acquired two or three different tongues. In this manner I had been traveling for a considerable time, when one evening, to my great surprise, whom should I see brought to the house where I was but my dear sister! As soon as she saw me, she gave a loud shriek and ran into my arms. I was quite overpowered; neither of us could speak, but, for a considerable time, clung to each other in mutual embraces, unable to do anything but weep. Our meeting affected all who saw us; and indeed I must acknowledge, in honor of those sable destroyers of human rights, that I never met with any ill treatment or saw any offered to their slaves except tying them, when necessary, to keep them from running away. When these people knew we were brother and sister they indulged us to be together; and the man to whom I supposed we belonged lay with us, he in the middle, while she and I held one another by the hands across his breast all night.

Thus for a while we forgot our misfortunes in the joy of being together. But even this small comfort was soon to have an end; for scarcely had the fatal morning appeared, when she was again torn from me for ever! I was now more miserable, if possible, than before. The small relief which her presence gave me from pain was gone, and the wretchedness of my situation was redoubled by my anxiety after her fate and my apprehensions lest her sufferings should be greater than mine when I could not be with her to alleviate them. Yes, thou dear partner of all my childish sports! thou sharer of my joys and sorrows! happy should I have ever esteemed myself to encounter every misery for you and to procure your freedom by the sacrifice of my own! Though you were early forced from my arms, your image has been always riveted in my heart, from which neither *time nor fortune* have been able to remove it. So that, while the thoughts of your sufferings have damped my prosperity, they have mingled with adversity and increased its bitterness. To that Heaven which protects the weak from the strong, I commit the care of your innocence and virtues if they have not already received their full reward and if your youth and delicacy have not long since fallen victims to the violence of the African trader, the pestilential stench of a Guinea ship, the seasoning in the European colonies, or the lash and lust of a brutal and unrelenting overseer.

I did not long remain after my sister. I was again sold and carried through a number of places till, after traveling a considerable time, I came to a town called Tinmah, in the most beautiful country I had yet seen in Africa. It was extremely rich, and there were many rivulets which flowed through it and supplied a large pond in the center of the town, where the people washed. Here I first saw and tasted cocoa nuts, which I thought superior to any nuts I had ever tasted before. And the trees, which were loaded, were interspersed amongst the houses, which had commodious shades adjoining and were in the same manner as ours, the insides being neatly plastered and whitewashed. Here I also saw and tasted for the first time sugarcane. Their money consisted of little white shells, the size of the finger nail. I was sold here for one hundred and seventy-two of them by a merchant who lived and brought me there.

I had been about two or three days at his house, when a wealthy widow, a neighbor of his, came there one evening and brought with her an only son, a young gentleman about my own age and size. Here they saw me, and, having taken a fancy to me, I was bought of the merchant and went home with them. Her house and premises were situated close to one of those rivulets I have mentioned and were the finest I ever saw in Africa. They were very extensive, and she had a number of slaves to attend her. The next day I was washed and perfumed and when mealtime came, I was led into the presence of my mistress, and ate and drank before her with her son. This filled me with astonishment. I could scarce help expressing my surprise that the young gentleman should suffer me, who was bound, to eat with him who was free, and not only so, but that he would not at any time either eat or drink till I had taken first, because I was the eldest, which was agreeable to our custom. Indeed everything here and all their treatment of me made me forget that I was a slave. The language of these people resembled ours so nearly that we understood each other perfectly. They had also the very same customs as we. There were likewise slaves daily to attend us, while my young master and I with other boys sported with our darts and bows and arrows, as I had been used to do at home.

In this resemblance to my former happy state, I passed about two months. I now began to think I was to be adopted into the family and was beginning to be reconciled to my situation and forget by degrees my misfortunes, when all at once the delusion vanished; for, without the least previous knowledge, one morning early, while my dear master and companion was still asleep, I was awakened out of my reverie to fresh sorrow and hurried away even amongst the uncircumcised.

Thus, at the very moment I dreamed of the greatest happiness, I found myself most miserable, and it seemed as if fortune wished to give me this taste of joy, only to render the reverse more poignant. The change I now experienced was as painful as it was sudden and unexpected. It was a change indeed from a state of bliss to a scene which is inexpressible by me, as it discovered to me an element I had never before beheld and till then had no idea of and wherein such instances of hardship and cruelty continually occurred as I can never reflect on but with horror.

All the nations and people I had hitherto passed through resembled our own in their manners, customs, and language. But I came at length to a country the inhabitants of which differed from us in all those particulars. I was very much struck with this difference, especially when I came among a people who did not circumcise and eat without washing their hands. They cooked also in iron pots and had European cutlasses and cross bows, which were unknown to us, and fought with their fists amongst themselves. Their women were not so modest as ours, for they ate and drank and slept with their men. But above all, I was amazed to see no sacrifices or offerings among them. In some of those places the people ornamented themselves with scars and likewise filed their teeth very sharp. They wanted sometimes to ornament me in the same manner, but I would not suffer them, hoping that I might some time be among a people who did not thus disfigure themselves, as I thought they did. At last I came to the banks of a large river that was covered with canoes, in which the people appeared to live with their household utensils and provisions of all kinds. I was beyond measure astonished at this, as I had never before seen any water larger than a pond or a rivulet, and my surprise was mingled with no small fear when I was put into one of these canoes and we began to paddle and move along the river.

We continued going on thus till night. And when we came to land and made fires on the banks, each family by themselves, some dragged their canoes on shore, others stayed and cooked in theirs and laid in them all night. Those on the land had mats, of which they made tents, some in the shape of little houses. In these we slept, and after the morning meal, we embarked again and proceeded as before. I was often very much astonished to see some of the women, as well as the men, jump into the water, dive to the bottom, come up again, and swim about. Thus I continued to travel, sometimes by land, sometimes by water, through different countries and various nations till, at the end of six or seven months after I had been kidnapped, I arrived at the sea coast. It would be tedious and uninteresting to relate all the incidents which befell me during this journey, and which I have not yet forgotten, of the various hands I passed through, and the manners and customs of all the different people among whom I lived. I shall therefore only observe that in all the places where I was, the soil was exceedingly rich; the pumpkins, aedas, plantains, yams, etc. were in great abundance, and of incredible size. There were also vast quantities of different gums, though not used for any purpose, and everywhere a great deal of tobacco. The cotton even grew quite wild, and there was plenty of redwood. I saw no mechanics whatever in all the way, except such as I have mentioned. The chief employment in all these countries was agriculture, and both the males and females, as with us, were brought up to it and trained in the arts of war.

The first object which saluted my eyes when I arrived on the coast was the sea and a slave ship, which was then riding at anchor and waiting for its cargo. These filled me with astonishment, which was soon converted into terror when I was carried on board. I was immediately handled and tossed up to see if I were sound by some of the crew. I was now persuaded that I had gotten into a world of bad spirits, and that they were going to kill me. Their complexions, too, differing so much from ours, their long hair, and the language they spoke (which was very different from any I had ever heard) united to confirm me in this belief.

Indeed such were the horrors of my views and fears at the moment that, if ten thousand worlds had been my own, I would have freely parted with them all to have exchanged my condition with that of the meanest slave in my own country. When I looked round the ship too and saw a large furnace or copper boiling and a multitude of black people of every description chained together, every one of their countenances expressing dejection and sorrow, I no longer doubted of my fate, and, quite overpowered with horror and anguish, I fell motionless on the deck and fainted. When I recovered a little I found some black people about me, who I believed were some of those who brought me on board and had been receiving their pay. They talked to me in order to cheer me, but all in vain. I asked them if we were not to be eaten by those white men with horrible looks, red faces, and long hair. They told me I was not, and one of the crew brought me a small portion of spirituous liquor in a wine glass; but, being afraid of him, I would not take it out of his hand. One of the blacks therefore took it from him and gave it to me. I took a little down my palate, which, instead of reviving me as they thought it would, threw me into the greatest consternation at the strange feeling it produced, having never tasted any such liquor before. Soon after this, the blacks who brought me on board went off and left me abandoned to despair.

I now saw myself deprived of all chance of returning to my native country or even the least glimpse of hope of gaining the shore, which I now considered as friendly. I even wished for my former slavery in preference to my present situation, which was filled with horrors of every kind, still heightened by my ignorance of what I was to undergo. I was not long suffered to indulge my grief. I was soon put down under the decks, and there I received such a salutation in my nostrils as I had never experienced in my life; so that, with the loathsomeness of the stench and crying together, I became so sick and low that I was not able to eat, nor had I the least desire to taste anything. I now wished for the last friend, death, to relieve me. But soon, to my grief, two of the white men offered me eatables, and, on my refusing to eat, one of them held me fast by the hands and laid me across, I think, the windlass and tied my feet, while the other flogged me severely. I had never experienced anything of this kind before. And although not being used to the water, I naturally feared that element the first time I saw it; yet, nevertheless, could I have got over the nettings, I would have jumped over the side. But I could not; and, besides, the crew used to watch us very closely who were not chained down to the decks, lest we should leap into the water. I have seen some of these poor African prisoners most severely cut for attempting to do so and hourly whipped for not eating. This indeed was often the case with me.

A little time after, amongst the poor chained men, I found some of my own nation, which in a small degree gave ease to my mind. I inquired of these what was to be done with us? They gave me to understand we were to be carried to these white people's country to work for them. I then was a little revived and thought: if it were no worse than working, my situation was not so desperate. Still I feared I should be put to death: the white people looked and acted, as I thought, in so savage a manner, for I had never seen among any people such instances of brutal cruelty, and this not only shown towards us blacks, but also to some of the whites themselves. One white man in particular I saw, when we were permitted to be on deck, flogged so unmercifully with a large rope near the foremast that he died in consequence of it, and they tossed him over the side as they would have done a brute. This made me fear these people the more, and I expected nothing less than to be treated in the same manner. I could not help expressing my fears and apprehensions to some of my countrymen. I asked them if these people had no country, but lived in this hollow place (the ship)? They told me they did not, but came from a distant one. "Then," said I, "how comes it in all our country we never heard of them?" They told me because they lived so very far off. I then asked where were their women? had they any like themselves? I was told they had. "And why," said I, "do we not see them?" They answered, because they were left behind. I asked how the vessel could go? They told me they could not tell, but that there was cloth put upon the masts by the help of the ropes I saw, and then the vessel went on. And the white men had some spell or magic they put in the water when they liked in order to stop the vessel. I was exceedingly amazed at this account and really thought they were spirits. I therefore wished much to be from amongst them, for I expected they would sacrifice me. But my wishes were vain, for we were so quartered that it was impossible for any of us to make our escape.

While we stayed on the coast I was mostly on deck, and one day to my great astonishment, I saw one of these vessels coming in with the sails up. As soon as the whites saw it, they gave a great shout, at which we were amazed, and the more so as the vessel appeared larger by approaching nearer. At last she came to an anchor in my sight, and when the anchor was let go I and my countrymen who saw it were lost in astonishment to observe the vessel stop, and were now convinced it was done by magic. Soon after this the other ship got her boats out, and they came on board of us, and the people of both ships seemed very glad to see each other. Several of the strangers also shook hands with us black people and made motions with their hands signifying, I suppose, we were to go to their country; but we did not understand them. At last, when the ship we were in had got in all her cargo, they made ready with many fearful noises, and we were all put under deck so that we could not see how they managed the vessel. But this disappointment was the least of my sorrow. The stench of the hold while we were on the coast was so intolerably loathsome that it was dangerous to remain there for any time, and some of us had been permitted to stay on the deck for the fresh air; but now that the whole ship's cargo were confined together, it became absolutely pestilential. The closeness of the place, and the heat of the climate, added to the number in the ship, which was so crowded that each had scarcely room to turn himself, almost suffocated us. This produced copious perspirations, so that the air soon became unfit for respiration—from a variety of loathsome smells—and brought on a sickness among the slaves of which many died, thus falling victims to the improvident avarice, as I may call it, of their purchasers. This wretched situation was again aggravated by the galling of the chains, now become insupportable, and the filth of the necessary tubs, into which the children often fell and were almost suffocated. The shrieks of the women and the groans of the dying rendered the whole a scene of horror almost inconceivable. Happily perhaps for myself, I was soon reduced so low here that it was thought necessary to keep me almost always on deck, and from my extreme youth I was not put in fetters.

In this situation I expected every hour to share the fate of my companions, some of whom were almost daily brought upon deck at the point of death, which I began to hope would soon put an end to my miseries. Often did I think many of the inhabitants of the deep much more happy than myself. I envied them the freedom they enjoyed, and as often wished I could change my condition for theirs. Every circumstance I met with served only to render my state more painful and heighten my apprehensions and my opinion of the cruelty of the whites. One day they had taken a number of fishes; and when they had killed and satisfied themselves with as many as they thought fit, to our astonishment who were on the deck, rather than give any of them to us to eat, as we expected, they tossed the remaining fish into the sea again, although we begged and prayed for some as well as we could, but in vain. Some of my countrymen, being pressed by hunger, took an opportunity, when they thought no one saw them, of trying to get a little privately; but they were discovered, and the attempt procured them some very severe floggings.

One day, when we had a smooth sea and moderate wind, two of my wearied countrymen who were chained together (I was near them at the time), preferring death to such a life of misery, somehow made through the nettings and jumped into the sea. Immediately, another quite dejected fellow, who on account of his illness was suffered to be out of irons, also followed their example. I believe many more would very soon have done the same if they had not been prevented by the ship's crew, who were instantly alarmed. Those of us that were the most active were in a moment put down under the deck, and there was such a noise and confusion amongst the people of the ship to stop her and get the boat out to go after the slaves as I never heard before. However, two of the wretches were drowned; but they got the other, and afterwards flogged him unmercifully for thus attempting to prefer death to slavery.

In this manner we continued to undergo more hardships than I can now relate, hardships which are inseparable from this accursed trade. Many a time we were near suffocation from the want of fresh air, which we were often without for whole days together. This and the stench of the necessary tubs carried off many. During our passage I first saw flying fish, which surprised me very much. They used frequently to fly across the ship, and many of them fell on the deck. I also now first saw the use of the quadrant; I had often with astonishment seen the mariners make observations with it, and I could not think what it meant. They at last took notice of my surprise, and one of them, willing to increase it, as well as to gratify my curiosity, made me one day look through it. The clouds appeared to me to be land, which disappeared as they passed along. This heightened my wonder, and I was now more persuaded than ever that I was in another world and that every thing about me was magic.

At last we came in sight of the island of Barbados, at which the whites on board gave a great shout and made many signs of joy to us. We did not know what to think of this. But as the vessel drew nearer we plainly saw the harbor and other ships of different kinds and sizes, and we soon anchored amongst them off Bridge Town. Many merchants and planters now came on board, though it was in the evening. They put us in separate parcels and examined us attentively. They also made us jump and pointed to the land, signifying we were to go there. We thought by this we should be eaten by these ugly men, as they appeared to us, and, when soon after we were all put down under the deck again, there was much dread and trembling among us and nothing but bitter cries to be heard all the night from these apprehensions, insomuch that at last the white people got some old slaves from the land to pacify us. They told us we were not to be eaten, but to work and were soon to go on land, where we should see many of our country people.

This report eased us much; and, sure enough, soon after we were landed, there came to us Africans of all languages. We were conducted immediately to the merchant's yard, where we were all pent up together like so many sheep in a fold, without regard to sex or age. As every object was new to me everything I saw filled me with surprise. What struck me first was that the houses were built with bricks and stories, and in every other respect different from those I had seen in Africa. But I was still more astonished on seeing people on horseback. I did not know what this could mean; and indeed I thought these people were full of nothing but magical arts. While I was in astonishment one of my fellow prisoners spoke to a countryman of his about the horses, who said they were the same kind they had in their country. I understood them, though they were from a distant part of Africa, and I thought it odd I had not seen any horses there; but afterwards, when I came to converse with different Africans, I found they had many horses amongst them and much larger than those I then saw. We were not many days in the merchant's custody before we were sold after their usual manner, which is this: On a signal given (as the beat of a drum), the buyers rush at once into the yard where the slaves are confined and make a choice of that parcel they like best. The noise and clamor with which this is attended and the eagerness visible in the countenances of the buyers serve not a little to increase the apprehension of the terrified Africans, who may well be supposed to consider them as the ministers of that destruction to which they think themselves devoted. In this manner, without scruple, are relations and friends separated, most of them never to see each other again. I remember in the vessel in which I was brought over, in the men's apartment, there were several brothers who, in the sale, were sold in different lots, and it was very moving on this occasion to see and hear their cries at parting. O, ye nominal Christians! might not an African ask you, learned you this from your God, who says unto you, Do unto all men as you would men should do unto you? Is it not enough that we are torn from our country and friends to toil for your luxury and lust of gain? Must every tender feeling be likewise sacrificed to your avarice? Are the dearest friends and relations, now rendered more dear by their separation from their kindred, still to be parted from each other and thus prevented from cheering the gloom of slavery with the small comfort of being together and mingling their sufferings and sorrows? Why are parents to lose their children, brothers their sisters, or husbands their wives? Surely this is a new refinement in cruelty, which, while it has no advantage to atone for it, thus aggravates distress and adds fresh horrors even to the wretchedness of slavery.

NAT TURNER

Nat Turner was the leader of the most famous slave uprising in the history of the South. The revolt began in Southampton County, Virginia, on August 31, 1831, and went on unchecked for three days and three nights. Turner and his band of about seventy slaves killed fifty-five whites. The uprising was put down by three companies of artillery from Fort Monroe and by two warships. The insurgents were hanged, and a bloody, indiscriminate massacre of Negroes followed. Turner, captured two months later, was brought to trial and hanged. His confession was taken down by Colonel Thomas R. Gray while Turner was in prison. Thomas Gray presents Nat's confession from the point of view of the slaveholding class. He views the uprising as the work of an inhuman fiend and religious fanatic. Here we have attempted to reproduce in so far as possible the factual details which Gray records. Gray described Turner as follows: "He is below the ordinary stature, though strong and active, having the true Negro face, every feature of which is strongly marked." The Nat Turner rebellion caused great fear throughout the South. More stringent laws designed to control slaves and free blacks and forbidding antislavery propaganda were quickly passed. Nat Turner has been the subject of a number of poems, plays, and novels—such as William Styron's *Confessions of Nat Turner*. The following passage is a part of the original work, *The Confessions of Nat Turner, The Leader of The Late Insurrection in Southampton, Virginia, as Fully and Voluntarily Made to Thomas R. Gray*, Baltimore, 1831.

The Southampton Rebellion

Sir, you have asked me to give a history of the motives which induced me to undertake the late insurrection, as you call it. To do so I must go back to the days of my infancy and even before I was born. I was thirty-one years of age the 2nd of October last, and born the property of Benjamin Turner of this county. In my childhood a circumstance occurred which made an indelible impression on my mind and laid the groundwork of that enthusiasm which has terminated so fatally to many, both white and black, and for which I am about to atone at the gallows. It is here necessary to relate this circumstance. Trifling as it may seem, it was the commencement of that belief which has grown with time and even now, sir, in this dungeon, helpless and forsaken as I am, I cannot divest myself of. Being at play with other children, when three or four years old, I was telling them something, which my mother overhearing, said it had happened before I was born. I stuck to my story, however, and related some things which went, in her opinion, to confirm it. Others being called on were greatly astonished, knowing that these things had happened, and it caused them to say, in my hearing, I surely would be a prophet, as the Lord had shown me things that had happened before my birth. And my father and mother strengthened me in this my first impression, saying, in my presence, I was intended for some great purpose, which they had always thought from certain marks on my head and breast. [A parcel of excrescences which I believe are not at all uncommon, particularly among Negroes, as I have seen several with the same. In this case he has either cut them off or they have nearly disappeared.] My grandmother, who was very religious, and to whom I was much attached; my master, who belonged to the church; and other religious persons who visited the house, and whom I often saw at prayers, noticing the singularity of my manners, I suppose, and my uncommon intelligence for a child, remarked I had too much sense to be raised (and if I was, I would never be of any service to anyone) as a slave.

To a mind like mine, restless, inquisitive, and observant of everything that was passing, it is easy to suppose that religion was the subject to which it would be directed; and although this subject principally occupied my thoughts, there was nothing that I saw or heard of to which my attention was not directed. The manner in which I learned to read and write not only had great influence on my own mind—as I acquired it with the most perfect ease, so much so that I have no recollection whatever of learning the alphabet, but, to the astonishment of the family, one day when a book was shown to me to keep me from crying, I began spelling the names of different objects—this was a source of wonder to all in the neighborhood, particularly the blacks, and this learning was constantly improved at all opportunities. When I got large enough to go to work, while employed I was reflecting on many things that would present themselves to my imagination, and whenever an opportunity occurred of looking at a book, when the school children were getting their lessons, I would find many things that the fertility of my own imagination had depicted to me before. All my time, not devoted to my master's service, was spent either in prayer or in making experiments in casting different things in molds made of earth, in attempting to make paper, gunpowder, and many other experiments that, although I could not perfect, convinced me of their practicability if I had the means. [When questioned as to the manner of manufacturing those different articles, he was found well informed on the subject.]

I was not addicted to stealing in my youth, nor have I ever been; yet such was the confidence of the Negroes in the neighborhood, even at this early period of my life, in my superior judgment that they would often carry me with them when they were going on any roguery, to plan for them.

Growing up among them with this confidence in my superior judgment, and when this in their opinions was perfected by divine inspiration from the circumstances already alluded to in my infancy, and which belief was ever afterwards zealously inculcated by the austerity of my life and manners, which became the subject of remark by white and black. Having soon discovered to be great, I must appear so, and therefore studiously avoided mixing in society and wrapped myself in mystery, devoting my time to fasting and prayer.

By this time, having arrived to man's estate and hearing the scriptures commented on at meetings, I was struck with that particular passage which says: "Seek ye the kingdom of Heaven and all things shall be added unto you." I reflected much on this passage, and prayed daily for light on this subject. As I was praying one day at my plough, the spirit spoke to me, saying, "Seek ye the kingdom of Heaven and all things shall be added unto you."

Q: What do you mean by the Spirit?

A: The Spirit that spoke to the prophets in former days.

And I was greatly astonished and for two years prayed continually, whenever my duty would permit; and then again I had the same revelation, which fully confirmed me in the impression that I was ordained for some great purpose in the hands of the Almighty.

Several years rolled round, in which many events occurred to strengthen me in this my belief. At this time I reverted in my mind to the remarks made of me in my childhood, and the things that had been shown me—and as it had been said of me in my childhood by those by whom I had been taught to pray, both white and black, and in whom I had the greatest confidence, that I had too much sense to be raised, and if I was I would never be of any use to anyone as a slave. Now finding I had arrived to man's estate and was a slave, and these revelations being made known to me, I began to direct my attention to this great object, to fulfil the purpose for which, by this time, I felt assured I was intended. Knowing the influence I had obtained over the minds of my fellow servants, not by the means of conjuring and such like tricks—for to them I always spoke of such things with contempt—but by the communion of the Spirit whose revelations I often communicated to them, and they believed and said my wisdom came from God, I now began to prepare them for my purpose by telling them something was about to happen that would terminate in fulfilling the great promise that had been made to me.

About this time I was placed under an overseer, from whom I ran away. And, after remaining in the woods thirty days, I returned, to the astonishment of the Negroes on the plantation, who thought I had made my escape to some other part of the country as my father had done before. But the reason of my return was that the Spirit appeared to me and said I had my wishes directed to the things of this world and not to the kingdom of Heaven, and that I should return to the service of my earthly master: "For he who knoweth his Master's will, and doeth it not, shall be beaten with many stripes, and thus have I chastened you." And the Negroes found fault and murmured against me, saying that if they had my sense they would not serve any master in the world. And about this time I had a vision—and I saw white spirits and black spirits engaged in battle, and the sun was darkened—the thunder rolled in the Heavens, and blood flowed in streams—and I heard a voice saying, "Such is your luck, such you are called to see, and let it come rough or smooth, you must surely bear it. I now withdrew myself, as much as my situation would permit, from the intercourse of my fellow servants, for the avowed purpose of serving the Spirit more fully. And it appeared to me and reminded me of the things it had already shown me, and that it would then reveal to me the knowledge of the elements, the revolution of the planets, the operation of tides, and changes of the seasons.

After this revelation in the year of 1825 and the knowledge of the elements being made known to me, I sought more than ever to obtain true holiness before the great day of judgment should appear, and then I began to receive the true knowledge of faith. And from the first steps of righteousness until the last, was I made perfect; and the Holy Ghost was with me, and said, "Behold me as I stand in the Heavens." And I looked and saw the forms of men in different attitudes—and there were lights in the sky to which the children of darkness gave other names than what they really were—for they were the lights of the Savior's hands, stretched forth from east to west, even as they were extended on the cross on Calvary for the redemption of sinners. And I wondered greatly at these miracles, and prayed to be informed of a certainty of the meaning thereof—and shortly afterwards, while laboring in the field, I discovered drops of blood on the corn as though it were dew from Heaven—and I communicated it to many, both white and black, in the neighborhood—and I then found on the leaves in the woods hieroglyphic characters and numbers with the forms of men in different attitudes, portrayed in blood and representing the figures I had seen before in the heavens. And now the Holy Ghost revealed itself to me and made plain the miracles it had shown me. For as the blood of Christ had been shed on this earth and had ascended to Heaven for the salvation of sinners and was now returning to earth again in the form of dew, and as the leaves on the trees bore the impression of the figures I had seen in the Heavens, it was plain to me that the Savior was about to lay down the yoke he had borne for the sins of men, and the great day of judgment was at hand.

About this time I told these things to a white man (Etheldred T. Brantley) on whom it had a wonderful effect—and he ceased from his wickedness and was attacked immediately with a cutaneous eruption, and blood oozed from the pores of his skin, and, after praying and fasting nine days, he was healed. And the Spirit appeared to me again and said, as the Savior had been baptized so should we be also—and when the white people would not let us be baptized by the church, we went down into the water together, in the sight of many who reviled us, and were baptized by the Spirit. After this I rejoiced greatly and gave thanks to God. And on the 12th of May, 1828, I heard a loud noise in the Heavens, and the Spirit instantly appeared to me and said the Serpent was loosened and Christ had laid down the yoke he had borne for the sins of men, and that I should take it on and fight against the Serpent, for the time was fast approaching when the first should be last and the last should be first.

Q. Do you not find yourself mistaken now?

A. Was not Christ crucified?

And by signs in the Heavens that it would make known to me when I should commence the great work—and until the first sign appeared, I should conceal it from the knowledge of men. And on the appearance of the sign (the eclipse of the sun last February), I should arise and prepare myself, and slay my enemies with their own weapons. And immediately on the sign appearing in the Heavens, the seal was removed from my lips, and I communicated the great work laid out for me to do to four in whom I had the greatest confidence (Henry, Hark, Nelson, and Sam). It was intended by us to have begun the work of death on the 4th July last. Many were the plans formed and rejected by us, and it affected my mind to such a degree that I fell sick, and the time passed without our coming to any determination how to commence. Still forming new schemes and rejecting them, the sign appeared again, which determined me not to wait longer.

Since the commencement of 1830, I had been living with Mr. Joseph Travis, who was to me a kind master and placed the greatest confidence in me; in fact, I had no cause to complain of his treatment to me. On Saturday evening, the 20th of August, it was agreed between Henry,

Hark, and myself to prepare a dinner the next day for the men we expected, and then to concert a plan, as we had not yet determined on any. Hark, on the following morning, brought a pig, and Henry, brandy, and being joined by Sam, Nelson, Will and Jack, they prepared in the woods a dinner, where, about three o'clock, I joined them.

Q. Why were you so backward in joining them?

A. The same reason that had caused me not to mix with them for years before.

I saluted them on coming up, and asked Will how came he there. He answered, his life was worth no more than others, and his liberty as dear to him. I asked him if he thought to obtain it? He said he would, or lose his life. This was enough to put him in full confidence. Jack, I knew, was only a tool in the hands of Hark.

It was quickly agreed we should commence at home (Mr. J. Travis's) on that night, and, until we had armed and equipped ourselves and gathered sufficient force, neither age nor sex was to be spared (which was invariably adhered to). We remained at the feast until about two hours in the night, when we went to the house and found Austin; they all went to the cider press and drank, except myself. On returning to the house, Hark went to the door with an axe for the purpose of breaking it open, as we knew we were strong enough to murder the family if they were awaked by the noise; but, reflecting that it might create an alarm in the neighborhood, we determined to enter the house secretly and murder them whilst sleeping. Hark got a ladder and set it against the chimney, on which I ascended and, hoisting a window, entered and came down stairs, unbarred the door, and removed the guns from their places. It was then observed that I must spill the first blood. On which, armed with a hatchet and accompanied by Will, I entered my master's chamber. It being dark, I could not give a death blow; the hatchet glanced from his head, he sprang from the bed and called his wife, it was his last word, Will laid him dead with a blow of his axe, and Mrs. Travis shared the same fate as she lay in bed. The murder of this family, five in number, was the work of a moment; not one of them awoke. There was a little infant sleeping in a cradle that was forgotten until we had left the house and gone some distance, when Henry and Will returned and killed it. We got here four guns that would shoot and several old muskets with a pound or two of powder.

We remained some time at the barn, where we paraded; I formed them in a line as soldiers and, after carrying them through all the maneuvers I was master of, marched them off to Mr. Salathul Francis's, about six hundred yards distant. Sam and Will went to the door and knocked. Mr. Francis asked who was there; Sam replied it was him and he had a letter for him; on which he got up and came to the door; they immediately seized him and, dragging him out a little from the door, he was dispatched by repeated blows on the head; there was no other white person in the family.

We started from there for Mrs. Reese's, maintaining the most perfect silence on our march, where, finding the door unlocked, we entered and murdered Mrs. Reese in her bed while sleeping; her son awoke, but it was only to sleep the sleep of death; he had only time to say who is that, and he was no more. From Mrs. Reese's we went to Mrs. Turner's, a mile distant, which we reached about sunrise on Monday morning. Henry, Austin, and Sam went to the still, where, finding Mr. Peebles, Austin shot him; and the rest of us went to the house. As we approached, the family discovered us, and shut the door. Vain hope! Will, with one stroke of his axe opened it, and we entered and found Mrs. Turner and Mrs. Newsome in the middle of a room, almost frightened to death. Will immediately killed Mrs. Turner with one blow of his axe. I took Mrs. Newsome by the hand, and, with the sword I had when I was apprehended, I struck her several blows over the head, but not being able to kill her, as the sword was dull. Will turning around and discovering it, dispatched her also. A general destruction of property and search for money and ammunition always succeeded the murders.

By this time my company amounted to fifteen. Nine men mounted, who started for Mrs. Whitehead's (the other six were to go through a byway to Mr. Bryant's and rejoin us at Mrs. Whitehead's). As we approached the house we discovered Mr. Richard Whitehead standing in the cotton patch near the lane fence; we called him over into the lane, and Will, the executioner, was near at hand with his fatal axe to send him to an untimely grave. As we pushed on to the house, I discovered someone run round the garden, and, thinking it was some of the white family, I pursued them; but finding it was a servant girl belonging to the house, I returned to commence the work of death; but they whom I left had not been idle; all the family were already murdered but Mrs. Whitehead and her daughter Margaret. As I came round to the door I saw Will pulling Mrs. Whitehead out of the house, and at the step he nearly severed her head from her body with his broad axe. Miss Margaret, when I discovered her, had concealed herself in the corner formed by the projection of cellar cap from the house; on my approach she fled but was soon overtaken, and, after repeated blows with a sword, I killed her by a blow on the head with a fence rail. By this time, the six who had gone by Mr. Bryant's rejoined us and informed me they had done the work of death assigned them.

We again divided: part going to Mr. Richard Porter's and from thence to Nathaniel Francis's, the others to Mr. Howell Harris's and Mr. T. Doyle's. On my reaching Mr. Porter's, he had escaped with his family. I understood there that the alarm had already spread, and I immediately returned to bring up those sent to Mr. Doyle's and Mr. Howell Harris's; the party I left going on to Mr. Francis's, having told them I would join them in that neighborhood. I met those sent to Mr. Doyle's and Mr. Harris's returning, having met Mr. Doyle on the road and killed him. Learning from some who joined them that Mr. Harris was from home, I immediately pursued the course taken by the party gone on before; but knowing they would complete the work of death and pillage, at Mr. Francis's before I could get there, I went to Mr. Peter Edwards's, expecting to find them there; but they had been here also. I then went to Mr. John T. Barrow's; they had been here and murdered him. I pursued on their track to Capt. Newit Harris's, where I found the greater part mounted and ready to start; the men, now amounting to about forty, shouted and hurrahed as I rode up; some were in the yard, loading their guns, others drinking. They said Captain Harris and his family had escaped; the property in the house they destroyed, robbing him of money and other valuables. I ordered them to mount and march instantly; this was about nine or ten o'clock, Monday morning.

I proceeded to Mr. Levi Waller's, two or three miles distant. I took my station in the rear, and, as it was my object to carry terror and devastation wherever we went, I placed fifteen or twenty of the best armed and most relied on in front, who generally approached the houses as fast as their horses could run; this was for two purposes: to prevent escape and strike terror to the inhabitants. On this account I never got to the houses, after leaving Mrs. Whitehead's, until the murders were committed, except in one case. I sometimes got in sight in time to see the work of death completed, viewed the mangled bodies as they lay, in silent satisfaction, and immediately started in quest of other victims.

Having murdered Mrs. Waller and ten children, we started for Mr. William Williams's—having killed him and two little boys that were there. While engaged in this, Mrs. Williams fled and got some distance from the house; but she was pursued, overtaken, and compelled to get up behind one of the company, who brought her back, and, after showing her the mangled body of her lifeless husband, she was told to get down and lay by his side, where she was shot dead. I then started for Mr. Jacob Williams's, where the family were murdered. Here we found a young man named Drury, who had come on business with Mr. Williams; he was pursued, overtaken, and shot. Mrs. Vaughan's was the next place we visited, and, after murdering the family here, I determined on starting for Jerusalem.

Our number amounted now to fifty or sixty, all mounted and armed with guns, axes, swords and clubs. On reaching Mr. James W. Parker's gate, immediately on the road leading to Jerusalem and about three miles distant, it was proposed to me to call there; but I objected, as I knew he was gone to Jerusalem and my object was to reach there as soon as possible; but some of the men having relations at Mr. Parker's it was agreed that they might call and get his people. I remained at the gate on the road with seven or eight; the others going across the field to the house, about half a mile off.

After waiting some time for them, I became impatient and started to the house for them. On our return we were met by a party of white men who had pursued our blood-stained track, and who had fired on those at the gate and dispersed them, which I knew nothing of, not having been at that time rejoined by any of them. Immediately on discovering the whites, I ordered my men to halt and form, as they appeared to be alarmed. The white men, eighteen in number, approached us in about one hundred yards, when one of them fired. [This was against the positive orders of Captain Alexander P. Peete, who commanded and who had directed the men to reserve their fire until within thirty paces.] And I discovered about half of them retreating; I then ordered my men to fire and rush on them; the few remaining stood their ground until we approached within fifty yards, when they fired and retreated. We pursued and overtook some of them who we thought we left dead (they were not killed); after pursuing them about two hundred yards and rising a little hill, I discovered they were met by another party, and had halted and were reloading their guns. [This was a small party from Jerusalem who knew the Negroes were in the field and had just tied their horses to await their return to the road, knowing that Mr. Parker and family were in Jerusalem, but knowing nothing of the party that had gone in with Captain Peete; on hearing the firing they immediately rushed to the spot and arrived just in time to arrest the progress of these barbarous villains and save the lives of their friends and fellow citizens.] Thinking that those who retreated first, and the party who fired on us at fifty or sixty yards distant, had all fallen back to meet others with ammunition. As I saw them reloading their guns, and more coming up than I saw at first, and several of my bravest men being wounded, the others became panic struck and squandered over the field; the white men pursued and fired on us several times. Hark had his horse shot under him, and I caught another for him as it was running by me; five or six of my men were wounded, but none left on the field; finding myself defeated here, I instantly determined to go through a private way and cross the Nottoway river at the Cypress Bridge, three miles below Jerusalem, and attack that place in the rear, as I expected they would look for me on the other road, and I had a great desire to get there to procure arms and ammunition.

After going a short distance in this private way, accompanied by about twenty men, I overtook two or three who told me the others were dispersed in every direction. After trying in vain to collect a sufficient force to proceed to Jerusalem, I determined to return, as I was sure they would make back to their old neighborhood, where they would rejoin me, make new recruits, and come down again. On my way back, I called at Mrs. Thomas's, Mrs. Spencer's, and several other places; the white families having fled, we found no more victims to gratify our thirst for blood. We stopped at Major Ridley's quarter for the night; and being joined by four of his men, with the recruits made since my defeat, we mustered now about forty strong. After placing out sentinels, I laid down to sleep, but was quickly roused by a great racket; starting up, I found some mounted and others in great confusion; one of the sentinels having given the alarm that we were about to be attacked, I ordered some to ride round and reconnoiter. On their return the others being more alarmed, not knowing who they were, fled in different ways, so that I was reduced to about twenty again; with this I determined to attempt to recruit and proceed on to rally in the neighborhood I had left. Dr. Blunt's was the nearest house, which we reached just before day; on riding up the yard, Hark fired a gun. We expected Dr. Blunt and his family were at Major Ridley's, as I knew there was a company of men there; the gun was fired to ascertain if any of the family were at home; we were immediately fired upon and retreated, leaving several of my men. I do not know what became of them, as I never saw them afterwards. Pursuing our course back and coming in sight of Captain Harris's, where we had been the day before, we discovered a party of white men at the house; on which all deserted me but two (Jacob and Nat); we concealed ourselves in the woods until near night, when I sent them in search of Henry, Sam, Nelson, and Hark and directed them to rally all they could at the place we had had our dinner the Sunday before, where they would find me; and I accordingly returned there as soon as it was dark and remained until Wednesday evening, when discovering white men riding around the place as though they were looking for someone and none of my men joining me, I concluded Jacob and Nat had been taken and compelled to betray me.

On this I gave up all hope for the present; and on Thursday night, after having supplied myself with provisions from Mr. Travis's, I scratched a hole under a pile of fence rails in a field, where I concealed myself for six weeks, never leaving my hiding place but for a few minutes in the dead of night to get water which was very near. Thinking by this time I could venture out, I began to go about in the night and eavesdrop the houses in the neighborhood—pursuing this course for about a fortnight and gathering little or no intelligence, afraid of speaking to any human being, and returning every morning to my cave before the dawn of day.

I know not how long I might have led this life, if accident had not betrayed me; a dog in the neighborhood passing by my hiding place one night while I was out, was attracted by some meat I had in my cave and crawled in and stole it, and was coming out just as I returned. A few nights after, two Negroes having started to go hunting with the same dog and passing that way, the dog came again to the place and, having just gone out to walk about, discovered me and barked; on which, thinking myself discovered, I spoke to them to beg concealment. On making myself known they fled from me. Knowing then they would betray me, I immediately left my hiding place and was pursued almost incessantly until I was taken a fortnight afterwards by Mr. Benjamin Phipps in a little hole I had dug out with my sword, for the purpose of concealment, under the top of a fallen tree. On Mr. Phipps's discovering the place of my concealment, he cocked his gun and aimed at me. I requested him not to shoot and I would give up, upon which he demanded my sword. I delivered it to him, and he brought me to prison. During the time I was pursued, I had many hair breadth escapes, which your time will not permit you to relate. I am here loaded with chains, and willing to suffer the fate that awaits me.

MOSES ROPER

The son of a North Carolina slaveholder, Moses Roper was sold from his mother at the age of six because his father found their resemblance embarrassing. Indeed his master's jealous white wife had attempted to stab little Moses. He led a difficult life laboring under cruel overseers and masters. He was a chronic runaway. For attempting to escape, he was whipped, chained, and forced to work long hours. On one occasion after his recapture his master put a long chain weighing twenty-five pounds around his neck and forced him to work while chained. Roper finally succeeded in escaping to Savannah, where a northern sea captain employed him as a steward on a vessel bound for New York. Well over six feet tall, Roper was of Caucasian, African, and Indian descent. The account of his life from which these chapters come, *A Narrative of the Adventures and Escape of Moses Roper from American Slavery*, appeared in London in 1839.

Chronic Runaway

This was the first time I attempted to run away, knowing that I should get a flogging. I was then between thirteen and fourteen years of age, I ran away to the woods half-naked, I was caught by a slaveholder, who put me in Lancaster Gaol. When they put slaves in gaol, they advertise for their masters to own them; but if the master does not claim his slave in six months from the time of imprisonment the slave is sold for gaol fees. When the slave runs away, the master always adopts a more rigorous system of flogging. This was the case in the present instance. After this, having determined from my youth to gain my freedom, I made several attempts, was caught, and got a severe flogging of 100 lashes each time. Mr. Hammans was a very severe and cruel master, and his wife still worse. She used to tie me up and flog me while naked.

After Mr. Hammans saw that I was determined to die in the woods and not live with him, he tried to obtain a piece of land from his father-in-law, Mr. Gooch. Not having the means of purchasing it, he ˊ :- changed me for the land.

As soon as Mr. Gooch had possession of me again, knowing that I was averse of going back to him, he chained me by the neck to his chaise. In this manner, he took me to his home at MacDaniel's Ferry, in the county of Chester, a distance of fifteen miles. After which, he put me into a swamp to cut trees—the heaviest work, which men of twenty-five or thirty years of age have to do, I being but sixteen. Here I was on very short allowance of food and, having heavy work, was too weak to fulfill my tasks. For this, I got many severe floggings, and, after I had got my irons off, I made another attempt at running away. He took my irons off in the full anticipation that I could never get across the Catarba River, even when at liberty. On this, I procured a small Indian canoe, which was tied to a tree, and ultimately got across the river in it. I then wandered through the wilderness for several days without any food and but a drop of water to allay my thirst, till I became so starved that I was obliged to go to a house to beg for something to eat, when I was captured and again imprisoned.

Mr. Gooch, having heard of me through an advertisement, sent his son after me. He tied me up, and took me back to his father. Mr. Gooch then obtained the assistance of another slaveholder and tied me up in his blacksmith's shop and gave me fifty lashes with a cowhide. He then put a log chain, weighing twenty-five pounds, round my neck and sent me into a field, into which he followed me with the cowhide, intending to set his slaves to flog me again. Knowing this, and dreading to suffer again in this way, I gave him the slip and got out of his sight, he having stopped to speak with the other slaveholder.

I got to a canal on the Catarba River, on the banks of which, and near to a lock, I procured a stone and a piece of iron, with which I forced the ring off my chain and got it off, and then crossed the river and walked about twenty miles, when I fell in with a slaveholder, named Ballad, who had married the sister of Mr. Hammans. I knew that he was not so cruel as Mr. Gooch and, therefore, begged of him to buy me. Mr. Ballad, who was one of the best planters in the neighborhood, said that he was not able to buy me and stated that he was obliged to take me back to my master on account of the heavy fine attaching to a man harboring a slave. Mr. Ballad proceeded to take me back. As we came in sight of Mr. Gooch's, all the treatment that I had met with there came forcibly upon my mind, the powerful influence of which is beyond description. On my knees, with tears in my eyes, with terror in my countenance, and fervency in all my features I implored Mr. Ballad to buy me, but he again refused and I was taken back to my dreaded and cruel master.

Having reached Mr. Gooch's, he proceeded to punish me. This he did by first tying my wrists together and placing them over the knees; he then put a stick through, under my knees and over my arms; and having thus secured my arms, he proceeded to flog me and gave me 500 lashes on my bare back. This may appear incredible, but the marks which they left at present remain on my body, a standing testimony to the truth of this statement of his severity. He then chained me down in a logpen with a forty-pound chain and made me lie on the damp earth all night. In the morning, after his breakfast, he came to me and, without giving me any breakfast, tied me to a large heavy harrow, which is usually drawn by a horse, and made me drag it to the cotton field for the horse to use in the field. Thus, the reader will see that it was of no possible use to my master to make me drag it to the field and not through it. His cruelty went so far as actually to make me the slave of his horse and thus to degrade me. He then flogged me again and set me to work in the corn field the whole of that day, and at night he chained me down in the logpen as before. The next morning, he took me to the cotton field and gave me a third flogging and set me to hoe cotton. At this time, I was dreadfully sore and weak with the repeated floggings and harsh treatment I had endured. He put me under a black man, with orders that if I did not keep my row up in hoeing with this man, he was to flog me. The reader must recollect here, that not being used to this kind of work, having been a domestic slave, it was quite impossible for me to keep up with him and, therefore, I was repeatedly flogged during the day.

Mr. Gooch had a female slave about eighteen years old, who also had been a domestic slave and, through not being able to fulfill her task, had run away; which slave he was at this time punishing for that offence. On the third day, he chained me to this female slave, with a large chain of forty pounds weight around the neck. It was most harrowing to my feelings thus to be chained to a young female slave, for whom I would rather have suffered a hundred lashes than that she should have been thus treated. He kept me chained to her during the week and repeatedly flogged us both while thus chained together, and forced us to keep up with the other slaves, although retarded by the heavy weight of the log-chain.

Here again, words are insufficient to describe the misery which possessed both body and mind whilst under this treatment, and which was most dreadfully increased by the sympathy which I felt for my poor, degraded fellow sufferer. On the Friday morning, I entreated my master to set me free from my chains and promised him to do the task which was given me and more, if possible, if he would desist from flogging me. This he refused to do until Saturday night, when he did set me free. This must rather be ascribed to his own interest in preserving me from death, as it was very evident I could no longer have survived under such treatment.

After this, though still determined in my own mind to escape, I stayed with him several months during which he frequently flogged me, but not so severely as before related. During this time, I had opportunity for recovering my health and using means to heal my wounds. My master's cruelty was not confined to me; it was his general conduct to all his slaves. I might relate many instances to substantiate this, but will confine myself to one or two. Mr. Gooch, it is proper to observe, was a member of a Baptist church, called Black Jack Meeting House, in Cashaw county, which church I attended for several years, but was never inside. This is accounted for by the fact that the colored population are not permitted to mix with the white population. In the Roman Catholic church no distinction is made. Mr. Gooch had a slave named Phil, who was a member of a Methodist church. This man was between seventy and eighty years of age; he was so feeble that he could not accomplish his tasks, for which his master used to chain him round the neck and run him down a steep hill; this treatment he never relinquished to the time of his death. Another case was that of a slave named Peter, who, for not doing his task, he flogged nearly to death and afterwards pulled out his pistol to shoot him; but his (Mr. Gooch's) daughter snatched the pistol from his hand. Another mode of punishment which this man adopted was that of using iron horns with bells attached to the back of the slave's neck, as shown on the following page.

This instrument he used to prevent the Negroes running away, being a very ponderous machine, several feet in height, and the cross pieces being two, four, and six feet in length. This custom is generally adopted among the slaveholders in South Carolina and some other slave states. One morning, about an hour before day break, I was going on an errand for my master. Having proceeded about a quarter of a mile, I came up to a man named King (Mr. Sumlin's overseer), who had caught a young girl that had run away with the above machine on her. She had proceeded four miles from her station, with the intention of getting into the hands of a more humane master. She came up with this overseer nearly dead and could get no farther. He immediately secured her and took her back to her master, a Mr. Johnston.

Having been in the habit of going over many slave states with my master, I had good opportunities of witnessing the harsh treatment

which was adopted by masters towards their slaves. As I have never read nor heard of anything connected with slavery so cruel as what I have myself witnessed, it will be well to mention a case or two.

A large farmer, Colonel M'Quiller, in Cashaw county, South Carolina, was in the habit of driving nails into a hogshead so as to leave the point of the nail just protruding in the inside of the cask. Into this he used to put his slaves for punishment, and roll them down a very long and steep hill. I have heard from several slaves (though I had no means of ascertaining the truth of the statement) that in this way he killed six or seven of his slaves. This plan was first adopted by a Mr. Perry, who lived on the Catarba River, and has since been adopted by several planters.

Another was that of a young lad who had been hired by Mr. Bell, a member of a Methodist church, to hoe three-quarters of an acre of cotton per day. Having been brought up as a domestic slave, he was not able to accomplish the task assigned to him. On the Saturday night, he left three or four rows to do on the Sunday. On the same night it rained very hard, by which the master could tell that he had done some of the rows on Sunday. On Monday, his master took and tied him up to a tree in the field and kept him there the whole of that day and flogged him at intervals. At night, when he was taken down, he was so weak that he could not get home, having a mile to go. Two white men, who were employed by Mr. Bell, put him on a horse, took him home, and threw him down on the kitchen floor, while they proceeded to their supper. In a little time, they heard some deep groans proceeding from the kitchen. They went to see him die; he had groaned his last. Thus, Mr. Bell flogged this poor boy, even to death. For what? For breaking the Sabbath, when he (his master) had set him a task, on Saturday, which it was not possible for him to do, and which if he did not do no mercy would be extended towards him. So much for the regard of this Methodist for the observance of the Sabbath. The general custom in this respect is that if a man kills his own slave, no notice is taken of it by the civil functionaries; but if a man kills a slave belonging to another master, he is compelled to pay the worth of the slave. In this case, a jury met, returned a verdict of "willful murder" against this man, and ordered him to pay the value.

FREDERICK DOUGLASS

The most famous fugitive slave and black leader of the late nineteenth century was Frederick Douglass. He was born on the
Eastern Shore of Maryland, the son of his white master. Douglass's life story is one of the most interesting historical accounts,
providing us with a picture of the slaveholding system, the slave
owner, and the reactions of the slaves. Douglass learned to read
while still a slave and worked as a ship's caulker in Baltimore.
When a "slave breaker" attempted to whip him, he boldly defended himself. He escaped from slavery in a sailor's uniform
with borrowed papers by taking the train from Baltimore to New
York. In the North he became an agent of the Anti-Slavery Society and was much in demand as a speaker here and abroad. A
close friend of John Brown, Douglass helped many fugitives escape to Canada. An associate of William Lloyd Garrison, he
broke with the great abolitionist on questions of strategy and
published his own antislavery newspaper *The North Star*. After
the Civil War Douglass was an advisor to presidents of the
United States and a leader in the struggle for full equality for
black people. An extraordinary orator and courageous leader,
Douglass never faltered in his devotion to the highest democratic
ideals. He wrote the first account of his life, *The Narrative of*

Frederick Douglass and published it in 1845. Other autobiographies of Douglass appeared in 1855 and 1882. The following passages are from the 1882 edition, *The Life and Times of Frederick Douglass.*

Breaking a Slave Breaker

It was generally supposed that slavery in the state of Maryland existed in its mildest form, and that it was totally divested of those harsh and terrible peculiarities which characterized the slave system in the southern and southwestern states of the American Union. The ground of this opinion was the contiguity of the free states, and the influence of their moral, religious, and humane sentiments. Public opinion was, indeed, a measurable restraint upon the cruelty and barbarity of masters, overseers, and slavedrivers, whenever and wherever it could reach them; but there were certain secluded and out-of-the-way places, even in the state of Maryland, fifty years ago, seldom visited by a single ray of healthy public sentiment, where slavery, wrapt in its own congenial darkness, could and did develop all its malign and shocking characteristics, where it could be indecent without shame, cruel without shuddering, and murderous without apprehension or fear of exposure or punishment. Just such a secluded, dark, and out-of-the-way place was the home plantation of Colonel Edward Lloyd, in Talbot County, Eastern Shore of Maryland. It was far away from all the great thoroughfares of travel and commerce, and proximate to no town or village. There was neither schoolhouse nor townhouse in its neighborhood. The schoolhouse was unnecessary, for there were no children to go to school. The children and grandchildren of Colonel Lloyd were taught in the house by a private tutor (a Mr. Page from Greenfield, Massachusetts, a tall, gaunt sapling of a man, remarkably dignified, thoughtful, and reticent, and who did not speak a dozen words to a slave in a whole year). The overseer's children went off somewhere in the state to school, and therefore could bring no foreign or dangerous influence from abroad to embarrass the natural operation of the slave system of the place. Here, not even the commonest mechanics, from whom there might have been an occasional outburst of honest and telling indignation at cruelty and wrong on other plantations, were white men. Its whole public was made up of and divided into three classes: slaveholders, slaves, and overseers. Its blacksmiths, wheelwrights, shoemakers, weavers, and coopers were slaves.

Not even commerce, selfish and indifferent to moral considerations as it usually is, was permitted within its secluded precincts. Whether with a view of guarding against the escape of its secrets, I know not, but it is a fact that every leaf and grain of the products of this plantation and those of the neighboring farms belonging to Colonel Lloyd were transported to Baltimore in his own vessels, every man and boy on board of which, except the captain, were owned by him as his property. In return, everything brought to the plantation came through the same channel. To make this isolation more apparent, it may be stated that the estates adjoining Colonel Lloyd's were owned and occupied by friends of his, who were as deeply interested as himself in maintaining the slave system in all its rigor. These were the Tilgmans, the Goldboroughs, the Lockermans, the Pacas, the Skinners, Gibsons, and others of lesser affluence and standing.

Public opinion in such a quarter, the reader must see, was not likely to be very efficient in protecting the slave from cruelty. To be a restraint upon abuses of this nature, opinion must emanate from humane and virtuous communities, and to no such opinion or influence was Colonel Lloyd's plantation exposed. It was a little nation by itself, having its own language, its own rules, regulations, and customs. The troubles and controversies arising here were not settled by the civil power of the state. The overseer was the important dignitary. He was generally accuser, judge, jury, advocate, and executioner. The criminal was always dumb, and no slave was allowed to testify other than against his brother slave.

There were, of course, no conflicting rights of property, for all the people were the property of one man, and they could themselves own no property. Religion and politics were largely excluded. One class of the population was too high to be reached by the common preacher, and the other class was too low in condition and ignorance to be much cared for by religious teachers; and yet some religious ideas did enter this dark corner.

This, however, is not the only view which the place presented. Though civilization was, in many respects, shut out, nature could not be. Though separated from the rest of the world, though public opinion, as I have said, could seldom penetrate its dark domain, though the whole place was stamped with its own peculiar iron-like individuality, and though crimes, high-handed and atrocious, could be committed there with strange and shocking impunity; it was, to outward seeming, a most strikingly interesting place, full of life, activity, and spirit, and presented a very favorable contrast to the indolent monotony and languor of Tuckahoe. It resembled, in some respects, descriptions I have since read of the old baronial domains of Europe. Keen as was my regret and great as was my sorrow at leaving my old home, I was not long in adapting myself to this my new one. A man's troubles are always half disposed of when he finds endurance the only alternative. I found myself here, there was no getting away, and naught remained for me but to make the best of it. Here were plenty of children to play with and plenty of pleasant resorts for boys of my age and older. The little tendrils of affection, so rudely broken from the darling objects in and around my grandmother's home, gradually began to extend and twine themselves around the new surroundings. Here, for the first time, I saw a large windmill, with its wide-sweeping white wings, a commanding object to a child's eye. This was situated on what was called Long Point —a tract of land dividing Miles River from the Wye. I spent many hours here watching the wings of this wondrous mill. In the river, or what was called the "Swash," at a short distance from the shore, quietly lying at anchor, with her small rowboat dancing at her stern, was a large sloop, the *Sally Lloyd*, called by that name in honor of the favorite daughter of the Colonel. These two objects, the sloop and mill, awakened, as I remember, thoughts, ideas, and wondering. Then here were a great many houses, human habitations full of the mysteries of life at every stage of it. There was the little red house up the road, occupied by Mr. Seveir, the overseer. A little nearer to my old master's stood a long, low, rough building literally alive with slaves of all ages, sexes, conditions, sizes, and colors. This was called the long quarter. Perched upon a hill east of our house was a tall, dilapidated old brick building, the architectural dimensions of which proclaimed its creation for a different purpose, now occupied by slaves in a similar manner to the long quarters. Besides these, there were numerous other slave houses and huts scattered around in the neighborhood, every nook and corner of which were completely occupied.

Old master's house, a long brick building, plain but substantial, was centrally located and was an independent establishment. Besides these houses there were barns, stables, storehouses, tobacco houses, blacksmith shops, wheelwright shops, cooper shops; but above all there stood the grandest building my young eyes had ever beheld, called by every one on the plantation the *great* house. This was occupied by Colonel Lloyd and his family. It was surrounded by numerous and variously shaped outbuildings. There were kitchens, washhouses, dairies, summer houses, greenhouses, hen houses, turkey houses, pigeon houses and arbors of many sizes and devices, all neatly painted or whitewashed, interspersed with grand old trees, ornamental and primitive, which afforded delightful shade in summer and imparted to the scene a high degree of stately beauty. The *great* house itself was a large white wooden building with wings on three sides of it. In front, extending the entire length of the building and supported by a long range of columns, was a broad portico, which gave to the Colonel's home an air of great dignity and grandeur. It was a treat to my young and gradually opening mind to behold this elaborate exhibition of wealth, power, and beauty.

The carriage entrance to the house was by a large gate, more than a quarter of a mile distant. The intermediate space was a beautiful lawn, very neatly kept and tended. It was dotted thickly over with trees and flowers. The road or lane from the gate to the great house was richly paved with white pebbles from the beach and in its course formed a complete circle around the lawn. Outside this select enclosure were parks, as about the residences of the English nobility, where rabbits, deer, and other wild game might be seen peering and playing about, with "none to molest them or make them afraid." The tops of the stately poplars were often covered with redwinged blackbirds, making all nature vocal with the joyous life and beauty of their wild, warbling notes. These all belonged to me as well as to Colonel Edward Lloyd, and, whether they did or not, I greatly enjoyed them.

Not far from the great house were the stately mansions of the dead Lloyds—a place of somber aspect. Vast tombs, embowered beneath the weeping willow and the fir tree, told of the generations of the family, as well as of their wealth. Superstition was rife among the slaves about this family burying-ground. Strange sights had been seen there by some of the older slaves, and I was often compelled to hear stories of shrouded ghosts, riding on great black horses, and of balls of fire which had been seen to fly there at midnight, and of startling and dreadful sounds that had been repeatedly heard. Slaves knew enough of the orthodox theology of the time to consign all bad slaveholders to hell, and they often fancied such persons wishing themselves back again to wield the lash. Tales of sights and sounds strange and terrible, connected with the huge black tombs, were a great security to the grounds about them, for few of the slaves had the courage to approach them during the daytime. It was a dark, gloomy, and forbidding place, and it was difficult to feel that the spirits of the sleeping dust there deposited reigned with the blest in the realms of eternal peace.

At Lloyd's was transacted the business of twenty or thirty different farms, which—with the slaves upon them, numbering in all not less than a thousand—all belonged to Colonel Lloyd. Each farm was under the management of an overseer, whose word was law.

Mr. Lloyd was, at this time, very rich. His slaves alone, numbering as I have said not less than a thousand, were an immense fortune and, though scarcely a month passed without the sale to the Georgia traders of one or more lots, there was no apparent diminution in the number of his human stock. The selling of any to the state of Georgia was a sore and mournful event to those left behind, as well as to the victims themselves.

The reader has already been informed of the handicrafts carried on here by the slaves. "Uncle" Toney was the blacksmith, "Uncle" Harry the cartwright, and "Uncle" Abel was the shoemaker, and these had assistants in their several departments. These mechanics were called "Uncles" by all the younger slaves, not because they really sustained that relationship to any, but, according to plantation etiquette, as a mark of respect, due from the younger to the older slaves. Strange and even ridiculous as it may seem, among a people so uncultivated and with so many stern trials to look in the face, there is not to be found among any people a more rigid enforcement of the law of respect to elders than is maintained among them. I set this down as partly constitutional with the colored race and partly conventional. There is no better material in the world for making a gentleman than is furnished in the African.

Among other slave notabilities, I found here one called by everybody, white and colored, "Uncle" Isaac Copper. It was seldom that a slave, however venerable, was honored with a surname in Maryland, and so completely has the South shaped the manners of the North in this respect that their right to such honor is tardily admitted even now. It goes sadly against the grain to address and treat a Negro as one would address and treat a white man. But once in a while, even in a slave state, a Negro had a surname fastened to him by common consent. This was the case with "Uncle" Isaac Copper. When the "Uncle" was dropped, he was called Doctor Copper. He was both our Doctor of Medicine and our Doctor of Divinity. Where he took his degree I am unable to say, but he was too well established in his profession to permit question as to his native skill or attainments. One qualification he certainly had. He was a confirmed cripple, wholly unable to work, and was worth nothing for sale in the market. Though lame, he was no sluggard. He made his crutches do him good service, and was always on the alert looking up the sick, and such as were supposed to need his aid and counsel. His remedial prescriptions embraced four articles. For diseases of the body, epsom salts and castor oil; for those of the soul, the "Lord's Prayer," and a few stout hickory switches.

I was, with twenty or thirty other children, early sent to Doctor Isaac Copper to learn the Lord's Prayer. The old man was seated on a huge three-legged oaken stool, armed with several large hickory switches, and from the point where he sat, lame as he was, he could reach every boy in the room. After our standing a while to learn what was expected of us, he commanded us to kneel down. This done, he told us to say everything he said. "Our Father"—this we repeated after him with promptness and uniformity—"who art in Heaven" was less promptly and uniformly repeated, and the old gentleman paused in the prayer to give us a short lecture and to use his switches on our backs.

Everybody in the South seemed to want the privilege of whipping somebody else. Uncle Isaac, though a good old man, shared the common passion of his time and country. I cannot say I was much edified by attendance upon his ministry. There was in my mind, even at that time, something a little inconsistent and laughable in the blending of prayer with punishment.

I was not long in my new home before I found that the dread I had conceived of Captain Anthony was in a measure groundless. Instead of leaping out from some hiding-place and destroying me, he hardly seemed to notice my presence. He probably thought as little of my arrival there as of an additional pig to his stock. He was the chief agent of his employer. The overseers of all the farms composing the Lloyd estate were in some sort under him. The Colonel himself seldom addressed an overseer, or allowed himself to be addressed by one. To Captain Anthony, therefore, was committed the headship of all the farms. He carried the keys of all the storehouses; weighed and measured the allowances of each slave at the end of each month; superintended the storing of all goods brought to the storehouse; dealt out the raw material to the different handicraftsmen; shipped the grain, tobacco, and all other salable produce of the numerous farms to Baltimore; and had a general oversight of all the workshops of the place. In addition to all this, he was frequently called abroad to Easton and elsewhere in the discharge of his numerous duties as chief agent of the estate.

The family of Captain Anthony consisted of two sons—Andrew and Richard—and his daughter Lucretia and her newly-married husband, Captain Thomas Auld. In the kitchen were Aunt Katy, Aunt Esther, and ten or a dozen children, most of them older than myself. Captain Anthony was not considered a rich slaveholder, though he was pretty well off in the world. He owned about thirty slaves and three farms in the Tuckahoe district. The more valuable part of his property was in slaves, of whom he sold one every year, which brought him in seven or eight hundred dollars, besides his yearly salary and other revenue from his lands.

I have been often asked, during the earlier part of my free life at the North, how I happened to have so little of the slave accent in my speech. The mystery is in some measure explained by my association with Daniel Lloyd, the youngest son of Colonel Edward Lloyd. The law of compensation holds here as well as elsewhere. While this lad could not associate with ignorance without sharing its shade, he could not give his black playmates his company without giving them his superior intelligence as well. Without knowing this, or caring about it at the time, I, for some cause or other, was attracted to him and was much his companion.

I had little to do with the older brothers of Daniel—Edward and Murray. They were grown up and were fine-looking men. Edward was especially esteemed by the slave children, and by me among the rest— not that he ever said anything to us or for us which could be called particularly kind. It was enough for us that he never looked or acted scornfully toward us. The idea of rank and station was rigidly maintained on this estate. The family of Captain Anthony never visited the great house, and the Lloyds never came to our house. Equal nonintercourse was observed between Captain Anthony's family and the family of Mr. Seveir, the overseer.

Such, kind readers, was the community and such the place in which my earliest and most lasting impressions of the workings of slavery were received, of which impressions you will learn more in the after coming chapters of this book.

Sleep does not always come to the relief of the weary in body and broken in spirit; especially is it so when past troubles only foreshadow coming disasters. My last hope had been extinguished. My master, who I did not venture to hope would protect me *as a man,* had now refused to protect me *as his property* and had cast me back, covered with reproaches and bruises, into the hands of one who was a stranger to that mercy which is the soul of the religion he professed. May the reader never know what it is to spend such a night as to me was that which heralded my return to the den of horrors from which I had made a temporary escape.

I remained—sleep I did not—all night at St. Michaels, and in the morning (Saturday) I started off, obedient to the order of Master Thomas, feeling that I had no friend on earth and doubting if I had one in heaven. I reached Covey's about nine o'clock, and just as I stepped into the field, before I had reached the house, true to his snakish habits, Covey darted out at me from a fence corner, in which he had secreted himself for the purpose of securing me. He was provided with a cowskin and a rope, and he evidently intended to tie me up and wreak his vengeance on me to the fullest extent. I should have been an easy prey had he succeeded in getting his hands upon me, for I had taken no refreshment since noon on Friday and this, with the other trying circumstances, had greatly reduced my strength. I, however, darted back into the woods before the ferocious hound could reach me and buried myself in a thicket, where he lost sight of me. The cornfield afforded me shelter in getting to the woods. But for the tall corn, Covey would have overtaken me and made me his captive. He was much chagrined that he did not, and gave up the chase very reluctantly, as I could see by his angry movements as he returned to the house.

For a little time I was clear of Covey and his lash. I was in the wood, buried in its somber gloom and hushed in its solemn silence, hidden from all human eyes, shut in with nature and with nature's God, and absent from all human contrivances. Here was a good place to pray, to pray for help, for deliverance—a prayer I had often made before. But how could I pray? Covey could pray—Captain Auld could pray. I would fain pray; but doubts arising, partly from my neglect of the means of grace and partly from the sham religion which everywhere prevailed, there was awakened in my mind a distrust of all religion and the conviction that prayers were unavailing and delusive.

Life in itself had almost become burdensome to me. All my outward relations were against me. I must stay here and starve, or go home to Covey's and have my flesh torn to pieces and my spirit humbled under his cruel lash. These were the alternatives before me. The day was long and irksome. I was weak from the toils of the previous day and from want of food and sleep, and I had been so little concerned about my appearance that I had not yet washed the blood from my garments. I was an object of horror, even to myself. Life in Baltimore, when most oppressive, was a paradise to this. What had I done, what had my parents done, that such a life as this should be mine? That day, in the woods, I would have exchanged my manhood for the brutehood of an ox.

Night came. I was still in the woods and still unresolved what to do. Hunger had not yet pinched me to the point of going home, and I laid myself down in the leaves to rest, for I had been watching for hunters all day; but not being molested by them during the day, I expected no disturbance from them during the night. I had come to the conclusion that Covey relied upon hunger to drive me home, and in this I was quite correct, for he made no effort to catch me after the morning.

During the night I heard the step of a man in the woods. He was coming toward the place where I lay. A person lying still in the woods in the daytime has the advantage over one walking, and this advantage is much greater at night. I was not able to engage in a physical struggle, and I had recourse to the common resort of the weak. I hid myself in the leaves to prevent discovery. But as the night rambler in the woods drew nearer I found him to be a friend, not an enemy, a slave of Mr. William Groomes of Easton, a kindhearted fellow named "Sandy." Sandy lived that year with Mr. Kemp, about four miles from St. Michaels. He, like myself, had been hired out, but unlike myself had not been hired out to be broken. He was the husband of a free woman who lived in the lower part of Poppie Neck, and he was now on his way through the woods to see her and to spend the Sabbath with her.

As soon as I had ascertained that the disturber of my solitude was not an enemy, but the good-hearted Sandy—a man as famous among the slaves of the neighborhood for his own good nature as for his good sense—I came out from my hiding-place and made myself known to him. I explained the circumstances of the past two days which had driven me to the woods, and he deeply compassionated my distress. It was a bold thing for him to shelter me, and I could not ask him to do so, for had I been found in his hut he would have suffered the penalty of thirty-nine lashes on his bare back, if not something worse. But Sandy was too generous to permit the fear of punishment to prevent his relieving a brother bondman from hunger and exposure, and therefore, on his own motion, I accompanied him home to his wife—for the house and lot were hers, as she was a free woman. It was about midnight, but his wife was called up, a fire was made, some Indian meal was soon mixed with salt and water, and an ash cake was baked in a hurry, to relieve my hunger. Sandy's wife was not behind him in kindness; both seemed to esteem it a privilege to succor me; for although I was hated by Covey and by my master, I was loved by the colored people because they thought I was hated for my knowledge and persecuted because I was feared. I was the only slave in that region who could read or write. There had been one other man, belonging to Mr. Hugh Hamilton, who could read; but he, poor fellow, had, shortly after coming into the neighborhood, been sold off to the Far South. I saw him in the cart, to be carried to Easton for sale, ironed and pinioned like a yearling for the slaughter. My knowledge was now the pride of my brother slaves, and no doubt Sandy felt on that account something of the general interest in me. The supper was soon ready, and though over the sea I have since feasted with honorables, lord mayors, and aldermen, my supper on ash cake and cold water with Sandy was the meal of all my life most sweet to my taste and now most vivid to my memory.

Supper over, Sandy and I went into a discussion of what was possible for me, under the perils and hardships which overshadowed my path. The question was: must I go back to Covey, or must I attempt to run away? Upon a careful survey the latter was found to be impossible, for I was on a narrow neck of land, every avenue from which would bring me in sight of pursuers. There was Chesapeake Bay to the right, and "Pot-pie" River to the left, and St. Michaels and its neighborhood occupied the only space through which there was any retreat.

I found Sandy an old adviser. He was not only a religious man, but he professed to believe in a system for which I have no name. He was a genuine African, and had inherited some of the so-called magical powers said to be possessed by the eastern nations. He told me that he could help me, that in those very woods there was an herb, which in the morning might be found, possessing all the powers required for my protection (I put his words in my own language), and that if I would take his advice he would procure me the root of the herb of which he spoke. He told me, further, that if I would take that root and wear it on my right side it would be impossible for Covey to strike me a blow, and that, with this root about my person, no white man could whip me. He said he had carried it for years and that he had fully tested its virtues. He had never received a blow from a slaveholder since he carried it, and he never expected to receive one, for he meant always to carry that root for protection. He knew Covey well, for Mrs. Covey was the daughter of Mrs. Kemp, and he (Sandy) had heard of the barbarous treatment to which I had been subjected, and he wanted to do something for me.

Now all this talk about the root was to me very absurd and ridiculous, if not positively sinful. I at first rejected the idea that the simple carrying a root on my right side (a root, by the way, over which I walked every time I went into the woods) could possess any such magic power as he ascribed to it, and I was, therefore, not disposed to cumber my pocket with it. I had a positive aversion to all pretenders to "divination." It was beneath one of my intelligence to countenance such dealings with the devil as this power implied. But with all my learning—it was really precious little—Sandy was more than a match for me. "My book-learning," he said, "had not kept Covey off me" (a powerful argument just then), and he entreated me, with flashing eyes, to try this. If it did me no good it could do me no harm, and it would cost me nothing any way. Sandy was so earnest and so confident of the good qualities of this weed that, to please him, I was induced to take it. He had been to me the good Samaritan, and had, almost providentially, found me and helped me when I could not help myself; how did I know but that the hand of the Lord was in it? With thoughts of this sort I took the roots from Sandy and put them in my right-hand pocket.

This was of course Sunday morning. Sandy now urged me to go home with all speed and to walk up bravely to the house, as though nothing had happened. I saw in Sandy, with all his superstition, too deep an insight into human nature not to have some respect for his advice, and perhaps, too, a slight gleam or shadow of his superstition had fallen on me. At any rate, I started off toward Covey's, as directed. Having, the previous night, poured my griefs into Sandy's ears and enlisted him in my behalf, having made his wife a sharer in my sorrows, and having also become well refreshed by sleep and food, I moved off quite courageously toward the dreaded Covey's. Singularly enough, just as I entered the yard-gate I met him and his wife on their way to church, dressed in their Sunday best and looking as smiling as angels. His manner perfectly astonished me. There was something really benignant in his countenance. He spoke to me as never before, told me that the pigs had got into the lot and he wished me to go to drive them out, inquired how I was, and seemed an altered man. This extraordinary conduct really made me begin to think that Sandy's herb had more virtue in it than I, in my pride, had been willing to allow; and had the day been other than Sunday, I should have attributed Covey's altered manner solely to the power of the root. I suspected, however, that the Sabbath, not the root, was the real explanation of the change. His religion hindered him from breaking the Sabbath, but not from breaking my skin on any other day than Sunday. He had more respect for the day than for the man for whom the day was mercifully given, for while he would cut and slash my body during the week, he would on Sunday teach me the value of my soul and the way of life and salvation by Jesus Christ.

All went well with me till Monday morning, and then, whether the root had lost its virtue, or whether my tormentor had gone deeper into the black art than I had (as was sometimes said of him), or whether he had obtained a special indulgence for his faithful Sunday's worship, it is not necessary for me to know or to inform the reader; but this much I may say, the pious and benignant smile which graced the face of Covey on Sunday wholly disappeared on Monday.

Long before daylight I was called up to go feed, rub, and curry the horses. I obeyed the call, as I should have done had it been made at an earlier hour, for I had brought my mind to a firm resolve during that Sunday's reflection to obey every order, however unreasonable, if it were possible, and if Mr. Covey should then undertake to beat me to defend and protect myself to the best of my ability. My religious views on the subject of resisting my master had suffered a serious shock by the savage persecution to which I had been subjected, and my hands were no longer tied by my religion. Master Thomas's indifference had severed the last link. I had backslidden from this point in the slaves' religious creed, and I soon had occasion to make my fallen state known to my Sunday-pious brother, Covey.

While I was obeying his order to feed and get the horses ready for the field, and when I was in the act of going up the stable loft, for the purpose of throwing down some blades, Covey sneaked into the stable, in his peculiar way, and seizing me suddenly by the leg, he brought me to the stable floor, giving my newly-mended body a terrible jar. I now forgot all about my roots and remembered my pledge to stand up in my own defense. The brute was skillfully endeavoring to get a slipknot on my legs before I could draw up my feet. As soon as I found what he was up to, I gave a sudden spring (my two days' rest had been of much service to me) and by that means, no doubt, he was able to bring me to the floor so heavily. He was defeated in his plan of tying me. While down, he seemed to think that he had me very securely in his power. He little thought he was—as the rowdies say—in for a rough and tumble fight, but such was the fact. Whence came the daring spirit necessary to grapple with a man who, eight-and-forty hours before, could, with his slightest word, have made me tremble like a leaf in a storm, I do not know; at any rate, I was resolved to fight, and what was better still, I actually was hard at it. The fighting madness had come upon me, and I found my strong fingers firmly attached to the throat of the tyrant, as heedless of consequences, at the moment, as if we stood as equals before the law. The very color of the man was forgotten. I felt supple as a cat, and was ready for him at every turn. Every blow of his was parried, though I dealt no blows in return. I was strictly on the defensive, preventing him from injuring me, rather than trying to injure him. I flung him on the ground several times when he meant to have hurled me there. I held him so firmly by the throat that his blood followed my nails. He held me, and I held him.

All was fair thus far, and the contest was about equal. My resistance was entirely unexpected and Covey was taken all aback by it. He trembled in every limb. "Are you going to resist, you scoundrel?" said he. To which I returned a polite "Yes, sir," steadily gazing my interrogator in the eye, to meet the first approach or dawning of the blow which I expected my answer would call forth. But the conflict did not long remain equal. Covey soon cried lustily for help, not that I was obtaining any marked advantage over him, or was injuring him, but because he was gaining none over me, and was not able, single-handed, to conquer me. He called for his cousin Hughes to come to his assistance, and now the scene was changed. I was compelled to give blows, as well as to parry them, and since I was in any case to suffer for resistance, I felt (as the musty proverb goes) that I might as well be hanged for an old sheep as a lamb. I was still defensive toward Covey, but aggressive toward Hughes, on whom, at his first approach, I dealt a blow which fairly sickened him. He went off, bending over with pain, and manifesting no disposition to come again within my reach. The poor fellow was in the act of trying to catch and tie my right hand and, while flattering himself with success, I gave him the kick which sent him staggering away in pain at the same time that I held Covey with a firm hand.

Taken completely by surprise, Covey seemed to have lost his usual strength and coolness. He was frightened and stood puffing and blowing, seemingly unable to command words or blows. When he saw that Hughes was standing half bent with pain, his courage quite gone, the cowardly tyrant asked if I meant to persist in my resistance. I told him I did mean to resist, come what might, that I had been treated like a brute during the last six months, and that I should stand it no longer. With that he gave me a shake and attempted to drag me toward a stick of wood that was lying just outside the stable door. He meant to knock me down with it, but, just as he leaned over to get the stick, I seized him with both hands by the collar and with a vigorous and sudden snatch brought my assailant harmlessly, his full length, on the not over-clean ground, for we were now in the cowyard. He had selected the place for the fight, and it was but right that he should have all the advantages of his own selection.

By this time Bill, the hired man, came home. He had been to Mr. Helmsley's to spend Sunday with his nominal wife. Covey and I had been skirmishing from before daybreak till now. The sun was shooting his beams almost over the eastern woods, and we were still at it. I could not see where the matter was to terminate. He evidently was afraid to let me go, lest I should again make off to the woods; otherwise he would probably have obtained arms from the house to frighten me. Holding me, he called upon Bill to assist him. The scene here had something comic about it. Bill, who knew precisely what Covey wished him to do, affected ignorance and pretended he did not know what to do. "What shall I do, Master Covey?" said Bill. "Take hold of him! Take hold of him!" cried Covey. With a toss of his head, peculiar to Bill, he said, "Indeed, Master Covey, I want to go to work." "This is your work," said Covey, "take hold of him." Bill replied, with spirit, "My master hired me here to work, and not to help you whip Frederick." It was my turn to speak. "Bill," said I, "don't put your hands on me." To which he replied, "My God, Frederick, I ain't goin' to tech ye"; and Bill walked off, leaving Covey and myself to settle our differences as best we might.

But my present advantage was threatened when I saw Caroline (the slave woman of Covey) coming to the cowyard to milk, for she was a powerful woman and could have mastered me easily, exhausted as I was.

As soon as she came near, Covey attempted to rally her to his aid. Strangely and fortunately, Caroline was in no humor to take a hand in any such sport. We were all in open rebellion that morning. Caroline answered the command of her master to "take hold of me" precisely as Bill had done, but in her it was at far greater peril, for she was the slave of Covey, and he could do what he pleased with her. It was not so with Bill, and Bill knew it. Samuel Harris, to whom Bill belonged, did not allow his slaves to be beaten unless they were guilty of some crime which the law would punish. But poor Caroline, like myself, was at the mercy of the merciless Covey, nor did she escape the dire effects of her refusal: he gave her several sharp blows.

At length (two hours had elapsed) the contest was given over. Letting go of me, puffing and blowing at a great rate, Covey said, "Now, you scoundrel, go to your work; I would not have whipped you half so hard if you had not resisted." The fact was, he had not whipped me at all. He had not, in all the scuffle, drawn a single drop of blood from me. I had drawn blood from him and should even without this satisfaction have been victorious, because my aim had not been to injure him, but to prevent his injuring me.

During the whole six months that I lived with Covey after this transaction, he never again laid the weight of his finger on me in anger. He would occasionally say he did not want to have to get hold of me again —a declaration which I had no difficulty in believing—and I had a secret feeling which answered, "You had better not wish to get hold of me again, for you will be likely to come off worse in a second fight than you did in the first."

This battle with Mr. Covey, undignified as it was and as I fear my narration of it is, was the turning-point in my "life as a slave." It rekindled in my breast the smoldering embers of liberty. It brought up my Baltimore dreams and revived a sense of my own manhood. I was a changed being after that fight. I was nothing before—I was a man now.

It recalled to life my crushed self-respect and my self-confidence, and inspired me with a renewed determination to be a free man. A man without force is without the essential dignity of humanity. Human nature is so constituted, that it cannot honor a helpless man, though it can pity him, and even this it cannot do long if signs of power do not arise.

He only can understand the effect of this combat on my spirit, who has himself incurred something, or hazarded something, in repelling the unjust and cruel aggressions of a tyrant. Covey was a tyrant and a cowardly one withal. After resisting him, I felt as I had never felt before. It was a resurrection from the dark and pestiferous tomb of slavery, to the heaven of comparative freedom. I was no longer a servile coward, trembling under the frown of a brother worm of the dust, but my long-cowed spirit was roused to an attitude of independence. I had reached the point at which I was *not afraid to die*. This spirit made me a freeman in *fact*, though I still remained a slave in *form*. When a slave cannot be flogged, he is more than half free. He has a domain as broad as his own manly heart to defend, and he is really "a power on earth." From this time until my escape from slavery, I was never fairly whipped. Several attempts were made, but they were always unsuccessful. Bruised I did get, but the instance I have described was the end of the brutification to which slavery had subjected me.

The reader may like to know why, after I had so grievously offended Mr. Covey, he did not have me taken in hand by the authorities; indeed, why the law of Maryland, which assigned hanging to the slave who resisted his master, was not put in force against me; at any rate why I was not taken up, as was usual in such cases, and publicly whipped as an example to other slaves and as a means of deterring me from again committing the same offence. I confess that the easy manner in which I got off was always a surprise to me, and even now I cannot fully explain the cause, though the probability is that Covey was ashamed to have it known that he had been mastered by a boy of sixteen. He enjoyed the unbounded and very valuable reputation of being a first-rate overseer and Negro breaker, and by means of this reputation he was able to procure his hands at very trifling compensation and with very great ease. His interest and his pride would mutually suggest the wisdom of passing the matter by in silence. The story that he had undertaken to whip a lad and had been resisted would of itself be damaging to him in the estimation of slaveholders.

It is perhaps not altogether creditable to my natural temper that after this conflict with Mr. Covey I did, at times, purposely aim to provoke him to an attack, by refusing to keep with the other hands in the field, but I could never bully him to another battle. I was determined on doing him serious damage if he ever again attempted to lay violent hands on me.

Hereditary bondmen, know ye not
Who would be free, themselves must strike the blow?

LUNSFORD LANE

Born a slave, Lunsford Lane earned money by preparing tobacco for market and succeeded in buying his freedom. He set up business in Raleigh, North Carolina. But he was forced, as a free black man, to leave the state and traveled to New York and Boston where he spoke to abolitionist audiences. When he returned to Raleigh to settle his affairs and buy the freedom of his wife and children, he was jailed, tarred and feathered, and driven out once more. An able man, with many influential white friends, he was nevertheless brutally and unjustly treated and barely escaped with his life. *The Narrative of Lunsford Lane*, from which the following passages come, was published in 1845. A later edition prepared by Reverend William G. Hawkins appeared in 1863.

Tar and Feathers

The small city of Raleigh, North Carolina, it is known, is the capital of the state, situated in the interior and containing about thirty-six hundred inhabitants. Here lived Mr. Sherwood Haywood: a man of considerable respectability, a planter, and the cashier of a bank. He owned three plantations—at the distances, respectively, of seventy-five, thirty, and three miles from his residence in Raleigh. He owned in all about two hundred and fifty slaves, among the rest my mother, who was a house servant to her master and, of course, a resident in the city. My father was a slave to a near neighbor. The apartment where I was born, and where I spent my childhood and youth, was called "the kitchen," situated some fifteen or twenty rods from the "great house." Here the house servants lodged and lived, and here the meals were prepared for the people in the mansion. The "field hands," of course, reside upon the plantation.

On the 30th of May, 1803, I was ushered into the world; but I did not begin to see the rising of its dark clouds, nor fancy how they might be broken and dispersed, until some time afterwards. My infancy was spent upon the floor in a rough cradle, or sometimes in my mother's arms; my early boyhood, in playing with the other boys and girls, colored and white, in the yard, and occasionally doing such little matters of labor as one of so young years could. I knew no difference between myself and the white children; nor did they seem to know any in turn. Sometimes my master would come out and give a biscuit to me, and another to one of his own white boys; but I did not perceive the difference between us. I had no brothers or sisters, but there were other colored families living in the same kitchen and children playing in the same yard with me and my mother.

When I was ten or eleven years old, my master set me regularly to cutting wood in the yard in the winter and working in the garden in the summer. And when I was fifteen years of age, he gave me the care of the pleasure horses and made me his carriage driver; but this did not exempt me from other labor, especially in the summer. Early in the morning, I used to take his three horses to the plantation and turn them into the pasture to graze, and myself into the cotton or cornfield, with a hoe in my hand, to work through the day. After sunset, I would take these horses back to the city (a distance of three miles), feed them, and then attend to any other business my master or any of his family had for me to do until bed time, when, with my blanket in my hand, I would go into the dining room to rest through the night. The next day the same round of labor would be repeated, unless some of the family wished to ride out, in which case I must be on hand with the horses to wait upon them and in the meantime to work about the yard. On Sunday I had to drive to church twice, which, with other things necessary to be done, took the whole day. So my life went wearily on from day to day, from night to night, and from week to week.

When I began to work, I discovered the difference between myself and my master's white children. They began to order me about and were told to do so by my master and mistress. I found, too, that they had learned to read, while I was not permitted to have a book in my hand. To be in the possession of anything written or printed was regarded as an offense. And then there was the fear that I might be sold away from those who were dear to me and conveyed to the far south. I had learned that being a slave, I was subject to this worst (to us) of all calamities, and I knew of others in similar situations to myself thus sold away. My friends were not numerous, but in proportion as they were few they were dear; and the thought that I might be separated from them forever was like that of having the heart torn from its socket; while the idea of being conveyed to the far south seemed infinitely worse than the terrors of death. To know, also, that I was never to consult my own will, but was, while I lived, to be entirely under the control of another was another state of mind hard for me to bear. Indeed, all things now made me *feel*, what I had before known only in words, that *I was a slave.* Deep was this feeling, and it preyed upon my heart like a never-dying worm. I saw no prospect that my condition would ever be changed. Yet I used to plan in my mind from day to day, and from night to night, how I might be free.

One day, while I was in this state of mind, my father gave me a small basket of peaches. I sold them for thirty cents, which was the first money I ever had in my life. Afterwards, I won some marbles and sold them for sixty cents, and some weeks after Mr. Hog, from Fayetteville, came to visit my master and on leaving gave me one dollar. After that, Mr. Bennahan, from Orange county, gave me a dollar, and a son of my master fifty cents. These sums and the hope that then entered my mind of purchasing at some future time my freedom made me long for money; and plans for money-making took the principal possession of my thoughts. At night I would steal away with my axe, get a load of wood to cut for twenty-five cents, and the next morning hardly escape a whipping for the offense. But I persevered until I had obtained twenty dollars. Now I began to think seriously of becoming able to buy myself; and, cheered by this hope, I went on from one thing to another, laboring "at dead of night," after the long weary day's toil for my master was over, till I found I had collected one hundred dollars. This sum I kept hid, first in one place and then in another, as I dare not put it out, for fear I should lose it.

After this, I lit upon a plan which proved of great advantage to me. My father suggested a mode of preparing smoking tobacco, different from any then or since employed. It had the double advantage of giving the tobacco a peculiarly pleasant flavor and of enabling me to manufacture a good article out of a very indifferent material. I improved somewhat upon his suggestion, and commenced the manufacture, doing, as I have before said, all my work in the night. The tobacco I put up in papers of about a quarter of a pound each, and sold them at fifteen cents. But the tobacco could not be smoked without a pipe, and, as I had given the former a flavor peculiarly grateful, it occurred to me that I might so construct a pipe as to cool the smoke in passing through it and thus meet the wishes of those who are more fond of smoke than heat. This I effected by means of a reed that grows plentifully in that region. I made a passage through the reed with a hot wire, polished it, and attached a clay pipe to the end so that the smoke should be cooled in flowing through the stem, like whiskey or rum in passing from the boiler through the worm of the still. These pipes I sold at ten cents a piece. In the early part of the night I would sell my tobacco and pipes, and manufacture them in the latter part. As the Legislature sat in Raleigh every year, I sold these articles considerably to the members, so that I became known, not only in the city but in many parts of the state, as a tobacconist.

Perceiving that I was getting along so well, I began, slave as I was, to think about taking a wife. So I fixed my mind upon Miss Lucy Williams, a slave of Thomas Devereaux, Esq., an eminent lawyer in the place, but failed in my undertaking. Then I thought I never would marry; but at the end of two or three years my resolution began to slide away, till, finding I could not keep it longer, I set out once more in pursuit of a wife. So I fell in with her to whom I am now united, Miss Martha Curtis, and the bargain between *us* was completed. I next went to her master, Mr. Boylan, and asked him, according to the custom, if I might "marry his woman." His reply was, "Yes, if you will behave yourself." I told him I would. "And make her behave herself?" To this I also assented and then proceeded to ask the approbation of my master, which was granted. So in May, 1828, I was bound as fast in wedlock as a slave can be. God may at any time sunder that band in a freeman; either master may do the same at pleasure in a slave. The bond is not recognized in law. But in my case it has never been broken, and now it cannot be, except by a higher power.

When we had been married nine months and one day, we were blessed with a son, and two years afterwards with a daughter. My wife also passed from the hands of Mr. Boylan into those of Mr. Benjamin B. Smith, a merchant, a member and class leader in the Methodist church, and in much repute for his deep piety and devotion to religion. But grace (of course) had not wrought in the same *manner* upon the heart of Mr. Smith as nature had done upon that of Mr. Boylan, who made no religious profession. This latter gentleman used to give my wife, who was a favorite slave (her mother nursed every one of his own children), sufficient food and clothing to render her comfortable, so that I had to spend for her but little, except to procure such small articles of extra comfort as I was prompted to from time to time. Indeed, Mr. Boylan was regarded as a very kind master to all the slaves about him—that is, to his house servants. Nor did he personally inflict much cruelty, if any, upon his field hands. The overseer on his nearest plantation (I know but little about the rest) was a very cruel man. In one instance, as it was said among the slaves, he whipped a man to death. But, of course, he denied that the man died in consequence of the whipping. Still, it was the choice of my wife to pass into the hands of Mr. Smith, as she had become attached to him in consequence of belonging to the same church and receiving his religious instruction and counsel as her class leader, and in consequence of the peculiar devotedness to the cause of religion for which he was noted, and which he always seemed to manifest. But when she became his slave, he withheld, both from her and her children, the needful food and clothing, while he exacted from them to the uttermost all the labor they were able to perform. Almost every article of clothing worn either by my wife or children, especially every article of much value, I had to purchase; while the food he furnished the family amounted to less than a meal a day and that of the coarser kind. I have no remembrance that he ever gave us a blanket or any other article of bedding, although it is considered a rule at the South that the master shall furnish each of his slaves with one blanket a year. So that, both as to food and clothing, I had in fact to support both my wife and the children, while he claimed them as his property and received all their labor. She was a house servant to Mr. Smith, sometimes cooked the food for his family, and usually took it from the table. But her mistress was so particular in giving it out to be cooked, or so watched it, that she always knew whether it was all returned, and when the table was cleared away, the stern old lady would sit by and see that every dish (except the very little she would send into the kitchen) was put away, and then she would turn the key upon it so as to be sure her slaves should not die of gluttony. This practice is common with some families in that region, but with others it is not. It was not so in that of her less pious master, Mr. Boylan, nor was it precisely so at my master's. We used to have corn bread enough and some meat. When I was a boy, the pot liquor, in which the meat was boiled for the "great house," together with some little cornmeal balls that had been thrown in just before the meat was done, was poured into a tray and set in the middle of the yard, and a clamshell or pewter spoon given to each of us children, who would fall upon the delicious fare as greedily as pigs. It was not generally as much as we wanted; consequently, it was customary for some of the white persons who saw us from the piazza of the house where they were sitting to order the more stout and greedy ones to eat slower, that those more young and feeble might have a chance. But it was not so with Mr. Smith; such luxuries were more than he could afford, kind and Christian man as he was considered to be. So that, by the expense of providing for my wife and children, all the money I had earned and could earn, by my night labor, was consumed, till I found myself reduced to five dollars, and this I lost one day in going to the plantation. My light of hope now went out. My prop seemed to have given way from under me. Sunk in the very night of despair respecting my freedom, I discovered myself, as though I had never known it before, a husband, the father of two children, a family looking up to me for bread, and I a slave, penniless, and well watched by my master, his wife, and his children lest I should, perchance, catch the friendly light of the stars to make something in order to supply the cravings of nature in those with whom my soul was bound up, or lest some plan of freedom might lead me to trim the light of diligence after the day's labor was over, while the rest of the world were enjoying the hours in pleasure or sleep.

At this time an event occurred, which, while it cast a cloud over the prospects of some of my fellow slaves, was a rainbow over mine. My master died and his widow, by the will, became sole executrix of his property. To the surprise of all, the bank of which he had been cashier presented a claim against the estate for forty thousand dollars. By a compromise, this sum was reduced to twenty thousand dollars, and my mistress, to meet the amount, sold some of her slaves and hired out others. I hired my time of her,° for which I paid her a price varying from one hundred dollars to one hundred and twenty dollars per year. This was a privilege which comparatively few slaves at the South enjoy, and in this I felt truly blessed.

I commenced the manufacture of pipes and tobacco on an enlarged scale. I opened a regular place of business, labelled my tobacco in a conspicuous manner with the names of "Edward and Lunsford Lane," and of some of the persons who sold it for me—establishing agencies for the sale in various parts of the State: one at Fayetteville, one at Salisbury, one at Chapel Hill, and so on—sold my articles from my place of business and about town also deposited them in stores on commission. And thus, after paying my mistress for my time and rendering such support as was necessary to my family, I found in the space of some six or

---

° It is contrary to the laws of the state for a slave to have command of his own time in this way, but in Raleigh it is sometimes winked at. I knew one slave-man, who was *doing well for himself*, taken up by the public authorities and hired out for the public good, three times in succession for this offense. The time of hiring in such a case is one year. The master is subject to a fine. But generally, as I have said, if the slave is *orderly* and appears to be *making nothing*, neither he nor the master is interfered with.

eight years that I had collected the sum of one thousand dollars. During this time I had found it politic to go shabbily dressed and to appear to be very poor, but to pay my mistress for my services promptly. I kept my money hid, never venturing to put out a penny, nor to let anybody but my wife know that I was making any. The thousand dollars was what I supposed my mistress would ask for me, and so I determined now what I would do.

I went to my mistress and inquired what was her price for me. She said a thousand dollars. I then told her that I wanted to be free and asked her if she would sell me to be made free. She said she would, and accordingly I arranged with her and with the master of my wife, Mr. Smith, already spoken of, for the latter to take my money° and buy of her my freedom, as I could not legally purchase it and as the laws forbid emancipation except for "meritorious services." This done, Mr. Smith endeavored to emancipate me formally and to get my manumission recorded. I tried also, but the court judged that I had done nothing "meritorious," and so I remained, nominally only, the slave of Mr. Smith for a year. Feeling unsafe in that relation, I accompanied him to New York, whither he was going to purchase goods, and was there regularly and formally made a freeman, and there my manumission was recorded. I returned to my family in Raleigh and endeavored to do by them as a freeman should. I had known what it was to be a slave, and I knew what it was to be free.

But I am going too rapidly over my story. When the money was paid to my mistress and the conveyance fairly made to Mr. Smith, I felt that I was free. And a queer and a joyous feeling it is to one who has been a slave. I cannot describe it; only it seemed as though I was in heaven. I used to lie awake whole nights thinking of it. And oh, the strange thoughts that passed through my soul, like so many rivers of light—deep and rich were their waves as they rolled. These were more to me than sleep, more than soft slumber after long months of watching over the decaying, fading frame of a friend and the loved one laid to rest in the dust. But I cannot describe my feelings to those who have never been slaves; then why should I attempt it? He who has passed from spiritual death to life and received the witness within his soul that his sins are

---

° *Legally*, my money belonged to my mistress; and she could have taken it and refused to grant me my freedom. But she was a very kind woman for a slave owner, and she would under the circumstances scorn to do such a thing. I have known of slaves, however, served in this way.

forgiven may possibly form some distant idea, like the ray of the setting sun from the far off mountain top, of the emotions of an emancipated slave. That opens heaven. To break the bonds of slavery opens up at once both earth and heaven. Neither can be truly seen by us while we are slaves.

And now will the reader take with me a brief review of the road I had trodden. I cannot here dwell upon its dark shades, though some of these were black as the pencilings of midnight, but upon the light that had followed my path from my infancy up, and had at length conducted me quite out of the deep abyss of bondage. There is a hymn opening with the following stanza, which very much expresses my feelings:

> When all thy mercies, Oh my God,
>   My rising soul surveys,
> Transported with the view, I'm lost
>   In wonder, love, and praise.

I had endured what a freeman would indeed call hard fare. But my lot, on the whole, had been a favored one for a slave. It is known that there is a wide difference in the situations of what are termed house servants, and plantation hands. I, though sometimes employed upon the plantation, belonged to the former, which is the favored class. My master, too, was esteemed a kind and humane man. Altogether, I fared quite differently from many poor fellows whom it makes my blood run chill to think of: confined to the plantation, with not enough of food and that little of the coarsest kind to satisfy the gnawings of hunger; compelled oftentimes to hie away in the nighttime, when worn down with work, and *steal* (if it be stealing) and privately devour such things as they can lay their hands upon; made to feel the rigors of bondage with no cessation; torn away sometimes from the few friends they love, friends doubly dear because they are few, and transported to a climate where in a few hard years they die; or, at best, conducted heavily and sadly to their resting place under the sod, upon their old master's plantation; sometimes, perhaps, enlivening the air with merriment, but a forced merriment that comes from a stagnant or a stupefied heart. Such as this is the fate of the plantation slaves generally; but such was not my lot. My way was comparatively light and, what is better, it conducted to freedom. And my wife and children were with me. After my master died, my mistress sold a number of her slaves from their families and friends—but not me. She sold several children from their parents—but

my children were with me still. She sold two husbands from their wives
—but I was still with mine. She sold one wife from her husband—but
mine had not been sold from me. The master of my wife, Mr. Smith,
had separated members of families by sale—but not of mine. With me
and my house the tenderer tendrils of the heart still clung to where the
vine had entwined; pleasant was its shade and delicious its fruits to our
taste, though we knew and, what is more, we *felt* that we were slaves.
But all around I could see where the vine had been torn down, and its
bleeding branches told of vanished joys and of new wrought sorrows
such as, slave though I was, had never entered into my practical experience.

I had never been permitted to learn to read, but I used to attend
church and there I received instruction which I trust was of some
benefit to me. I trusted, too, that I had experienced the renewing in-
fluences of the gospel, and, after obtaining from my mistress a written
permit (a thing *always* required in such a case), I had been baptized
and received into fellowship with the Baptist denomination. So that in
religious matters I had been indulged in the exercise of my own conscience—a favor not always granted to slaves. Indeed I, with others,
was often told by the minister how good God was in bringing us over to
this country from dark and benighted Africa and permitting us to listen
to the sound of the gospel. To me, God also granted temporal freedom,
which man, without God's consent, had stolen away.

I often heard select portions of the scriptures read. And on the Sabbath there was one sermon preached expressly for the colored people
that was generally my privilege to hear. I became quite familiar with
the texts, "Servants be obedient to your masters," "Not with eye service
as men pleasers," "He that knoweth his master's will and doeth it not,
shall be beaten with many stripes," and others of this class, for they
formed the basis of most of these public instructions to us. The first
commandment impressed upon our minds was to obey our masters, and
the second was like unto it, namely, to do as much work when they or
the overseers were not watching us as when they were. But connected
with these instructions there was more or less that was truly excellent,
though mixed up with much that would sound strangely in the ears of
freedom. There was one very kindhearted Episcopal minister whom I
often used to hear; he was very popular with the colored people. But
after he had preached a sermon to us in which he argued from the Bible
that it was the will of heaven from all eternity we should be slaves and

our masters be our owners, most of us left him. For, like some of the faint hearted disciples in early times, we said, "This is a hard saying, who can bear it?"

My manumission, as I shall call it—that is, the bill of sale conveying me to Mr. Smith, was dated September 9, 1835. I continued in the tobacco and pipe business as already described, to which I added a small trade in a variety of articles. Also, some two years before I left Raleigh, I entered into a considerable business in wood, which I used to purchase by the acre standing, cut it, haul it into the city, deposit it in a yard, and sell it out as I advantageously could. Also, I was employed about the office of the Governor, as I shall hereafter relate. I used to keep one or two horses and various vehicles, by which I did a variety of work at hauling about town. Of course, I had to hire more or less help to carry on my business.

In the manufacture of tobacco I met with considerable competition, but none that materially injured me. The method of preparing it having originated with me and my father, we found it necessary, in order to secure the advantage of the invention, to keep it to ourselves and decline, though often solicited, going into partnership with others. Those who undertook the manufacture could neither give the article a flavor so pleasant as ours nor manufacture it so cheaply; so they either failed in it, or succeeded but poorly.

Not long after obtaining my own freedom, I began seriously to think about purchasing the freedom of my family. The first proposition was that I should buy my wife, and that we should jointly labor to obtain the freedom of the children afterwards, as we were able. But that idea was abandoned when her master, Mr. Smith, refused to sell her to me for less than one thousand dollars, a sum which then appeared too much for me to raise.

Afterwards, however, I conceived the idea of purchasing at once the entire family. I went to Mr. Smith to learn his price, which he put at *three thousand dollars* for my wife and six children, the number we then had. This seemed a large sum, both because it was a great deal for me to raise, and also because Mr. Smith, when he bought my wife and *two* children, had actually paid but five hundred and sixty dollars for them and had received, ever since, their labor; while I had almost entirely supported them, both as to food and clothing. Altogether, therefore, the case seemed a hard one, but as I was entirely in his power I must do the best I could. At length he concluded, perhaps partly of his own motion and partly through the persuasion of a friend, to sell the family for twenty-five hundred dollars, as I wished to free them, though he contended still that they were worth three thousand dollars. Perhaps they would at that time have brought this larger sum, if sold for the southern market. The arrangement with Mr. Smith was made in December 1838. I gave him five notes of five hundred dollars each, the first due in January 1840, and one in January each succeeding year; for which he transferred my family into my own possession, with a bond to give me a bill of sale when I should pay the notes. With this arrangement, we found ourselves living in our own house—a house which I had previously purchased—in January, 1839.

After moving my family, my wife was for a short time sick, in consequence of her labor and the excitement in moving and her excessive joy. I told her that it reminded me of a poor shoemaker in the neighborhood who purchased a ticket in a lottery. Not expecting to draw, the fact of his purchasing it had passed out of his mind. But one day, as he was at work on his last, he was informed that his ticket had drawn the liberal prize of ten thousand dollars, and the poor man was so overjoyed that he fell back on his seat and immediately expired.

In this new and joyful situation we found ourselves getting along very well, until September 1840, when, to my surprise, as I was passing the street one day, engaged in my business, the following note was handed me. "Read it," said the officer, "or if you cannot read, get some white man to read it to you." Here it is, verbatim:

To Lunsford Lane, a free man of Color:

Take notice, that whereas complaint has been made to us, two Justices of the Peace for the county of Wake and State of North Carolina, that you are a free Negro from another State, who has migrated into this State contrary to the provisions of the act of assembly concerning free Negroes and mulattoes, now notice is given you that unless you leave and remove out of this State within twenty days, that you will be proceeded against for the penalty prescribed by said act of assembly, and be otherwise dealt with as the law directs. Given under our hands and seals this the 5th Sept. 1840.

WILLIS SCOTT, JP (Seal)
JORDAN WOMBLE, JP (Seal)

This was a terrible blow to me, for it prostrated at once all my hopes in my cherished object of obtaining the freedom of my family and led me to expect nothing but a separation from them forever.

In order that the reader may understand the full force of the foregoing notice, I will copy the law of the State under which it was issued:

Sec. 65. It shall not be lawful for any free Negro or mulatto to migrate into this State: and if he or she shall do so, contrary to the provisions of this act, and being thereof informed, shall not, within twenty days thereafter, remove out of the State, he or she being thereof convicted in the manner hereafter directed, shall be liable to a penalty of five hundred dollars; and upon failure to pay the same, within the time prescribed in the judgment awarded against such person or persons, he or she shall be liable to be held in servitude and at labor a term of time not exceeding ten years, in such manner and upon such terms as may be provided by the court awarding such sentence, and the proceeds arising therefrom shall be paid over to the county trustee for county purposes: Provided, that in case any free Negro or mulatto shall pay the penalty of five hundred dollars, according to the provisions of this act, it shall be the duty of such free Negro or mulatto to remove him or herself out of this State within twenty days thereafter, and for every such failure, he or she shall be subject to the like penalty as is prescribed for a failure to remove in the first instance.—*Revised Statutes North Carolina, chap.* 111.

The next section provides that if the free person of color so notified does not leave within the twenty days after receiving the notice, he may be arrested on a warrant from any Justice and be held to bail for his appearance at the next county court, when he will be subject to the penalties specified above, or, in case of his failure to give bonds, he may be sent to jail.

I made known my situation to my friends, and, after taking legal counsel, it was determined to induce, if possible, the complainants to prosecute no farther at present, and then as the legislature of the state was to sit in about two months, to petition that body for permission to remain in the state until I could complete the purchase of my family. After which, I was willing, if necessary, to leave.

From January 1, 1837, I had been employed, as I have mentioned, in the office of the governor of the state, principally under the direction of his private secretary, in keeping the office in order, taking the letters to the Post Office, and doing such other duties of the sort as occurred from time to time. This circumstance, with the fact of the high standing in the city of the family of my former master and of the former masters of my wife, had given me the friendship of the first people in the place generally, who from that time forward acted towards me the friendly part.

Mr. Battle, then private secretary to Governor Dudley, addressed the following letter to the prosecuting attorney in my behalf:

Raleigh, Nov. 3, 1840

DEAR SIR:—Lunsford Lane, a free man of color, has been in the employ of the State under me since my entering on my present situation. I understand that under a law of the State, he has been notified to leave, and that the time is now at hand.

In the discharge of the duties I had from him, I have found him prompt, obedient and faithful. At this particular time, his absence to me would be much regretted, as I am now just fixing up my books and other papers in the new office, and I shall not have time to learn another what he can already do so well. With me the period of the Legislature is a very busy one, and I am compelled to have a servant who understands the business I want done, and one I can trust. I would not wish to be an obstacle in the execution of any law, but the enforcing of the one against him will be doing me a serious inconvenience, and the object of this letter is to ascertain whether I could not procure a suspension of the sentence till after the adjournment of the Legislature, say about 1st January, 1841.

I should feel no hesitation in giving my word that he will conduct himself orderly and obediently.

I am, most respectfully,
Your obedient servant,
C. C. Battle

G. W. Haywood
Attorney at Law, Raleigh, N. C.

To the above letter the following reply was made:

Raleigh, Nov. 3, 1840

MY DEAR SIR:—I have no objection, so far as I am concerned, that all further proceedings against Lunsford should be postponed until after the adjournment of the Legislature.

The process now out against him is one issued by two magistrates, Messrs. Willis Scott and Jordan Womble, over which I have no control. You had better see them to-day, and perhaps, at your request, they will delay further action on the subject.

Respectfully yours,
Geo. W. Haywood

Mr. Battle then enclosed the foregoing correspondence to Messrs. Scott and Womble, requesting their "favorable consideration." They returned the correspondence, but neglected to make any reply.

In consequence, however, of this action on the part of my friends, I was permitted to remain without further interruption until the day the Legislature commenced its session. On that day a warrant was served upon me, to appear before the county court, to answer for the sin of having remained in the place of my birth for the space of twenty days and more after being warned out. I escaped going to jail through the kindness of Mr. Haywood, a son of my former master, and Mr. Smith, who jointly became security for my appearance at court.

This was on Monday. On Wednesday I appeared before the court, but as my prosecutors were not ready for the trial, the case was laid over three months, to the next term.

I then proceeded to get up a petition to the Legislature. It required much hard labor and persuasion on my part to start it. But after that, I readily obtained the signatures of the principal men in the place. Then I went round to the members, many of whom were known to me, calling upon them at their rooms and urging them for my sake, for humanity's sake, for the sake of my wife and little ones, whose hopes had been excited by the idea that they were even now free. I appealed to them as husbands, fathers, brothers, sons, to vote in favor of my petition and allow me to remain in the state long enough to purchase my family. I was doing well in business and it would be but a short time before I could accomplish the object. Then, if it was desired, I and my wife and children, redeemed from bondage, would together seek a more friendly home, beyond the dominion of slavery. The following is the petition presented, endorsed as the reader will see:

To the Hon. General Assembly of the State of North Carolina

GENTLEMEN:—The petition of Lunsford Lane humbly shews—That about five years ago he purchased his freedom from his mistress, Mrs. Sherwood Haywood, and by great economy and industry has paid the purchase money; that he has a wife and seven children, whom he has agreed to purchase, and for whom he has paid a part of the purchase money; but not having paid in full, is not yet able to leave the State, without parting with his wife and children.

Your petitioner prays your Honorable Body to pass a law allowing him to remain a limited time within the State, until he can remove his family also. Your petitioner will give bond and good security for his good behavior while he remains.

Your petitioner will ever pray, &c.

Lunsford Lane

The undersigned are well acquainted with Lunsford Lane, the petitioner, and join in his petition to the Assembly for relief.

Charles Manly	Drury Lacy
R. W. Haywood	Will. Peck
Eleanor Haywood	W. A. Stith
William Hill	A. B. Stith
R. Smith	J. Brown
William Peace	William White
Jos. Peace	George Simpson
William M'Pheeters	Jno. I. Christophers
William Boylan	John Primrose
Fabius J. Haywood	Hugh M'Queen
D. W. Stone	Alex. J. Lawrence
T. Merideth	C. L. Hinton
A. J. Battle	

Lunsford Lane, the petitioner herein, has been servant to the Executive Office since the 1st of January, 1837, and it gives me pleasure to state that, during the whole time, without exception, I have found him faithful and obedient, in keeping every thing committed to his care in good condition. From what I have seen of his conduct and demeanor, I cheerfully join in the petition for his relief.

C. C. Battle, *P. Secretary to Gov. Dudley.*
Raleigh, Nov. 20, 1840.

The foregoing petition was presented to the Senate. It was there referred to a committee. I knew when the committee was to report and watched about the State House that I might receive the earliest news of the fate of my petition. I should have gone within the senate chamber, but no colored man has that permission. I do not know why, unless for fear he may hear the name of *Liberty*. By and by a member came out and as he passed me said, "Well, Lunsford, they have laid you out; the nigger bill is killed." I need not tell the reader that my feelings did not enter into the merriment of this honorable senator. To me, the fate of my petition was the last blow to my hopes. I had done all I could do, had said all I could say, laboring night and day to obtain a favorable reception to my petition; but all in vain. Nothing appeared before me but

I must leave the state and leave my wife and my children, never to see them more. My friends had also done all they could for me.

And why must I be banished? Ever after I entertained the first idea of being free, I had endeavored so to conduct myself as not to become obnoxious to the white inhabitants, knowing as I did their power and their hostility to the colored people. The two points necessary in such a case I had kept constantly in mind. First, I had made no display of the little property or money I possessed, but in every way I wore as much as possible the aspect of poverty. Second, I had never appeared to be even so intelligent as I really was. This all colored people at the South, free and slaves, find it peculiarly necessary to their own comfort and safety to observe.

I should, perhaps, have mentioned that on the same day I received the notice to leave Raleigh, similar notices were presented to two other free colored people who had been slaves, were trying to purchase their families, and were otherwise in a like situation to myself. And they took the same course I did to endeavor to remain a limited time. Isaac Hunter, who had a family with five children, was one, and Waller Freeman, who had six children, was the other. Mr. Hunter's petition went before mine, and a bill of some sort passed the Senate, that was so cut down in the Commons as to allow him only *twenty days* to remain in the State. He has since, however, obtained the freedom of his family, who are living with him in Philadelphia.

Mr. Freeman's petition received no better fate than mine. His family were the property of Judge Badger, who was afterwards made a member of Mr. Harrison's cabinet. When Mr. Badger removed to Washington, he took with him among other slaves this family, and Freeman removed also to that city. After this, when Mr. Badger resigned his office, with the other members of the cabinet, under President Tyler, he entered into some sort of contract with Freeman to sell him this family, which he left at Washington, while he took the rest of his slaves back to Raleigh. Freeman is now endeavoring to raise money to make the purchase.

It was now between two and three months to the next session of the court. I knew that before or at that time I must leave the state. I was bound to appear before the court, but it had been arranged between my lawyer and the prosecuting attorney that if I would leave the state and pay the costs of court, the case should be dropped so that my bondsmen should not be involved. I therefore concluded to stay as long as I possibly could and then leave. I also determined to appeal to the kindness of the friends of the colored man in the North for assistance, though I had but little hope of succeeding in this way. Yet it was the only course I could think of by which I could see any possible hope of accomplishing the object.

I had paid Mr. Smith six hundred and twenty dollars and had a house and lot worth five hundred dollars, which he had promised to take when I had raised the balance. He gave me also a bill of sale for one of my children, Laura, in consideration of two hundred and fifty dollars of the money already paid. Her I determined to take with me to the North. The costs of court, which I had to meet, amounted to between thirty and forty dollars, besides the fee of my lawyer.

On May 18, 1841, three days after the court commenced its session, I bid adieu to my friends in Raleigh and set out for the city of New York. I took with me a letter of introduction and recommendation from Mr. John Primrose (a very estimable man), a recommendatory certificate from Mr. Battle, and a letter from the church of which I was a member, together with such papers relating to the affair as I had in my possession. Also I received the following:

Raleigh, N. C., May, 1841

The bearer, Lunsford Lane, a free man of color, for some time a resident in this place, being about to leave North Carolina in search of a more favorable location to pursue his trade, has desired us to give him a certificate of his good conduct heretofore.

We take pleasure in saying that his habits are temperate and industrious, that his conduct has been orderly and proper, and that he has for these qualities been distinguished among his caste.

William Hill	R. Smith
Weston R. Gales	C. Dewey
C. L. Hinton	

The above was certified to officially in the usual form by the clerk of the Court of Common Pleas and Quarter Sessions.

My success in New York was at first small. But at length I fell in with two friends who engaged to raise for me three hundred dollars, provided I should first obtain from other sources the balance of the sum required, which balance would be one thousand and eighty dollars. Thus encouraged, I proceeded to Boston, and in the city and vicinity the needful sum was contributed by about April 1, 1842. My thanks I have endeavored to express in my poor way to the many friends who so kindly and liberally assisted me. I cannot reward them. I hope they will receive their reward in another world. If the limits of this publication would permit, I should like to record the names of many to whom I am very especially indebted for their kindness and aid, not only in contributing, but in introducing me, and opening various ways of access to others.

On the fifth of February, 1842, finding that I should soon have in my possession the sum necessary to procure my family, and fearing that there might be danger in visiting Raleigh for that purpose, in consequence of the strong opposition of many of the citizens against colored people, their opposition to me, and their previously persecuting me from the city, I wrote to Mr. Smith, requesting him to see the Governor and obtain, under his hand, a permit to visit the State for a sufficient time to accomplish this business. I requested Mr. Smith to publish the permit in one or two of the city papers and then to enclose the original to me. This letter he answered, under date of Raleigh, February 19, 1842, as follows:

Lunsford:—Your letter of the 5th inst. came duly to hand, and in reply I have to inform you, that owing to the absence of Gov. Morehead, I cannot send you the permit you requested, but this will make no difference, for you can come home, and after your arrival you can obtain one to remain long enough to settle up your affairs. You ought of course to apply to the Governor immediately on your arrival, before any malicious person would have time to inform against you; I don't think by pursuing this course you need apprehend any danger.

We are all alive at present in Raleigh on the subjects of temperance and religion. We have taken into the temperance societies about five hundred members, and about fifty persons have been happily converted. The work seems still to be spreading, and such a time I have never seen before in my life. Glorious times truly.

Do try to get all the religion in your heart you possibly can, for it is the only thing worth having after all.

Your, &c.

B. B. Smith

The way now appeared to be in a measure open. Also, I thought that the religious and temperance interest mentioned in the latter portion of Mr. Smith's letter augured a state of feeling which would be a protection to me. But fearing still that there might be danger in visiting Raleigh without the permit from the Governor or at least wishing to take every possible precaution, I addressed another letter to Mr. Smith and received under date of March 12th a reply, from which I copy as follows:

The Governor has just returned, and I called upon him to get the permit, as you requested, but he said he had no authority by law to grant one; and *he told me to say to you that you might in perfect safety come home* in a quiet manner, and remain twenty days without being interrupted. I also consulted Mr. Manly, (a lawyer,) and he *told me the same thing. Surely you need not fear any thing under these circumstances. You had therefore better come on just as soon as possible.*

I need not say, what the reader has already seen, that my life so far had been one of joy succeeding sorrow and sorrow following joy, of hope, of despair, of bright prospects, of gloom, and of as many hues as ever appear on the varied sky—from the black of midnight or of the deep brown of a tempest, to the bright warm glow of a clear noon day.

On the eleventh of April, it was noon with me. I left Boston on my way for Raleigh with high hopes, intending to pay over the money for my family and return with them to Boston, which I designed should be my future home. For there I had found friends, and there I would find a grave. The visit I was making to the South was to be a farewell one, and I did not dream that my old cradle, hard as it once had jostled me, would refuse to rock me a pleasant, or even an affectionate, good bye. I thought, too, that the assurances I had received from the Governor through Mr. Smith, and the assurances of other friends, were a sufficient guaranty that I might visit the home of my boyhood, of my youth, of my manhood, in peace, especially as I was to stay but for a few days and then to return. With these thoughts and with the thoughts of my family and freedom I pursued my way to Raleigh, and arrived there on the twenty-third of the month. It was Saturday, about four o'clock, p.m., when I found myself once more in the midst of my family. With them I remained over the Sabbath, as it was sweet to spend a little time with them after so long an absence, an absence filled with so much of interest to us, and as I could not do any business until the beginning of the week. On Monday morning, between eight and nine o'clock, while I was making ready to leave the house for the first time after my arrival, to go to the store of Mr. Smith, where I was to transact my business with him, two constables, Messrs. Murray and Scott, entered, accompanied by two other men, and summoned me to appear immediately before the police. I accordingly accompanied them to the City Hall, but as it was locked and the officers could not at once find the key, we were told that the court would be held in Mr. Smith's store, a large and commodious room. This was what is termed in common phrase, in Raleigh, a "call court." The Mayor, Mr. Loring, presided, assisted by William Boylan and Jonathan Busbye, Esqs., Justices of the Peace. There were a large number of people together—more than could obtain admission to the room—and a large company of mobocratic spirits crowded around the door. Mr. Loring read the writ, setting forth that I had been guilty of delivering abolition lectures in the State of Massachusetts. He asked me whether I was guilty or not guilty. I told him I did not know whether I had given abolition lectures or not, but if it pleased the court I would relate the course I had pursued during my absence from Raleigh. He then said that I was at liberty to speak.

The circumstances under which I left Raleigh, said I, are perfectly familiar to you. It is known that I had no disposition to remove from this city, but resorted to every lawful means to remain. After I found that I could not be permitted to stay, I went away, leaving behind everything I held dear with the exception of one child, whom I took with me after paying two hundred and fifty dollars for her. It is also known to you and to many other persons here present that I had engaged to purchase my wife and children of their master, Mr. Smith, for the sum of twenty-five hundred dollars, and that I had paid of this sum (including my house and lot) eleven hundred and twenty dollars, leaving a balance to be made up of thirteen hundred and eighty dollars. I had previously to that lived in Raleigh, a slave, the property of Mr. Sherwood Haywood, and had purchased my freedom by paying the sum of one thousand dollars. But being driven away—no longer permitted to live in this city to raise the balance of the money due on my family—my last resort was to call upon the friends of humanity in other places to assist me.

I went to the city of Boston, and there I related the story of my persecutions here, the same as I have now stated to you. The people gave ear to my statements and one of them, Reverend Mr. Neale, wrote back, unknown to me, to Mr. Smith, inquiring of him whether the statements made by me were correct. After Mr. Neale received the answer, he sent for me, informed me of his having written and read to me the reply. The letter fully satisfied Mr. Neale and his friends. He placed it in my hands, remarking that it would, in a great measure, do away the necessity of using the other documents in my possession. I then, with that letter in my hands, went out from house to house, from place of business to place of business, and from church to church, relating where I could gain an ear, the same heart rending and soul trying story which I am now repeating to you. In pursuing that course, the people, first one and then another, contributed, until I had succeeded in raising the amount alluded to, namely, thirteen hundred and eighty dollars. I may have had contributions from abolitionists, but I did not stop to ask those who assisted me whether they were antislavery or proslavery, for I considered that the money coming from either would accomplish the object I had in view. These are the facts. Now, sir, it remains for you to say whether I have been giving abolition lectures or not.

In the course of my remarks, I presented the letter of Mr. Smith to Mr. Neale, showing that I had acted the open part while in Massachusetts; also, I referred to my having written to Mr. Smith, requesting him to obtain for me the permit of the Governor; and I showed to the court Mr. Smith's letters in reply, in order to satisfy them that I had reason to believe I should be unmolested in my return.

Mr. Loring then whispered to some of the leading men, after which he remarked that he saw nothing in what I had done, according to my statements, implicating me in a manner worthy of notice. He called upon any present who might be in possession of information tending to disprove what I had said or to show any wrong on my part, to produce it. Otherwise, I should be set at liberty. No person appeared against me, so I was discharged.

I started to leave the house; but just before I got to the door I met Mr. James Litchford, who touched me on the shoulder, and I followed him back. He observed to me that if I went out of that room I should in less than five minutes be a dead man, for there was a mob outside waiting to drink my life. Mr. Loring then spoke to me again and said that notwithstanding I had been found guilty of nothing, yet public opinion was law, and he advised me to leave the place the next day. Otherwise, he was convinced I should have to suffer death. I replied, "Not tomorrow, but today." He answered that I could not go that day, because I had not done my business. I told him that I would leave my business in his hands and in those of other such gentlemen as himself, who might settle it for me and send my family to meet me at Philadelphia. This was concluded upon and a guard appointed to conduct me to the depot. I took my seat in the cars, when the mob that had followed us surrounded me and declared that the cars should not go if I were permitted to go in them. Mr. Loring inquired what they wanted of me. He told them that there had been an examination and nothing had been found against me; that they were at the examination invited to speak if they knew aught to condemn me, but they had remained silent; and that now it was but right I should be permitted to leave in peace. They replied that they wanted a more thorough investigation, that they wished to search my trunks (I had but one trunk) and see if I was not in possession of abolition papers.

It now became evident that I should be unable to get off in the cars, and my friends advised me to go the shortest way possible to jail, for my safety. They said they were persuaded that what the rabble wanted was to get me into their possession and then to murder me. The mob looked dreadfully enraged and seemed to lap for blood. The whole city was in an uproar. But the first men and the more wealthy were my friends, and they did everything in their power to protect me. Mr. Boylan, whose name has repeatedly occurred in this publication, was more than a father to me. And Mr. Smith and Mr. Loring and many other gentlemen, whose names it would give me pleasure to mention, were exceedingly kind.

The guard then conducted me through the mob to the prison, and I felt joyful that even a prison could protect me. Looking out from the prison window, I saw my trunk in the hands of Messrs. Johnson, Scott, and others, who were taking it to the City Hall for examination. I understood afterwards that they opened my trunk and as the lid flew up, Lo! a paper! a paper!! Those about seized it, three or four at once, as hungry dogs would a piece of meat after forty days famine. But the meat quickly turned to a stone, for the paper it happened, was one *printed in Raleigh* and edited by Weston R. Gales, a nice man to be sure, but no abolitionist. The only other printed or written things in the trunk were some business cards of a firm in Raleigh—not incendiary.

Afterwards I saw from the window Mr. Scott, accompanied by Mr. Johnson, lugging my carpetbag in the same direction my trunk had gone. It was opened at the City Hall and found actually to contain a pair of old shoes and a pair of old boots! But they did not conclude that these were incendiary.

Mr. Smith now came to the prison and told me that the examination had been completed and nothing found against me, but that it would not be safe for me to leave the prison immediately. It was agreed that I should remain in prison until after nightfall, and then steal secretly away, being let out by the keeper, and pass unnoticed to the house of my old and tried friend Mr. Boylan. Accordingly I was discharged between nine and ten o'clock. I went by the back way leading to Mr. Boylan's. But soon and suddenly a large company of men sprang upon me, and instantly I found myself in their possession. They conducted me sometimes high above ground and sometimes dragging me along, but as silently as possible, in the direction of the gallows, which is always kept standing upon the Common, or as it is called, "the pines," or, "piny old field." I now expected to pass speedily into the world of spirits. I thought of that unseen region to which I seemed to be hastening, and then my mind would return to my wife and children and the labors I had made to redeem them from bondage. Although I had the money to pay for them according to a bargain already made, it seemed to me some white man would get it, and they would die in slavery, without benefit from my exertions and the contributions of my friends. Then the thought of my own death, to occur in a few brief moments, would rush over me, and I seemed to bid adieu in spirit to all earthly things and to hold communion already with eternity. But at length I observed those who were carrying me away changed their course a little from the direct line to the gallows, and hope, a faint beaming, sprung up within me. But then as they were taking me to the woods, I thought they intended to murder me there, in a place where they would be less likely to be interrupted than in so public a spot as where the gallows stood. They conducted me to a rising ground among the trees and set me down. "Now," said they, "tell us the truth about those abolition lectures you have been giving at the North." I replied that I had related the circumstances before the court in the morning, and could only repeat what I had then said. "But that was not the truth—tell us the truth." I again said that any different story would be false, and, as I supposed I was in a few minutes to die, I would not, whatever they might think I would say under other circumstances, pass into the other world with a lie upon my lips. Said one, "you were always, Lunsford, when you were here, a clever fellow, and I did not think you would be engaged in such business as giving abolition lectures." To this and similar remarks I replied that the people of Raleigh had always said the abolitionists did not believe in buying slaves, but contended that their masters ought to free them without pay. I had been laboring to buy my family. How then could they suppose me to be in league with the abolitionists?

After other conversation of this kind, and after they seemed to have become tired of questioning me, they held a consultation in a low whisper among themselves. Then a bucket was brought and set down by my side. But what it contained, or for what it was intended, I could not divine. But soon, one of the number came forward with a pillow, and then hope sprung up, a flood of light and joy within me. The heavy weight on my heart rolled off; death had passed by and I unharmed. They commenced stripping me till every rag of clothes was removed. Then the bucket was set near, and I discovered it to contain tar. One man—I will do him the honor to record his name—Mr. William Andres, a journeyman printer, when he is anything except a tar-and-featherer, put his hands the first into the bucket and was about passing them to my face. "Don't put any in his face or eyes," said one.° So he desisted. But he, with three other "gentlemen," whose names I should be happy to record if I could recall them, gave me as nice a coat of tar all over, face only excepted, as any one would wish to see. Then they took the pillow and ripped it open at one end, and with the open end commenced the operation at the head and so worked downwards, putting a coat of its contents over that of the contents of the bucket. A fine escape from the hanging this will be, thought I, provided they do not with a match set fire to the feathers. I had some fear they would. But when the work was completed they gave me my clothes, and one of them handed me my watch, which he had carefully kept in his hands. They all expressed great interest in my welfare, advised me how to proceed with my business the next day, told me to stay in the place as long as I wished, and with other such words of consolation they bid me good night.

After I had returned to my family, to their inexpressible joy, as they had become greatly alarmed for my safety, some of the persons who had participated in this outrage, came in (probably influenced by a curiosity to see how the tar and feathers would be got off) and expressed great sympathy for me. They said they regretted that the affair had happened; that they had no objections to my living in Raleigh; I might feel perfectly safe to go out and transact my business preparatory to leaving; I should not be molested.

Meanwhile, my friends, understanding that I had been discharged from prison and perceiving I did not come to them, had commenced a regular search for me, on foot and on horseback, everywhere. Mr. Smith

---

° I think this was Mr. Burns, a blacksmith in the place, but I am not certain. At any rate, this man was my *friend* (if so he may be called) on this occasion; and it was fortunate for me that the company generally seemed to look up to him for wisdom.

called upon the Governor to obtain his official interference; and after my return a guard came to protect me. But I chose not to risk myself at my own house and so went to Mr. Smith's, where this guard kept me safely until morning. They seemed friendly indeed and were regaled with a supper during the night by Mr. Smith. My friend, Mr. Battle (late Private Secretary to the Governor), was with them, and he made a speech to them, setting forth the good qualities I had exhibited in my past life, particularly in my connection with the Governor's office.

In the morning, Mr. Boylan, true as ever and unflinching in his friendship, assisted me in arranging my business,° so that I should start with my family that day for the North. He furnished us with provisions more than sufficient to sustain the family to Philadelphia, where we intended to make a halt, and sent his own baggage wagon to convey our baggage to the depot, offering also to send his carriage for my family. But my friend, Mr. Malone, had been before him in this kind offer, which I had agreed to accept.

Brief and sorrowful was the parting from my kind friends. But the worst was the thought of leaving my mother. The cars were to start at ten o'clock in the morning. I called upon my old mistress, Mrs. Haywood, who was affected to weeping by the considerations that naturally came to her mind. She had been kind to me. The day before, she and her daughter, Mrs. Hogg, now present, had jointly transmitted a communication to the court, representing that in consequence of my good conduct from my youth, I could not be supposed to be guilty of any offense. And now, "with tears that ceased not flowing," they gave me their parting blessing. My mother was still Mrs. Haywood's slave, and I her only child. Our old mistress could not witness the sorrow that would attend the parting with my mother. She told her to go with me, and said that if I ever became able to pay two hundred dollars for her, I might. Otherwise it should be her loss. She gave her the following paper, which is in the ordinary form of a pass:

RALEIGH, N. C., April 26, 1842

Know all Persons by these Presents, That the bearer of this, Clarissa, a slave, belonging to me, hath my permission to visit the city of New York with her rela-

---

° Of course I was obliged to sacrifice much on my property, leaving in this hurried manner. And while I was in the North, a kind *friend* had removed from the woodlot wood that I had cut and corded, for which I expected to receive over one hundred dollars, thus saving me the trouble of making sale of it, or of being burdened with the money it would bring. I suppose I have no redress. I might add other things as bad.

tions, who are in company with her; and it is my desire that she may be protected and permitted to pass without molestation or hindrance, on good behavior. Witness my hand this 26th April, 1842.

Eleanor Haywood

Witness—J. A. Campbell.

On leaving Mrs. Haywood's, I called upon Mrs. Badger, another daughter and wife of Judge Badger, previously mentioned. She seemed equally affected. She wept as she gave me her parting counsel. She and Mrs. Hogg and I had been children together, playing in the same yard, while yet none of us had learned that they were of a superior and I of a subject race. And in those infant years there were pencilings made upon the heart, which time and opposite fortunes could not all efface. May these friends never be slaves as I have been, nor their bosom companions and their little ones be slaves like mine.

When the cars were about to start, the whole city seemed to be gathered at the depot, and, among the rest, the mobocratic portion, who appeared to be determined still that I should not go peaceably away. Apprehending this, it had been arranged with my friends and the conductor that my family should be put in the cars and that I should go a distance from the city on foot and be taken up as they passed. The mob, therefore, supposing that I was left behind, allowed the cars to start.

Mr. Whiting, known as the agent of the railroad company, was going as far as Petersburg, Va., and he kindly assisted in purchasing our tickets and enabling us to pass on unmolested. After he left, Captain Guyan, of Raleigh, performed the same kind office as far as Alexandria, D. C., and then he placed us in the care of a citizen of Philadelphia, whose name I regret to have forgotten, who protected us quite out of the land of slavery. But for this we should have been liable to be detained at several places on our way, much to our embarrassment, at least, if nothing had occurred of a more serious nature.

One accident only had happened. We lost at Washington a trunk containing most of our valuable clothing. This we have not recovered; but our lives have been spared to bless the day that conferred freedom upon us. I felt when my feet struck the pavements in Philadelphia as though I had passed into another world. I could draw in a full long breath, with no one to say to the ribs, "why do ye so?"

On reaching Philadelphia we found that our money had all been expended, but kind friends furnished us with the means of proceeding as far as New York. And thence we were with equal kindness aided on to Boston.

In Boston and in the vicinity are persons almost without number who have done me favors more than I can express. The thought that I was now in my loved, though recently acquired home; that my family were with me where the stern, cruel, hated hand of slavery could never reach us more; the greetings of friends; the interchange of feeling and sympathy; the kindness bestowed upon us, more grateful than rain to the thirsty earth; the reflections of the past that would rush into my mind. These and more almost overwhelmed me with emotion, and I had deep and strange communion with my own soul. Next to God from whom every good gift proceeds, I feel under the greatest obligations to my kind friends in Massachusetts. To be rocked in their cradle of Liberty. Oh, how unlike being stretched on the pillory of slavery! May that cradle rock forever. May many a poor careworn child of sorrow, many a spirit-bruised (worse than lash-mangled) victim of oppression there sweetly sleep to the lullaby of freedom, sung by Massachusetts' sons and daughters.

A number of meetings have been held at which friends have contributed to our temporal wants, and individuals have sent us various articles of provision and furniture and apparel, so that our souls have been truly made glad. There are now ten of us in the family: my wife, my mother, and myself, with seven children, and we expect soon to be joined by my father, who several years ago received his freedom by legacy. The wine fresh from the clustering grapes never filled so sweet a cup as mine. May I and my family be permitted to drink it, remembering whence it came!

MOSES GRANDY

An energetic and resourceful man, Moses Grandy led a most difficult life as a slave, yet he succeeded at last in gaining his liberty.
He was forced to labor long hours cutting lumber in the Dismal
Swamp and working in the fields. He was hired out and abused.
His brother and his wife were sold away from him. After years of
labor he accumulated his purchase price but was cheated by his
master out of his money. Finally, he succeeded in buying himself.
For a time he tried to live in the South as a free man, but he was
compelled for his safety to flee to Boston. The account of his experiences, *The Narrative of The Life of Moses Grandy, Late a
Slave in the United States of America,* was published in Boston in
1844. What follows is taken from that book.

Robbed of Freedom and Purchase Money

Next year I was hired by Mr. John Micheau, of the same county, who married my young mistress, one of the daughters of Mr. Grandy, and sister of my present owner. This master gave us very few clothes and but little to eat. I was almost naked. One day he came into the field and asked why no more work was done. The older people were afraid of him, so I said that the reason was, we were so hungry we could not work. He went home and told the mistress to give us plenty to eat, and at dinner-time we had plenty. We came out shouting for joy and went to work with delight. From that time we had food enough, and he soon found that he had a great deal more work done. The field was quite alive with people striving who should do most.

He hired me for another year. He was a great gambler. He kept me up five nights together, without sleep night or day, to wait on the gambling table. I was standing in the corner of the room, nodding for want of sleep, when he took up the shovel and beat me with it; he dislocated my shoulder and sprained my wrist and broke the shovel over me. I ran away and got another person to hire me.

This person was Mr. Richard Furley, who, after that, hired me at the court house every year till my master came of age. He gave me a pass to work for myself, so I obtained work by the piece where I could, and paid him out of my earnings what we had agreed on. I maintained myself on the rest, and saved what I could. In this way I was not liable to be flogged and ill used. He paid seventy, eighty, or ninety dollars a year for me, and I paid him twenty or thirty dollars a year more than that.

When my master came of age, he took all his colored people to himself. Seeing that I was industrious and persevering, and had obtained plenty of work, he made me pay him almost twice as much as I had paid Mr. Furley. At that time the English blockaded the Chesapeake, which made it necessary to send merchandise from Norfolk to Elizabeth City by the Grand Canal, so that it might get to sea by Pamlico Sound and Ocracock Inlet. I took some canal boats on shares; Mr. Grice, who married my other young mistress, was the owner of them. I gave him one-half of all I received for freight; out of the other half I had to victual and man the boats, and all over that expense was my own profit.

Some time before this, my brother Benjamin returned from the West Indies, where he had been two years with his master's vessel. I was very glad to hear of it, and got leave to go see him. While I was sitting with his wife and him, his wife's master came and asked him to fetch a can of water; he did so and carried it into the store. While I was waiting for him and wondering at his being so long away, I heard the heavy blows of a hammer; after a little while I was alarmed and went to see what was going on. I looked into the store, and saw my brother lying on his back on the floor, and Mr. Williams, who had bought him, driving staples over his wrists and ankles. An iron bar was afterwards put across his breast, which was also held down by staples. I asked what he had been doing, and was told that he had done nothing amiss, but that his master had failed, and he was sold towards paying the debts. He lay in that state all that night; next day he was taken to jail, and I never saw him again. This is the usual treatment under such circumstances. I had to go by my mother's next morning, but I feared to tell her what had happened to my brother. I got a boy to go and tell her. She was blind and very old, and was living in a little hut in the woods, after the usual manner of old, worn-out slaves. She was unable to go to my brother before he was taken away, and grieved after him greatly.

It was some time after this that I married a slave belonging to Mr. Enoch Sawyer, who had been so hard a master to me. I left her at home (that is, at his house) one Thursday morning, when we had been married about eight months. She was well, and seemed likely to be so. We were nicely getting together our little necessaries. On Friday as I was at work, as usual, with the boats, I heard a noise behind me, on the road which ran by the side of the canal. I turned to look, and saw a gang of slaves coming. When they came up to me, one of them cried out,

"Moses, my dear!" I wondered who among them should know me, and found it was my wife. She cried out to me, "I am gone!" I was struck with consternation. Mr. Rogerson was with them, on his horse, armed with pistols. I said to him, "For God's sake, have you bought my wife?" He said he had. When I asked him what she had done, he said she had done nothing, but that her master wanted money. He drew out a pistol and said that if I went near the wagon on which she was, he would shoot me. I asked for leave to shake hands with her, which he refused, but said I might stand at a distance and talk with her. My heart was so full that I could say very little. I asked leave to give her a dram. He told Mr. Burgess, the man who was with him, to get down and carry it to her. I gave her the little money I had in my pocket and bade her farewell. I have never seen or heard of her from that day to this. I loved her as I loved my life.

Mr. Grice found that I served him faithfully. He and my young mistress, his wife, advised me, as I was getting money fast, to try to buy myself. By their advice, I asked my master what he would take for me. He wanted $800; and when I said that was too much, he replied, he could get $1,000 for me any minute. Mr. Grice afterwards went with me to him. He said to him that I had already been more profitable to him than any five other of his Negroes, and reminded him that we had been playfellows. In this way he got him to consent to take $600 for me. I then went heartily to work, and whenever I paid him for my time, I paid him something, also, towards my freedom, for which he gave me receipts. When I made him the last payment of the $600 for my freedom, he tore up all the receipts. I told him he ought not to have done so. He replied it did not signify, for as soon as court day came he should give me my free papers. On Monday in court week, I went to him. He was playing at billiards, and would not go with me, but told me to come again the next day. The next day he did the same, and so on daily. I went to his sister, Mrs. Grice, and told her I feared that he did not mean to give them to me. She said she feared so too and sent for him. He was a very wicked young man: he came and cursed her, and went out of the house. Mr. Grice was away from home. On his return, he went to my master and told him he ought to give me my free papers: that I had paid for myself and it was court week, so that there was no excuse. He promised he would. Instead, he rode away and kept away till court was over. Before the next court came, he sold me to Mr. Trewitt for $600.

The way in which Mr. Trewitt came to buy me was this: I had left the boats, and had gone with a schooner collecting lumber in Albemarle Sound for the merchants. Coming to Elizabeth City, I found a new store had been opened by Mr. Grice, which Mr. Sutton was keeping. The latter gentleman was glad to see me, and was desirous that I should return to my old employment with the canal boats, as lumber was in great demand at Norfolk. I did so, and sold some cargoes to Mr. Moses Myers, of Norfolk. As I was waiting at the door of his store for settlement, he came up with Mr. Trewitt, whom I did not then know. Mr. Myers said to Mr. Trewitt, "Here is a captain doing business for you." Mr. Trewitt then asked me who had chartered the boats, and to whom I belonged. I told him Mr. Sutton had chartered me, and that I had belonged to Mr. James Grandy, but had bought myself. He said he would buy me, on which Mr. Myers told him he could not, as I had already bought myself, and further said I was one of their old war captains, and had never lost a single thing of the property intrusted to me. Mr. Trewitt said he would buy me, and would see about it as soon as he got to Elizabeth City. I thought no more about it. On my return voyage, I delivered a cargo at Elizabeth City for Mr. Trewitt. I had been at Mr. Grice's, the owner of the boats. On my going away from him to meet Mr. Trewitt for settlement, he said he would go with me, as he wanted money. Opposite the custom house we met Mr. Trewitt, who said, "Well, captain, I have bought you." Mr. Grice said, "Let us have no nonsense; go and settle with him." Angry words passed between them, one saying he had bought me, and the other denying that he had or could, as I had bought myself already. We all went to Mr. Grice's dwelling house. There Mr. Trewitt settled with me about the freight, and then, jumping up, said, "Now I will show you, Mr. Grice, whether I am a liar or not." He fetched the bill of sale. On reading it Mr. Grice's color changed, and he sent for Mrs. Grice. When she read it, she began to cry; seeing that, I began to cry too. She sent me to her brother, who was at Mr. Wood's boarding house. He was playing at billiards. I said to him, "Master James, have you sold me?" He said, "No." I said he had, when he turned round and went into another room. Crying, I followed him. All the gentlemen followed us, saying, "Captain Grandy, what is the matter?" I told them Master James had sold me again. They asked him why he had done it. He said it was because people had jeered him by saying I had more sense than he had. They would not suffer him to remain in the boarding house, but turned him out, there and then, with all his trunks and boxes. Mrs. Grice, his sister, sued him in my name for my liberty, but he gained the cause. The court maintained that I, and all I could do, belonged to him, and that he had a right to do as he pleased with me and all my earnings, as his own property, until he had taken me to the court house and given me my free papers, and until, besides that, I had been a year and a day in the Northern States to gain my residence.

So I was forced to go to Mr. Trewitt. He agreed that if I would pay him the same wages as I paid my late master and the $600 he gave for me, he would give me my free papers. He bought two canal boats, and, taking me out of Mr. Grice's employment, set me to work them on the same terms as I did for my former master. I was two years and a half in earning $600 to pay for myself the second time. Just when I had completed the payment, he failed. On Christmas eve he gave me a letter to take to Mr. Mews, at Newbegun Creek. I was rather unwilling to take it, wishing to go to my wife. I told him, too, I was going to his office to settle with him. He offered to give me two dollars to take the letter, and said he would settle when I came back. Then Mr. Shaw came from another room and said his vessel was ready loaded, but he had nobody he could trust with his goods. He offered me five dollars to take the vessel down and deliver the goods to Mr. Knox, who also was at Newbegun Creek. The wind was fair and the hands on board, so I agreed; it being Christmas eve, I was glad of something to carry to my wife. I ran the vessel down to the mouth of the creek and anchored. When the moon rose, I went up the river. I reached the wharf and commenced taking out the goods that night, and delivered them all safely to Mr. Knox next morning. I then took the letter to Mr. Mews, who read it and, looking up at me, said, "Well, you belong to me." I thought he was joking and said, "How? What way?" He said, "Don't you recollect when Trewitt chartered Wilson Sawyer's brig to the West Indies?" I said, I did. He told me Trewitt then came to him to borrow $600, which he would not lend, except he had a mortgage on me. Trewitt was to take it up at a certain time, but never did. I asked him whether he really took the mortgage on me. He replied that he certainly thought Trewitt would have taken up the mortgage, but he had failed and was not worth a cent, and he, Mews, must have his money. I asked him whether he had not helped me and my young mistress in the court house, when master James fooled me before. He said he did help me all he could, and that he should not have taken a mortgage on me, but that he thought Trewitt would take it up. Trewitt must have received some of the last pay-ments from me after he had given the mortgage and knew he should fail, for the mortgage was given two months before this time.

My head seemed to turn round and round; I was quite out of my senses; I went away towards the woods; Mr. Mews sent his waiter after me to persuade me to go back. At first I refused, but afterwards went. He told me he would give me another chance to buy myself, and I cer-tainly should have my freedom that time. He said Mr. Enoch Sawyer wanted to buy me, to be his overseer in the Swamp. I replied I would never try again to buy myself, and that they had already got $1,200 from me.

My wife° (this was my second wife) belonged to Mr. Sawyer. Mr. Mews told me that her master would not allow me to go to see her if I would not consent to what he now proposed, for any colored person going on the grounds of a white man, after being warned off, is liable to be flogged, or even shot. I thus found myself forced to go, although no colored man wishes to live at the house where his wife lives, for he has to endure the continual misery of seeing her flogged and abused, with-out daring to say a word in her defense.

In the service of Mr. Sawyer, I got into a fair way of buying myself again, for I undertook the lightering of shingles or boards out of the Dis-mal Swamp, and hired hands to assist me. But my master had become security for his two sons-in-law at Norfolk, who failed; on consequence of which he sold eighteen colored people, his share of the Swamp, and two plantations. I was one of the slaves he kept, and after that had to work in the cornfield the same as the rest. The overseer was a bad one; his name was Brooks. The horn was blown at sunrise. The colored peo-ple had then to march before the overseer to the field, he on horseback. We had to work, even in long summer days, till twelve o'clock before we tasted a morsel—men, women, and children all being served alike.

° It will be observed that the narrator married a second wife, without having heard of the decease of the first. To explain this feat, it is necessary to state that the frequent occur-rence of cases where husbands and wives, members of Christian societies, were finally separated by sale led the ministers, some years ago, to deliberate on the subject: they de-cided that such separation might be considered as the death of the parties to each other, and they therefore agreed to consider subsequent marriages not immoral. The practice is general. It is scarcely necessary to remark that a more unequivocal and impressive proof of the heinous nature of the system could hardly exist. It breaks up the fondest connec-tions, it tears up the holiest attachments, and induces the ministers of religion, as much as in them lies, to carve the divine law to a fitting with its own infernal exigencies.

At noon the cart appeared with our breakfast. It was in large trays, and was set on the ground. There was bread, of which a piece was cut off for each person; then there was small hominy boiled: that is, Indian corn ground in the hand mill; and besides this two herrings for each of the men and women, and one for each of the children. Our drink was the water in the ditches, whatever might be its state. If the ditches were dry, water was brought to us by the boys. The salt fish always made us thirsty, but no other drink than water was ever allowed. However thirsty a slave may be, he is not allowed to leave his employment for a moment to get water. He can only have it when the hands in working have reached the ditch, at the end of the rows. The overseer stood with his watch in his hand, to give us just an hour. When he said, "Rise," we had to rise and go to work again. The women who had children had them down the hedgerow, and gave them straws and other trifles to play with. Here they were in danger from snakes. I have seen a large snake found coiled round the neck and face of a child, when its mother went to suckle it at dinner-time. The hands work in a line by the side of each other: the overseer puts the swiftest hands in the fore row, and all must keep up with them. One black man is kept on purpose to whip the others in the field; if he does not flog with sufficient severity, he is flogged himself; he whips severely, to keep the whip from his own back. If a man have a wife in the same field with himself, he chooses a row by the side of hers that, with extreme labor, he may, if possible, help her. But he will not be in the same field if he can help it, for, with his hardest labor, he often cannot save her from being flogged, and he is obliged to stand by and see it. He is always liable to see her taken home at night, stripped naked, and whipped before all the men. On the estate I am speaking of, those women who had suckling children suffered much from their breasts becoming full of milk, the infants being left at home. They, therefore, could not keep up with the other hands. I have seen the overseer beat them with rawhide, so that blood and milk flowed mingled from their breasts. A woman who gives offense in the field and is large in the family way is compelled to lie down over a hole made to receive her corpulency, and is flogged with the whip or beat with a paddle that has holes in it. At every hole comes a blister. One of my sisters was so severely punished in this way that labor was brought on, and the child was born in the field. This very overseer, Mr. Brooks, killed in this manner a girl named Mary. Her father and mother were in the field at

the time. He killed, also, a boy about twelve years old. He had no punishment, or even trial, for either.

There was no dinner till dark, when he gave the order to knock off
and go home. The meal then was the same as in the morning, except
that we had meat twice a week.

On very few estates are the colored people provided with any bedding: the best masters give only a blanket; this master gave none. A
board, which the slave might pick up anywhere on the estate, was all he
had to lie on. If he wished to procure bedding, he could only do so by
working at nights. For warmth, therefore, the Negroes generally sleep
near a large fire, whether in the kitchen or in their log huts. Their legs
are often in this way blistered and greatly swelled, and sometimes badly
burnt. They suffer severely from this cause.

When the water mill did not supply meal enough, we had to grind
with the hand mill. The night was employed in this work, without any
thing being taken from the labor of the day. We had to take turns at it,
women as well as men. Enough was to be ground to serve for the following day.

I was eight months in the field. My master, Mr. Sawyer, agreed to
allow me eight dollars a month, while so employed, towards buying myself. It will be seen he did not give me even that. When I first went to
work in the corn field, I had paid him $230 towards this third buying of
my freedom. I told him, one night, I could not stand his field work any
longer. He asked why. I said I was almost starved to death, and had long
been unaccustomed to this severe labor. He wanted to know why I
could not stand it as well as the rest. I told him he knew well I had not
been used to it for a long time, that his overseer was the worst that had
ever been on the plantation, and that I could not stand it. He said he
would direct Mr. Brooks to give each of us a pint of meal or corn every
evening, which we might bake, and which would serve us next morning,
till our breakfast came at noon. The black people were much rejoiced
that I got this additional allowance for them. But I was not satisfied; I
wanted liberty.

On Sunday morning, as master was sitting in his porch, I went to
him and offered to give him the $230 I had already paid him if, besides
it, he would take for my freedom the $600 he had given for me. He
drove me away, saying I had no way to get the money. I sat down for a
time and went to him again. I repeated my offer to procure the $600,
and he again said I could not. He called his wife out of the room to the

porch and said to her, "Don't you think Moses has taken to getting drunk?" She asked me if it was so. I denied it. When she inquired what was the matter, Master replied, "Don't you think he wants me to sell him?" She said, "Moses, we would not take any money for you. Captain Cormack put a thousand dollars for you on the supper table last Friday night, and Mr. Sawyer would not touch it. He wants you to be overseer in the Dismal Swamp." I replied, "Captain Cormack never said any thing to me about buying me. I would cut my throat from ear to ear rather than go to him. I know what made him say so. He is courting Miss Patsey, and he did it to make himself look big!" Mistress laughed and turned away, and slammed to the door. Master shook himself with laughing, and put the paper he was reading before his face, knowing that I spoke the truth. Captain Cormack was an old man who went on crutches. Miss Patsey was the finest of master's daughters. Master drove me away from him again.

On Monday morning, Mr. Brooks, the overseer, blew the horn as usual for all to go to the field. I refused to go. I went to master and told him that if he would give me a paper, I would go and fetch the $600. He then gave me a paper stating that he was willing to take that sum for my freedom. So I hired an old horse and started for Norfolk, fifty miles off.

When I reached Deep Creek, I went to the house of Captain Edward Minner. He was very glad to see me, for in former days I had done much business for him. He said how sorry he had been to hear that I was at field work. He inquired where I was going. I said, to Norfolk, to get some of the merchants to let me have money to buy myself. He replied, "What did I always say to you? Was it not, that I would let you have the money at any time, if you would only tell me when you could be sold?" He called Mrs. Minner into the room and told her I could be sold for my freedom; she was rejoiced to hear it. He said, "Put up your horse at Mr. Western's tavern, for you need go no farther. I have plenty of old rusty dollars, and no man shall put his hand on your collar again to say you are a slave. Come and stay with me tonight, and in the morning I will get Mr. Garret's horse, and go with you."

Next morning we set off and found master at Major Farrence's, at the cross canal, where I knew he was to be that day, to sell his share of the canal. When I saw him, he told me to go forward home, for he would not sell me. I felt sick and sadly disappointed. Captain Minner stepped up to him, and showed him the paper he had given me, saying, "Mr. Sawyer, is not this your handwriting?" He replied, "Mistress said, the last word when I came away, I was not to sell him, but send him home again." Captain Minner said, "Mind, gentlemen, I do not want him for a slave. I want to buy him for freedom. He will repay me the money, and I shall not charge him a cent of interest for it. I would not have a colored person, to drag me down to hell, for all the money in the world." A gentleman who was by said it was a shame I should be so treated—I had bought myself so often that Mr. Sawyer ought to let me go. The very worst man as an overseer over the persons employed in digging the canal, Mr. Wiley M'Pherson, was there. He was never known to speak in favor of a colored person. Even he said that Mr. Sawyer ought to let me go, as I had been sold so often. At length, Mr. Sawyer consented I should go for $650, and would take no less. I wished Captain Minner to give the extra $50 and not stand about it. I believe it was what M'Pherson said that induced my master to let me go, for he was well known for his great severity to colored people, so that after even he had said so, master could not stand out. The Lord must have opened M'Pherson's heart to say it.

I have said this M'Pherson was an overseer where slaves were employed in cutting canals. The labor there is very severe. The ground is often very boggy; the Negroes are up to the middle, or much deeper, in mud and water, cutting away roots and baling out mud. If they can keep their heads above water, they work on. They lodge in huts or, as they are called, camps, made of shingles or boards. They lie down in the mud which has adhered to them, making a great fire to dry themselves and keep off the cold. No bedding whatever is allowed them. It is only by work done over his task that any of them can get a blanket. They are paid nothing, except for this overwork. Their masters come once a month to receive the money for their labor. Then, perhaps, some few very good masters will give them $2 each, some others $1, some a pound of tobacco, and some nothing at all. The food is more abundant than that of field slaves—indeed, it is the best allowance in America. It consists of a peck of meal and six pounds of pork per week. The pork is commonly not good: it is damaged, and is bought, as cheap as possible, at auctions.

M'Pherson gave the same task to each slave; of course, the weak ones often failed to do it. I have often seen him tie up persons and flog them in the morning, only because they were unable to get the previous day's task done. After they were flogged, pork or beef brine was put on their bleeding backs to increase the pain—he sitting by, resting himself, and seeing it done. After being thus flogged and pickled, the sufferers often remained tied up all day, the feet just touching the ground, the legs tied, and pieces of wood put between the legs. All the motion allowed was a slight turn of the neck. Thus exposed and helpless, the yellow flies and mosquitoes in great numbers would settle on the bleeding and smarting back and put the sufferer to extreme torture. This continued all day, for they were not taken down till night. In flogging, he would sometimes tie the slave's shirt over his head, that he might not flinch when the blow was coming. Sometimes he would increase his misery, by blustering and calling out that he was coming to flog again, which he did or did not, as happened. I have seen him flog them with his own hands till their entrails were visible, and I have seen the sufferers dead when they were taken down. He never was called to account in any way for it.

WILLIAM WELLS BROWN

Sired by one of his master's relatives, William Wells Brown was a house servant in Kentucky. At various times while he was a slave, he was employed by a doctor and a slave trader. His narrative is interesting for its account of the way slaves were prepared for auction. He also presents valuable insights into the slaveholding class. His master, for example, he describes as "a horse-racer, cock-fighter, gambler and withal an inveterate drunkard." After his escape from slavery, Brown became an agent of the New York Anti-Slavery Society. Later, as a close associate of William Lloyd Garrison, he was himself a prominent abolitionist, a delegate to the International Peace Congress in Paris, and the author of the first novel and the first play written by an Afro-American. *The Narrative of William Wells Brown*, which he wrote himself and from which these chapters are taken, appeared in Boston in 1848.

Preparing Slaves for Auction

I was born in Lexington, Kentucky. The man who stole me as soon as I was born recorded the births of all the infants that he claimed to be born his property in a book which he kept for that purpose. My mother's name was Elizabeth. She had seven children: Solomon, Leander, Benjamin, Joseph, Millford, Elizabeth, and myself. No two of us were children of the same father. My father's name, as I learned from my mother, was George Higgins. He was a white man, a relative of my master, and connected with some of the first families in Kentucky.

My master owned about forty slaves, twenty-five of whom were field hands. He removed from Kentucky to Missouri when I was quite young and settled thirty or forty miles above St. Charles, on the Missouri, where, in addition to his practice as a physician, he carried on milling, merchandising, and farming. He had a large farm, the principal productions of which were tobacco and hemp. The slave cabins were situated on the back part of the farm, with the house of the overseer, whose name was Grove Cook, in their midst. He had the entire charge of the farm and, having no family, was allowed a woman to keep house for him, whose business it was to deal out the provisions for the hands.

A woman was also kept at the quarters to do the cooking for the field hands, who were summoned to their unrequited toil every morning at four o'clock by the ringing of a bell hung on a post near the house of the overseer. They were allowed half an hour to eat their breakfast and get to the field. At half past four a horn was blown by the overseer, which was the signal to commence work; and everyone that was not on the spot at the time had to receive ten lashes from the Negro-whip, with which the overseer always went armed. The handle was about three feet long, with the butt-end filled with lead, and the lash, six or seven feet in length, made of cowhide, with platted wire on the end of it. This whip was put in requisition very frequently and freely, and a small offense on the part of a slave furnished an occasion for its use. During the time that Mr. Cook was overseer, I was a house servant—a situation preferable to that of a field hand, as I was better fed, better clothed, and not obliged to rise at the ringing of the bell, but about half an hour after. I have often laid and heard the crack of the whip and the screams of the slave. My mother was a field hand, and one morning was ten or fifteen minutes behind the others in getting into the field. As soon as she reached the spot where they were at work, the overseer commenced whipping her. She cried, "Oh pray!—Oh pray!—Oh pray!"—these are generally the words of slaves when imploring mercy at the hands of their oppressors. I heard her voice and knew it, and jumped out of my bunk and went to the door. Though the field was some distance from the house, I could hear every crack of the whip, and every groan and cry of my poor mother. I remained at the door, not daring to venture any further. The cold chills ran over me and I wept aloud. After giving her ten lashes, the sound of the whip ceased, and I returned to my bed and found no consolation but in my tears. Experience has taught me that nothing can be more heart-rending than for one to see a dear and beloved mother or sister tortured, and to hear their cries and not be able to render them assistance. But such is the position which an American slave occupies.

My master, being a politician, soon found those who were ready to put him into office, for the favors he could render them; and a few years after his arrival in Missouri he was elected to a seat in the legislature. In his absence from home everything was left in charge of Mr. Cook, the overseer, and he soon became more tyrannical and cruel. Among the slaves on the plantation was one by the name of Randall. He was a man about six feet high and well-proportioned, and known as a man of great strength and power. He was considered the most valuable and able-bodied slave on the plantation; but no matter how good or useful a slave may be, he seldom escapes the lash. But it was not so with Randall. He had been on the plantation since my earliest recollection, and I had never known of his being flogged. No thanks were due to the master or overseer for this. I had often heard him declare that no white man should ever whip him—that he would die first.

Cook, from the time that he came upon the plantation, had frequently declared that he could and would flog any nigger that was put into the field to work under him. My master had repeatedly told him not to attempt to whip Randall, but he was determined to try it. As soon as he was left sole dictator, he thought the time had come to put his threats into execution. He soon began to find fault with Randall, and threatened to whip him if he did not do better. One day he gave him a very hard task: more than he could possibly do; and at night, the task not being performed, he told Randall that he should remember him the next morning. On the following morning, after the hands had taken breakfast, Cook called out to Randall and told him that he intended to whip him, and ordered him to cross his hands and be tied. Randall asked why he wished to whip him. He answered, because he had not finished his task the day before. Randall said that the task was too great, or he should have done it. Cook said it made no difference—he should whip him. Randall stood silent for a moment, and then said, "Mr. Cook, I have always tried to please you since you have been on the plantation, and I find you are determined not to be satisfied with my work, let me do as well as I may. No man has laid hands on me, to whip me, for the last ten years, and I have long since come to the conclusion not to be whipped by any man living." Cook, finding by Randall's determined look and gestures that he would resist, called three of the hands from their work and commanded them to seize Randall and tie him. The hands stood still: they knew Randall—and they also knew him to be a powerful man and were afraid to grapple with him. As soon as Cook had ordered the men to seize him, Randall turned to them and said, "Boys, you all know me. You know that I can handle any three of you, and the man that lays hands on me shall die. This white man can't whip me himself, and therefore he has called you to help him." The overseer was unable to prevail upon them to seize and secure Randall, and finally ordered them all to go to their work together.

Nothing was said to Randall by the overseer for more than a week. One morning, however, while the hands were at work in the field, he came into it accompanied by three friends of his: Thompson, Woodbridge, and Jones. They came up to where Randall was at work, and Cook ordered him to leave his work, and go with them to the barn. He refused to go. Whereupon he was attacked by the overseer and his companions, when he turned upon them and laid them, one after another, prostrate on the ground. Woodbridge drew out his pistol and fired at him and brought him to the ground by a pistol ball. The others rushed upon him with their clubs and beat him over the head and face until they succeeded in tying him. He was then taken to the barn and tied to a beam. Cook gave him over one hundred lashes with a heavy cowhide, had him washed with salt and water, and left him tied during the day. The next day he was untied and taken to a blacksmith's shop and had a ball and chain attached to his leg. He was compelled to labor in the field and perform the same amount of work that the other hands did. When his master returned home, he was much pleased to find that Randall had been subdued in his absence.

Soon afterwards, my master removed to the city of St. Louis and purchased a farm four miles from there, which he placed under the charge of an overseer by the name of Friend Haskell. He was a regular Yankee from New England. The Yankees are noted for making the most cruel overseers.

My mother was hired out in the city, and I was also hired out there to Major Freeland, who kept a public house. He was formerly from Virginia, and was a horse-racer, cock-fighter, gambler, and withal an inveterate drunkard. There were ten or twelve servants in the house, and when he was present, it was cut and slash—knock down and drag out. In his fits of anger, he would take up a chair and throw it at a servant. In his more rational moments, when he wished to chastise one, he would tie them up in the smoke-house and whip them; after which, he would cause a fire to be made of tobacco stems and smoke them. This he called "Virginia play."

I complained to my master of the treatment which I received from Major Freeland; but it made no difference. He cared nothing about it, so long as he received the money for my labor. After living with Major Freeland five or six months, I ran away and went into the woods back of the city. When night came on, I made my way to my master's farm, but was afraid to be seen, knowing that if Mr. Haskell, the overseer, should discover me, I should be again carried back to Major Freeland. So I kept in the woods. One day, while in the woods, I heard the barking and howling of dogs, and in a short time they came so near that I knew them to be the bloodhounds of Major Benjamin O'Fallon. He kept five or six, to hunt runaway slaves with.

As soon as I was convinced that it was them, I knew there was no chance of escape. I took refuge in the top of a tree. The hounds were soon at its base and there remained until the hunters came up in a half or three-quarters of an hour afterwards. There were two men with the dogs, who, as soon as they came up, ordered me to descend. I came down, was tied, and taken to St. Louis jail. Major Freeland soon made his appearance and took me out and ordered me to follow him, which I did. After we returned home, I was tied up in the smokehouse and was very severely whipped. After the major had flogged me to his satisfaction, he sent out his son Robert, a young man eighteen or twenty years of age, to see that I was well smoked. He made a fire of tobacco stems, which soon set me to coughing and sneezing. This, Robert told me, was the way his father used to do to his slaves in Virginia. After giving me what they conceived to be a decent smoking, I was untied and again set to work.

Robert Freeland was a "chip of the old block." Though quite young, it was not infrequently that he came home in a state of intoxication. He is now, I believe, a popular commander of a steamboat on the Mississippi river. Major Freeland soon after failed in business, and I was put on board the steamboat Missouri, which plied between St. Louis and Galena. The commander of the boat was William B. Culver. I remained on her during the sailing season, which was the most pleasant time for me that I had ever experienced. At the close of navigation I was hired to Mr. John Colburn, keeper of the Missouri Hotel. He was from one of the free states, but a more inveterate hater of the Negro I do not believe ever walked God's green earth. This hotel was at that time one of the largest in the city, and there were employed in it twenty or thirty servants, mostly slaves.

Mr. Colburn was very abusive, not only to the servants, but to his wife also, who was an excellent woman, and one from whom I never knew a servant to receive a harsh word; but never did I know a kind one to a servant from her husband. Among the slaves employed in the hotel was one by the name of Aaron, who belonged to Mr. John F. Darby, a lawyer. Aaron was the knife-cleaner. One day, one of the knives was put on the table, not as clean as it might have been. Mr. Colburn, for this offense, tied Aaron up in the woodhouse and gave him over fifty lashes on the bare back with a cowhide. Afterwards, he made me wash him down with rum. This seemed to put him into more agony than the whipping. After being untied, he went home to his master and complained of the treatment which he had received. Mr. Darby would give no heed to anything he had to say, but sent him directly back. Colburn, learning that he had been to his master with complaints, tied him up again and gave him a more severe whipping than before. The poor fellow's back was literally cut to pieces; so much so, that he was not able to work for ten or twelve days.

There was also, among the servants, a girl whose master resided in the country. Her name was Patsey. Mr. Colburn tied her up one evening and whipped her until several of the boarders came out and begged him to desist. The reason for whipping her was this. She was engaged to be married to a man belonging to Major William Christy, who resided four or five miles north of the city. Mr. Colburn had forbid her to see John Christy. The reason of this was said to be the regard which he himself had for Patsey. She went to meeting that evening, and John returned home with her. Mr. Colburn had intended to flog John, if he came within the inclosure; but John knew too well the temper of his rival and kept at a safe distance. So he took vengeance on the poor girl. If all the slave drivers had been called together, I do not think a more cruel man than John Colburn—and he too a northern man—could have been found among them.

While living at the Missouri Hotel, a circumstance occurred which caused me great unhappiness. My master sold my mother and all her children, except myself. They were sold to different persons in the city of St. Louis.

On our arrival at St. Louis, I went to Dr. Young and told him that I did not wish to live with Mr. Walker any longer. I was heartsick at seeing my fellow creatures bought and sold. But the Doctor had hired me out for the year, and stay I must. Mr. Walker again commenced purchasing another gang of slaves. He bought a man of Colonel John O'Fallon, who resided in the suburbs of the city. This man had a wife and three children. As soon as the purchase was made, he was put in jail for safe keeping, until we should be ready to start for New Orleans. His wife visited him while there, several times; and several times when she went for that purpose was refused admittance.

In the course of eight or nine weeks Mr. Walker had his cargo of human flesh made up. There was in this lot a number of old men and women, some of them with gray locks. We left St. Louis in the steamboat Carlton (Captain Swan) bound for New Orleans. On our way down, and before we reached Rodney, the place where we made our first stop, I had to prepare the old slaves for market. I was ordered to have the old men's whiskers shaved off and the grey hairs plucked out where they were not too numerous, in which case he had a preparation of blacking to color it—and with a blacking brush we would put it on. This was new business to me, and was performed in a room where the passengers could not see us. After going through the blacking process they looked ten or fifteen years younger. These slaves were also taught how old they were by Mr. Walker. I am sure that some of those who purchased slaves of Mr. Walker were dreadfully cheated, especially in the ages of the slaves which they bought.

We landed at Rodney, and the slaves were driven to the pen in the back part of the village. Several were sold at this place, during our stay of four or five days. Then we proceeded to Natchez. There we landed at night, and the gang were put in the warehouse until morning, when they were driven to the pen. As soon as the slaves are put in these pens, swarms of planters may be seen in and about them. They knew when Walker was expected, as he always had the time advertised beforehand when he would be in Rodney, Natchez, and New Orleans. These were the principal places where he offered his slaves for sale.

When at Natchez the second time, I saw a slave very cruelly whipped. He belonged to a Mr. Broadwell, a merchant who kept a store on the wharf. The slave's name was Lewis. I had known him several years, as he was formerly from St. Louis. We were expecting a steamboat down the river, in which we were to take passage for New Orleans. Mr. Walker sent me to the landing to watch for the boat, ordering me to inform him on its arrival. While there I went into the store to see Lewis. I saw a slave in the store and asked him where Lewis was. Said he, "They have got Lewis hanging between the heavens and the earth." I asked him what he meant by that. He told me to go into the warehouse and see. I went in and found Lewis there. He was tied up to a beam, with his toes just touching the floor. As there was no one in the warehouse but himself, I inquired the reason of his being in that situation. He said Mr. Broadwell had sold his wife to a planter six miles from the city, and that he had been to visit her—that he went in the night, expecting to return before daylight, and went without his master's permission. The patrol had taken him up before he reached his wife. He was put in jail, and his master had to pay for his catching and keeping, and that was what he was tied up for.

Just as he finished his story, Mr. Broadwell came in and inquired what I was doing there. I knew not what to say, and while I was think-ing what reply to make he struck me over the head with the cowhide, the end of which struck me over my right eye, sinking deep into the flesh, leaving a scar which I carry to this day. Before I visited Lewis he had received fifty lashes. Mr. Broadwell gave him fifty lashes more after I came out, as I was afterwards informed by Lewis himself.

The next day we proceeded to New Orleans and put the gang in the same Negro-pen which we occupied before. In a short time the planters came flocking to the pen to purchase slaves. Before the slaves were ex-hibited for sale, they were dressed and driven out into the yard. Some were set to dancing, some to jumping, some to singing, and some to playing cards. This was done to make them appear cheerful and happy. My business was to see that they were placed in those situations before the arrival of the purchasers, and I have often set them to dancing when their cheeks were wet with tears. As slaves were in good demand at that time, they were all soon disposed of, and we again set out for St. Louis.

On our arrival, Mr. Walker purchased a farm five or six miles from the city. He had no family, but made a housekeeper of one of his female slaves. Poor Cynthia! I knew her well. She was a quadroon, and one of the most beautiful women I ever saw. She was a native of St. Louis and bore an irreproachable character for virtue and propriety of conduct. Mr. Walker bought her for the New Orleans market and took her down with him on one of the trips that I made with him. Never shall I forget the circumstances of that voyage! On the first night that we were on board the steamboat, he directed me to put her into a stateroom he had provided for her, apart from the other slaves. I had seen too much of the workings of slavery not to know what this meant. I accordingly watched him into the stateroom and listened to hear what passed between them. I heard him make his base offers, and her reject them. He told her that if she would accept his vile proposals, he would take her back with him to St. Louis and establish her as his housekeeper on his farm. But if she persisted in rejecting them, he would sell her as a field hand on the worst plantation on the river. Neither threats nor bribes prevailed, how-ever, and he retired, disappointed of his prey.

The next morning poor Cynthia told me what had passed, and be-wailed her sad fate with floods of tears. I comforted and encouraged her all I could; but I foresaw but too well what the result must be. Without entering into any further particulars, suffice it to say that Walker per-formed his part of the contract at that time. He took her back to St.

Louis, established her as his mistress and housekeeper at his farm, and, before I left, he had two children by her. But, mark the end! Since I have been at the North, I have been credibly informed that Walker has been married, and, as a previous measure, sold poor Cynthia and her four children (she having had two more since I came away) into hopeless bondage!

He soon commenced purchasing to make up the third gang. We took steamboat, and went to Jefferson City, a town on the Missouri river. Here we landed and took stage for the interior of the state. He bought a number of slaves as he passed the different farms and villages. After getting twenty-two or twenty-three men and women, we arrived at St. Charles, a village on the banks of the Missouri. Here he purchased a woman who had a child in her arms, appearing to be four or five weeks old.

We had been traveling by land for some days, and were in hopes to have found a boat at this place for St. Louis, but were disappointed. As no boat was expected for some days, we started for St. Louis by land. Mr. Walker had purchased two horses. He rode one, and I the other. The slaves were chained together, and we took up our line of march: Mr. Walker taking the lead, and I bringing up the rear. Though the distance was not more than twenty miles, we did not reach it the first day. The road was worse than any that I have ever traveled.

Soon after we left St. Charles, the young child grew very cross and kept up a noise during the greater part of the day. Mr. Walker complained of its crying several times, and told the mother to stop the child's d——d noise, or he would. The woman tried to keep the child from crying, but could not. We put up at night with an acquaintance of Mr. Walker, and in the morning, just as we were about to start, the child again commenced crying. Walker stepped up to her and told her to give the child to him. The mother tremblingly obeyed. He took the child by one arm, as you would a cat by the leg, walked into the house, and said to the lady, "Madam, I will make you a present of this little nigger; it keeps such a noise that I can't bear it."

"Thank you, sir," said the lady.

The mother, as soon as she saw that her child was to be left, ran up to Mr. Walker and, falling upon her knees, begged him to let her have her child; she clung around his legs, and cried, "Oh, my child! my child! master, do let me have my child! oh, do, do, do! I will stop its crying if you will only let me have it again." When I saw this woman crying for her child so piteously, a shudder—a feeling akin to horror—shot through my frame. I have often since in imagination heard her crying for her child:

> O, master, let me stay to catch
>   My baby's sobbing breath,
> His little glassy eye to watch,
>   And smooth his limbs in death,
>
> And cover him with grass and leaf,
>   Beneath the large oak tree:
> It is not sullenness, but grief—
>   O, master, pity me!
>
> The morn was chill—I spoke no word,
>   But feared my babe might die,
> And heard all day, or thought I heard,
>   My little baby cry.
>
> At noon, oh, how I ran and took
>   My baby to my breast!
> I lingered—and the long lash broke
>   My sleeping infant's rest.
>
> I worked till night—till darkest night,
>   In torture and disgrace;
> Went home and watched till morning light,
>   To see my baby's face.
>
> Then give me but one little hour—
>   O! do not lash me so!
> One little hour—one little hour—
>   And gratefully I'll go.

Mr. Walker commanded her to return into the ranks with the other slaves. Women who had children were not chained, but those that had none were. As soon as her child was disposed of, she was chained in the gang.

The following song I have often heard the slaves sing, when about to be carried to the Far South. It is said to have been composed by a slave.

> See these poor souls from Africa
> Transported to America;
> We are stolen, and sold to Georgia—
> Will you go along with me?

We are stolen, and sold to Georgia—
Come sound the jubilee!

See wives and husbands sold apart,
Their children's screams will break my heart;
There's a better day a coming—
Will you go along with me?
There's a better day a coming,
Go sound the jubilee!

O, gracious Lord! when shall it be,
That we poor souls shall all be free?
Lord, break them slavery powers—
Will you go along with me?
Lord, break them slavery powers,
Go sound the jubilee!

Dear Lord, dear Lord, when slavery'll cease,
Then we poor souls will have our peace;
There's a better day a coming—
Will you go along with me?
There's a better day a coming,
Go sound the jubilee!

We finally arrived at Mr. Walker's farm. He had a house built during our absence to put slaves in. It was a kind of domestic jail. The slaves were put in the jail at night, and worked on the farm during the day. They were kept here until the gang was completed, when we again started for New Orleans, on board the steamboat North America (Captain Alexander Scott). We had a large number of slaves in this gang. One, by the name of Joe, Mr. Walker was training up to take my place, as my time was nearly out, and glad was I. We made our first stop at Vicksburg, where we remained one week and sold several slaves.

Mr. Walker, though not a good master, had not flogged a slave since I had been with him, though he had threatened me. The slaves were kept in the pen, and he always put up at the best hotel and kept his wines in his room, for the accommodation of those who called to negotiate with him for the purchase of slaves. One day, while we were at Vicksburg, several gentlemen came to see him for that purpose, and as usual the wine was called for. I took the tray and started around with it, and, having accidentally filled some of the glasses too full, the gentlemen spilled the wine on their clothes as they went to drink. Mr. Walker apologized to them for my carelessness, but looked at me as though he would see me again on this subject.

After the gentlemen had left the room, he asked me what I meant by my carelessness and said that he would attend to me. The next morning he gave me a note to carry to the jailer and a dollar in money to give to him. I suspected that all was not right, so I went down near the landing, where I met with a sailor and, walking up to him, asked him if he would be so kind as to read the note for me. He read it over and then looked at me. I asked him to tell me what was in it. Said he, "They are going to give you hell."

"Why?" said I.

He said, "This is a note to have you whipped, and says that you have a dollar to pay for it."

He handed me back the note, and off I started. I knew not what to do, but was determined not to be whipped. I went up to the jail—took a look at it, and walked off again. As Mr. Walker was acquainted with the jailer, I feared that I should be found out if I did not go and be treated in consequence of it still worse.

While I was meditating on the subject, I saw a colored man about my size walk up, and the thought struck me in a moment to send him with my note. I walked up to him and asked him who he belonged to. He said he was a free man and had been in the city but a short time. I told him I had a note to go into the jail and get a trunk to carry to one of the steamboats, but was so busily engaged that I could not do it, although I had a dollar to pay for it. He asked me if I would not give him the job. I handed him the note and the dollar, and off he started for the jail.

I watched to see that he went in, and, as soon as I saw the door close behind him, I walked around the corner and took my station, intending to see how my friend looked when he came out. I had been there but a short time, when a colored man came around the corner and said to another colored man with whom he was acquainted:

"They are giving a nigger scissors in the jail."

"What for?" said the other.

The man continued, "A nigger came into the jail and asked for the jailer. The jailer came out, and he handed him a note and said he wanted to get a trunk. The jailer told him to go with him, and he would give him the trunk. So he took him into the room and told the nigger to give up the dollar. He said a man had given him the dollar to pay for getting the trunk. But that lie would not answer. So they made him strip himself, and then they tied him down and are now whipping him."

I stood by all the while listening to their talk and soon found out that the person alluded to was my customer. I went into the street opposite the jail and concealed myself in such a manner that I could not be seen by any one coming out. I had been there but a short time, when the young man made his appearance and looked around for me. I, unobserved, came forth from my hiding place behind a pile of brick, and he pretty soon saw me and came up to me complaining bitterly, saying that I had played a trick upon him. I denied any knowledge of what the note contained and asked him what they had done to him. He told me in substance what I heard the man tell who had come out of the jail.

"Yes," said he, "they whipped me and took my dollar and gave me this note."

He showed me the note which the jailer had given him, telling him to give it to his master. I told him I would give him fifty cents for it—that being all the money I had. He gave it to me and took his money. He had received twenty lashes on his bare back, with the Negro-whip.

I took the note and started for the hotel where I had left Mr. Walker. Upon reaching the hotel, I handed it to a stranger whom I had not seen before and requested him to read it to me. As near as I can recollect, it was as follows:

"DEAR SIR:—By your direction, I have given your boy twenty lashes. He is a very saucy boy, and tried to make me believe that he did not belong to you, and I put it on to him well for lying to me.

"I remain your obedient servant."

It is true that in most of the slave-holding cities, when a gentleman wishes his servants whipped, he can send him to the jail and have it done. Before I went in where Mr. Walker was, I wet my cheeks a little, as though I had been crying. He looked at me and inquired what was the matter. I told him that I had never had such a whipping in my life and handed him the note. He looked at it and laughed.

"And so you told him that you did not belong to me?"

"Yes, sir," said I. "I did not know that there was any harm in that."

He told me I must behave myself, if I did not want to be whipped again.

This incident shows how it is that slavery makes its victims lying and mean, for which vices it afterwards reproaches them and uses them as arguments to prove that they deserve no better fate. Had I entertained the same views of right and wrong which I now do, I am sure I should never have practiced the deception upon that poor fellow which I did. I know of no act committed by me while in slavery which I have regretted more than that, and I heartily desire that it may be at some time or other in my power to make him amends for his vicarious sufferings in my behalf.

At the end of a week, we left for New Orleans, the place of our final destination, which we reached in two days. Here the slaves were placed in a Negro-pen, where those who wished to purchase could call and examine them. The Negro-pen is a small yard, surrounded by buildings, from fifteen to twenty feet wide, with the exception of a large gate with iron bars. The slaves are kept in the buildings during the night and turned out into the yard during the day. After the best of the stock was sold at private sale at the pen, the balance were taken to the Exchange Coffee-House Auction Rooms, kept by Isaac L. McCoy, and sold at public auction. After the sale of this lot of slaves, we left New Orleans for St. Louis.

[In St. Louis William Wells Brown tried in vain to get his owner to hire him to someone other than the slavetrader, Walker. For he was "heart sick at seeing [his] fellow creatures bought and sold." However a gang of slaves was gathered in St. Louis and after some weeks during which Brown witnessed the flogging and mistreatment of slaves, they and their cargo left for New Orleans.]

In a few days we reached New Orleans. Arriving there in the night, we remained on board until morning. While at New Orleans this time, I saw a slave killed, an account of which has been published by Theodore D. Weld in his book entitled *Slavery As It Is*. The circumstances were as follows. In the evening, between seven and eight o'clock, a slave came running down the levee, followed by several men and boys. The whites were crying out, "Stop that nigger! stop that nigger!" While the poor panting slave, in almost breathless accents, was repeating, "I did not steal the meat—I did not steal the meat." The poor man at last took refuge in the river. The whites who were in pursuit of him ran on board one of the boats to see if they could discover him. They finally espied him under the bow of the steamboat Trenton. They got a pikepole, and tried to drive him from his hiding place. When they would strike at him he would dive under the water. The water was so cold that it soon became evident that he must come out or be drowned.

While they were trying to drive him from under the bow of the boat or drown him, he would in broken and imploring accents say, "I did not steal the meat; I did not steal the meat. My master lives up the river. I want to see my master. I did not steal the meat. Do let me go home to master." After punching him and striking him over the head for some time, he at last sunk in the water, to rise no more alive.

On the end of the pikepole with which they were striking him was a hook, which caught in his clothing; and they hauled him up on the bow of the boat. Some said he was dead; others said he was "playing possum"; while others kicked him to make him get up; but it was of no use —he was dead.

As soon as they became satisfied of this, they commenced leaving, one after another. One of the hands on the boat informed the captain that they had killed the man, and that the dead body was lying on the deck. The captain came on deck, and said to those who were remaining, "You have killed this nigger; now take him off of my boat." The captain's name was Hart. The dead body was dragged on shore and left there. I went on board of the boat where our gang of slaves were, and during the whole night my mind was occupied with what I had seen. Early in the morning, I went on shore to see if the dead body remained there. I found it in the same position that it was left the night before. I watched to see what they would do with it. It was left there until between eight and nine o'clock, when a cart, which takes up the trash out of the streets, came along, and the body was thrown in and in a few minutes more was covered over with dirt that they were removing from the streets. During the whole time, I did not see more than six or seven persons around it, who, from their manner, evidently regarded it as no uncommon occurrence.

During our stay in the city, I met with a young white man with whom I was well acquainted in St. Louis. He had been sold into slavery under the following circumstances. His father was a drunkard and very poor, with a family of five or six children. The father died and left the mother to take care of and provide for the children as best she might. The eldest was a boy, named Burrill, about thirteen years of age, who did chores in a store kept by Mr. Riley, to assist his mother in procuring a living for the family. After working with him two years, Mr. Riley took him to New Orleans to wait on him while in that city on a visit; and when he returned to St. Louis, he told the mother of the boy that he had died with the yellow fever. Nothing more was heard from him, no one supposing him to be alive. I was much astonished when Burrill told me his story. Though I sympathized with him I could not assist him. We were both slaves. He was poor, uneducated, and without friends, and, if living, is, I presume, still held as a slave.

After selling out this cargo of human flesh, we returned to St. Louis; and my time was up with Mr. Walker. I had served him one year, and it was the longest year I ever lived.

[Hired out to work on a steamboat between St. Louis and Independence, Missouri, Brown planned his escape.]

At last the time for action arrived. The boat landed at a point which appeared to me to be the place to start from. I found that it would be impossible to carry anything with me but what was upon my person. I had some provisions and a single suit of clothes, about half worn. When the boat was discharging her cargo and the passengers engaged carrying their baggage on and off shore, I improved the opportunity to convey myself with my little effects on land. Taking up a trunk, I went up the wharf and was soon out of the crowd. I made directly for the woods, where I remained until night, knowing well that I could not travel, even in the state of Ohio, during the day without danger of being arrested.

I had long since made up my mind that I would not trust myself in the hands of any man, white or colored. The slave is brought up to look upon every white man as an enemy to him and his race; and twenty-one years in slavery had taught me that there were traitors, even among colored people. After dark, I emerged from the woods into a narrow path that led me into the main traveled road. But I knew not which way to go. I did not know north from south, east from west. I looked in vain for the North Star; a heavy cloud hid it from my view. I walked up and down the road until near midnight, when the clouds disappeared and I welcomed the sight of my friend—truly the slave's friend—the North Star!

As soon as I saw it, I knew my course. Before daylight I traveled twenty or twenty-five miles. It being in the winter, I suffered intensely from the cold, being without an overcoat and my other clothes rather thin for the season. I was provided with a tinderbox, so I could make up a fire when necessary. And but for this, I should certainly have frozen to death, for I was determined not to go to any house for shelter. I knew of a man belonging to General Ashly of St. Louis, who had run away near Cincinnati, on the way to Washington, but had been caught and carried back into slavery. I felt that a similar fate awaited me should I be seen by any one. I traveled at night and lay by during the day.

On the fourth day my provisions gave out, and then what to do I could not tell. Have something to eat I must; but how to get it was the question! On the first night after my food was gone, I went to a barn on the roadside and there found some ears of corn. I took ten or twelve of them and kept on my journey. During the next day, while in the woods, I roasted my corn and feasted upon it, thanking God that I was so well provided for.

My escape to a land of freedom now appeared certain, and the prospects of the future occupied a great part of my thoughts. What should be my occupation was a subject of much anxiety to me. The next thing: what should be my name? I have before stated that my old master, Dr. Young, had no children of his own, but had with him a nephew, the son of his brother, Benjamin Young. When this boy was brought to Dr. Young, his name being William, the same as mine, my mother was ordered to change mine to something else. This, at the time, I thought to be one of the most cruel acts that could be committed upon my rights, and I received several very severe whippings for telling people that my name was William, after orders were given to change it. Though young, I was old enough to place a high appreciation upon my name. It was decided, however, to call me "Sandford," and this name I was known by, not only upon my master's plantation, but up to the time that I made my escape. I was sold under the name of Sandford.

But as soon as the subject came to my mind, I resolved on adopting my old name of William and let Sandford go by the board, for I always hated it. Not because there was anything peculiar in the name, but because it had been forced upon me. It is sometimes common, at the South, for slaves to take the name of their masters. Some have a legitimate right to do so. But I always detested the idea of being called by the name of either of my masters. And as for my father, I would rather have adopted the name of "Friday" and been known as the servant of some Robinson Crusoe than to have taken his name. So I was not only hunting for my liberty, but also hunting for a name—though I regarded the latter as of little consequence, if I could but gain the former. Traveling along the road, I would sometimes speak to myself, sounding my name over, by way of getting used to it, before I should arrive among civilized human beings. On the fifth or sixth day, it rained very fast and froze about as fast as it fell, so that my clothes were one glare of ice. I traveled on at night until I became so chilled and benumbed—the wind blowing into my face—that I found it impossible to go any further and accordingly took shelter in a barn, where I was obliged to walk about to keep from freezing.

I have ever looked upon that night as the most eventful part of my escape from slavery. Nothing but the providence of God, and that old barn, saved me from freezing to death. I received a very severe cold, which settled upon my lungs. From time to time, my feet had been frostbitten, so that it was with difficulty I could walk. In this situation I traveled two days, when I found that I must seek shelter somewhere, or die.

The thought of death was nothing frightful to me, compared with that of being caught and again carried back into slavery. Nothing but the prospect of enjoying liberty could have induced me to undergo such trials, for

> Behind I left the whips and chains,
> Before me were sweet Freedom's plains!

This, and this alone, cheered me onward. But I at last resolved to seek protection from the inclemency of the weather, and therefore I secured myself behind some logs and brush, intending to wait there until some one should pass by. I thought it probable that I might see some colored person or, if not, some one who was not a slaveholder, for I had an idea that I should know a slaveholder as far as I could see him.

The first person that passed was a man in a buggy-wagon. He looked too genteel for me to hail him. Very soon another passed by on horseback. I attempted to speak to him, but fear made my voice fail me. As he passed, I left my hiding-place and was approaching the road, when I observed an old man walking towards me, leading a white horse. He had on a broad-brimmed hat and a very long coat and was evidently walking for exercise. As soon as I saw him and observed his dress, I thought to myself, "You are the man that I have been looking for!" Nor was I mistaken. He was the very man!

On approaching me, he asked me "if I was not a slave." I looked at him some time and then asked him "if he knew of any one who would help me, as I was sick." He answered that he would, but again asked if I was not a slave. I told him I was. He then said I was in a very proslavery neighborhood, and if I would wait until he went home, he would get a covered wagon for me. I promised to remain. He mounted his horse and was soon out of sight.

After he was gone, I meditated whether to wait or not, being apprehensive that he had gone for some one to arrest me. But I finally concluded to remain until he should return, removing some few rods to watch his movements. After a suspense of an hour and a half or more, he returned with a two-horse covered wagon, such as are usually seen under the shed of a Quaker meeting-house on Sundays and Thursdays; for the old man proved to be a Quaker of the George Fox stamp.

He took me to his house; but it was some time before I could be induced to enter it. Not until the old lady came out, did I venture into the house. I thought I saw something in the old lady's cap that told me I was not only safe but welcome in her house. I was not, however, prepared to receive their hospitalities. The only fault I found with them was their being too kind. I had never had a white man to treat me as an equal, and the idea of a white lady waiting on me at the table was still worse! Though the table was loaded with the good things of this life, I could not eat. I thought if I could only be allowed the privilege of eating in the kitchen I should be more than satisfied!

Finding that I could not eat, the old lady, who was a "Thompsonian," made me a cup of "composition" or "number six"; but it was so strong and hot, that I called it *"number seven!"* However, I soon found myself at home in this family. On different occasions, when telling these facts, I have been asked how I felt upon finding myself regarded as a man by a white family, especially just having run away from one. I cannot say that I have ever answered the question yet.

The fact that I was in all probability a freeman sounded in my ears like a charm. I am satisfied that none but a slave could place such an appreciation upon liberty as I did at that time. I wanted to see mother and sister, that I might tell them "I was free!" I wanted to see my fellow-slaves in St. Louis and let them know that the chains were no longer upon my limbs. I wanted to see Captain Price and let him learn from my own lips that I was no more a chattel, but a man! I was anxious, too, to inform Mrs. Price that she must get another coachman. And I wanted to see Eliza more than I did either Mr. or Mrs. Price!

The fact that I was a freeman—could walk, talk, eat and sleep as a man, and no one to stand over me with the blood-clotted cowhide—all this made me feel that I was not myself.

The kind friend that had taken me in was named Wells Brown. He was a devoted friend of the slave, but was very old and not in the enjoyment of good health. After being by the fire awhile, I found that my feet had been very much frozen. I was seized with a fever that threatened to confine me to my bed. But my Thompsonian friends soon raised me, treating me as kindly as if I had been one of their own children. I remained with them twelve or fifteen days, during which time they made me some clothing, and the old gentleman purchased me a pair of boots.

I found that I was about fifty or sixty miles from Dayton, in the state of Ohio, and between one and two hundred miles from Cleveland, on Lake Erie—a place I was desirous of reaching on my way to Canada. This I know will sound strangely to the ears of people in foreign lands, but it is nevertheless true. An American citizen was fleeing from a democratic, republican, Christian government, to receive protection under the monarchy of Great Britain. While the people of the United States boast of their freedom, they at the same time keep three millions of their own citizens in chains; and while I am seated here in sight of Bunker Hill Monument writing this narrative, I am a slave, and no law, not even in Massachusetts, can protect me from the hands of the slaveholder!

Before leaving this good Quaker friend, he inquired what my name was besides William. I told him that I had no other name. "Well," said he, "thee must have another name. Since thee has got out of slavery, thee has become a man, and men always have two names."

I told him that he was the first man to extend the hand of friendship to me, and I would give him the privilege of naming me.

"If I name thee," said he, "I shall call thee Wells Brown, after myself."

"But," said I, "I am not willing to lose my name of William. As it was taken from me once against my will, I am not willing to part with it again upon any terms.

"Then," said he, "I will call thee William Wells Brown."

"So be it," said I; and I have been known by that name ever since I left the house of my first white friend, Wells Brown.

After giving me some little change, I again started for Canada. In four days I reached a public house and went in to warm myself. I there learned that some fugitive slaves had just passed through the place. The men in the barroom were talking about it, and I thought that it must have been myself they referred to. I was therefore afraid to start, fearing they would seize me. But I finally mustered courage enough, and took my leave. As soon as I was out of sight, I went into the woods and remained there until night, when I again regained the road and traveled on until next day.

Not having had any food for nearly two days, I was faint with hunger and was in a dilemma what to do, as the little cash supplied me by my adopted father, and which had contributed to my comfort, was now all gone. I however concluded to go to a farmhouse and ask for something to eat. On approaching the door of the first one presenting itself, I knocked, and was soon met by a man who asked me what I wanted. I told him that I would like something to eat. He asked me where I was from and where I was going. I replied that I had come some way and was going to Cleveland.

After hesitating a moment or two, he told me that he could give me nothing to eat, adding, "that if I would work, I could get something to eat."

I felt bad, being thus refused something to sustain nature, but did not dare tell him that I was a slave.

Just as I was leaving the door, with a heavy heart, a woman, who proved to be the wife of this gentleman, came to the door and asked her husband what I wanted. He did not seem inclined to inform her. She therefore asked me herself. I told her that I had asked for something to eat. After a few other questions, she told me to come in and that she would give me something to eat.

I walked up to the door, but the husband remained in the passage, as if unwilling to let me enter.

She asked him two or three times to get out of the way and let me in. But as he did not move, she pushed him on one side, bidding me walk in! I was never before so glad to see a woman push a man aside! Ever since that act, I have been in favor of "woman's rights!"

After giving me as much food as I could eat, she presented me with ten cents, all the money then at her disposal, accompanied with a note to a friend, a few miles further on the road. Thanking this angel of mercy from an overflowing heart, I pushed on my way and in three days arrived at Cleveland, Ohio.

Being an entire stranger in this place, it was difficult for me to find where to stop. I had no money, and the lake being frozen, I saw that I must remain until the opening of the navigation or go to Canada by way of Buffalo. But believing myself to be somewhat out of danger, I secured an engagement at the Mansion House, as a table waiter, in payment for my board. The proprietor, however, whose name was E. M. Segur, in a short time hired me for twelve dollars a month, on which terms I remained until spring, when I found good employment on board a lake steamboat.

I purchased some books and at leisure moments perused them with considerable advantage to myself. While at Cleveland, I saw, for the first time, an antislavery newspaper. It was the *Genius of Universal Emancipation*, published by Benjamin Lundy. Though I had no home, I subscribed for the paper. It was my great desire, being out of slavery myself, to do what I could for the emancipation of my brethren yet in chains and, while on Lake Erie, I found many opportunities of "helping their cause along."

It is well known that a great number of fugitives make their escape to Canada, by way of Cleveland. While on the lakes, I always made arrangement to carry them on the boat to Buffalo or Detroit and thus effect their escape to the "promised land." The friends of the slave, knowing that I would transport them without charge, never failed to have a delegation when the boat arrived at Cleveland. I have sometimes had four or five on board at one time.

In the year 1842, I conveyed, from the first of May to the first of December, sixty-nine fugitives over Lake Erie to Canada. In 1843, I visited Malden, in Upper Canada, and counted seventeen in that small village whom I had assisted in reaching Canada. Soon after coming north I subscribed for the *Liberator*, edited by that champion of freedom, William Lloyd Garrison. I had heard nothing of the antislavery movement while in slavery. As soon as I found that my enslaved countrymen had friends who were laboring for their liberation, I felt anxious to join them and give what aid I could to the cause.

I found that a temperance reformation was needed among my colored brethren, and I early embraced the temperance cause. In company with a few friends, I commenced a temperance reformation among the colored people in the city of Buffalo and labored three years, in which time a society was built up numbering over five hundred out of a population of less than seven hundred.

In the autumn, 1843, impressed with the importance of spreading antislavery truth as a means to bring about the abolition of slavery, I commenced lecturing as an agent of the western New York Anti-Slavery Society and have ever since devoted my time to the cause of my enslaved countrymen.

JAMES W. C. PENNINGTON

A slave in Maryland, James Pennington was a blacksmith. He was cruelly treated by overseers and masters and fled from bondage to Pennsylvania. There he was befriended by Quakers and worked on a farm. Two years after the emancipation of slaves in New York, he settled there, got a job, and attended evening school. "I now began to see," he wrote, "for the first time, the extent of the mischief slavery had done to me. Twenty-one years of my life were gone, never again to return, and I was as profoundly ignorant comparatively, as a child five years old. This was painful, annoying, and humiliating in the extreme." Pennington became an outstanding abolitionist and minister, recognized in Europe as well as in the United States. He performed the marriage of Frederick and Anna Douglass. The University of Heidelberg gave him an Honorary Doctor of Divinity degree. The passage which follows describes his experiences while fleeing from slavery. Published in London in 1849, the second edition of his autobiography used here is entitled *The Fugitive Blacksmith or Events in the History of James W. C. Pennington.*

Flight and Recapture

Hope, fear, dread, terror, love, sorrow, and deep melancholy were mingled in my mind together; my mental state was one of most painful distraction, when I looked at my numerous family—a beloved father and
mother, eleven brothers and sisters. But when I looked at slavery as
such, when I looked at it in its mildest form, with all its annoyances,
and, above all, when I remembered that one of the chief annoyances of
slavery, in the most mild form, is the liability of being at any moment
sold into the worst form, it seemed that no consideration, not even that
of life itself, could tempt me to give up the thought of flight. And then
when I considered the difficulties of the way—the reward that would be
offered—the human bloodhounds that would be set upon my track—
the weariness—the hunger—the gloomy thought of not only losing all
one's friends in one day, but of having to seek and to make new friends
in a strange world. . . . But, as I have said, the hour was come, and the
man must act or forever be a slave.

It was now two o'clock. I stepped into the quarter. There was a
strange and melancholy silence mingled with the destitution that was
apparent in every part of the house. The only morsel I could see in the
shape of food was a piece of Indian flour bread; it might be half-a-
pound in weight. This I placed in my pocket and, giving a last look at
the aspect of the house and at a few small children who were playing at
the door, I sallied forth thoughtfully and melancholy.

After crossing the barnyard, a few moments' walk brought me to a small cave, near the mouth of which lay a pile of stones and into which I had deposited my clothes. From this, my course lay through thick and heavy woods and back lands to ———— town, where my brother lived. This town was six miles distance. It was now near three o'clock. My object was to be neither seen on the road, nor to approach the town by daylight, as I was well-known there and any intelligence of my having been seen there would at once put the pursuers on my track. This first six miles of my flight, I not only travelled very slowly, therefore, so as to avoid carrying any daylight to this town, but during this walk another very perplexing question was agitating my mind. Shall I call on my brother as I pass through, and show him what I am about? My brother was older than I and we were much attached. I had been in the habit of looking to him for counsel.

I entered the town about dark resolved, all things in view, *not* to show myself to my brother. Having passed through the town without being recognized, I now found myself under cover of night, a solitary wanderer from home and friends. My only guide was the North Star. By this I knew my general course northward, but at what point I should strike Pennsylvania, or when and where I should find a friend, I knew not. Another feeling now occupied my mind. I felt like a mariner who has gotten his ship outside of the harbour and has spread his sails to the breeze. The cargo is on board—the ship is cleared—and the voyage I must make; besides, this being my first night, almost everything will depend upon my clearing the coast before the day dawns. In order to do this my flight must be rapid. I therefore set forth in sorrowful earnest, only now and then I was cheered by the wild hope that I should somewhere and at sometime be free.

The night was fine for the season, and I passed on with little interruption for want of strength until, about three o'clock in the morning, I began to feel the chilling effects of the dew.

At this moment, gloom and melancholy again spread through my whole soul. The prospect of utter destitution which threatened me was more than I could bear, and my heart began to melt. What substance is there in a piece of dry Indian bread? What nourishment is there in it to warm the nerves of one already chilled to the heart? Will this afford a sufficient sustenance after the toil of the night? But while these thoughts were agitating my mind, the day dawned upon me in the midst of an open extent of country, where the only shelter I could find, without risking my travel by daylight, was a corn shock but a few hundred yards from the road. Here I must pass my first day out. The day was an unhappy one; my hiding-place was extremely precarious. I had to sit in a squatting position the whole day, without the least chance to rest. But besides this, my scanty pittance did not afford me that nourishment which my hard night's travel needed. Night came again to my relief, and I sallied forth to pursue my journey. By this time, not a crumb of my crust remained, and I was hungry and began to feel the desperation of distress.

As I traveled I felt my strength failing and my spirits wavered; my mind was in a deep and melancholy dream. It was cloudy; I could not see my star and had serious misgivings about my course.

In this way the night passed away. Just at the dawn of day I found a few sour apples and took my shelter under the arch of a small bridge that crossed the road. Here I passed the second day in ambush.

This day would have been more pleasant than the previous. But the sour apples and a draught of cold water had produced anything but a favorable effect. Indeed, I suffered most of the day with severe symptoms of cramp. The day passed away again without any further incident. As I set out at nightfall, I felt quite satisfied that I could not pass another twenty-four hours without nourishment. I made but little progress during the night and often sat down and slept frequently fifteen or twenty minutes. At the dawn of the third day, I continued my travel. As I had found my way to a public turnpike road during the night, I came very early in the morning to a tollgate, where the only person I saw, was a lad about twelve years of age. I inquired of him where the road led to. He informed me it led to Baltimore. I asked him the distance. He said it was eighteen miles.

This intelligence was perfectly astounding to me. My master lived eighty miles from Baltimore. I was now sixty-two miles from home. That distance in the right direction would have placed me several miles across Mason and Dixon's line, but I was evidently yet in the state of Maryland.

I ventured to ask the lad at the gate another question—which is the best way to Philadelphia? Said he, you can take a road which turns off about half-a-mile below this and goes to Gettysburg, or you can go on to Baltimore and take the packet.

I made no reply, but my thought was that I was as near Baltimore and Baltimore packets as would answer my purpose.

In a few moments I came to the road to which the lad had referred, and felt some relief when I had gotten out of that great public highway, "The National Turnpike," which I found it to be.

When I had walked a mile on this road, and when it had now gotten to be about nine o'clock, I met a young man with a load of hay. He drew up his horses and addressed me in a very kind tone, when the following dialogue took place between us.

"Are you traveling any distance, my friend?"

"I am on my way to Philadelphia."

"Are you free?"

"Yes, sir."

"I suppose, then, you are provided with free papers?"

"No, sir. I have no papers."

"Well, my friend, you should not travel on this road; you will be taken up before you have gone three miles. There are men living on this road who are constantly on the lookout for your people. It is seldom that one escapes them who attempts to pass by day."

He then very kindly gave me advice where to turn off the road at a certain point and how to find my way to a certain house, where I would meet with an old gentleman who would further advise me whether I had better remain till night, or go on.

I left this interesting young man, and such was my surprise and chagrin at the thought of having so widely missed my way, and my alarm at being in such a dangerous position, that in ten minutes I had so far forgotten his directions as to deem it unwise to attempt to follow them, lest I should miss my way and get into evil hands.

I left the road, however, and went into a small piece of wood. But not finding a sufficient hiding-place, and it being a busy part of the day, when persons were at work about the fields, I thought I should excite less suspicion by keeping in the road—so I returned to the road. The events of the next few moments proved that I committed a serious mistake.

I went about a mile, making in all two miles from the spot where I met my young friend and about five miles from the tollgate to which I have referred, and I found myself at the twenty-four miles' stone from Baltimore. It was now about ten o'clock in the forenoon. My strength was greatly exhausted by reason of the want of suitable food, but the excitement that was then going on in my mind left me little time to think of my need of food. Under ordinary circumstances as a traveler, I should have been glad to see the "Tavern" which was near the milestone. But as the case stood with me, I deemed it a dangerous place to pass, much less to stop at. I was therefore passing it as quietly and as rapidly as possible—when from the lot just opposite the house or signpost, I heard a coarse stern voice cry, "Halloo!"

I turned my face to the left, the direction from which the voice came, and observed that it proceeded from a man who was digging potatoes. I answered him politely; when the following occurred:—

"Who do *you* belong to?"

"I am free, sir."

"Have you got papers?"

"No, sir."

"Well, you must stop here."

By this time he had got astride the fence, making his way into the road. I said, "My business is onward, sir, and I do not wish to stop."

"I will see then if you don't stop, you black rascal."

He was now in the middle of the road, making after me in a brisk walk.

I saw that a crisis was at hand. I had no weapons of any kind, not even a pocket-knife; but I asked myself, shall I surrender without a struggle. The instinctive answer was "No." What will you do? Continue to walk. If he runs after you, run. Get him as far from the house as you can, then turn suddenly and smite him on the knee with a stone. That will render him, at least, unable to pursue you.

This was a desperate scheme, but I could think of no other; and my habits as a blacksmith had given my eye and hand such mechanical skill, that I felt quite sure that if I could only get a stone in my hand and have time to wield it, I should not miss his kneepan.

He began to breathe short. He was evidently vexed because I did not halt, and I felt more and more provoked at the idea of being thus pursued by a man to whom I had not done the least injury. I had just began to glance my eye about for a stone to grasp, when he made a tiger-like leap at me. This of course brought us to running. At this moment he yelled out "Jake Shouster!" and at the next moment the door of a small house standing to the left was opened, and out jumped a shoemaker girded up in his leather apron, with his knife in hand. He sprang forward and seized me by the collar, while the other seized my arms behind. I was now in the grasp of two men, either of whom were larger bodied than myself, and one of whom was armed with a dangerous weapon.

Standing in the door of the shoemaker's shop was a third man, and in the potato lot I had passed was still a fourth man. Thus surrounded by superior physical force, the fortune of the day it seemed to me was gone.

My heart melted away. I sunk resistlessly into the hands of my captors, who dragged me immediately into the tavern which was near.

A few moments after I was taken into the barroom, the news having gone as by electricity, the house and yard were crowded with gossipers, who had left their business to come and see "the runaway nigger." This hastily assembled congregation consisted of men, women, and children. Each one had a look to give at, and a word to say about—the "nigger."

But among the whole, there stood one whose name I have never known, but who evidently wore the garb of a man whose profession bound him to speak for the dumb. It was he, standing head and shoulders above all that were round about, who spoke the first hard sentence against me. Said he, "That fellow is a runaway, I know. Put him in jail a few days, and you will soon hear where he came from." And then fixing a fiend-like gaze upon me, he continued. "If I lived on this road, you fellows would not find such clear running as you do. I'd trap more of you."

But now comes the pinch of the case: the case of conscience to me even at this moment. Emboldened by the cruel speech just recited, my captors enclosed me and said, "Come now, this matter may easily be settled without you going to jail. Who do you belong to, and where did you come from?"

The facts here demanded were in my breast. I knew according to the law of slavery who I belonged to and where I came from, and I must now do one of three things: I must refuse to speak at all, or I must communicate the fact, or I must tell an untruth. How would an untutored slave, who had never heard of such a writer as Archdeacon Paley, be likely to act in such a dilemma? The first point decided was: the facts in this case are my private property. These men have no more right to them than a highway robber has to my purse. What will be the consequence if I put them in possession of the facts. In forty-eight hours, I shall have received perhaps one hundred lashes and be on my way to the Louisiana cotton fields. Of what service will it be to them. They will get a paltry sum of two hundred dollars. Is not my liberty worth more to me than two hundred dollars are to them?

I resolved, therefore, to insist that I was free. This not being satisfactory without other evidence, they tied my hands and set out for a magistrate who lived about half a mile distant. It so happened that when we arrived at his house he was not at home. This was to them a disappointment, but to me it was a relief. However, I soon learned by their conversation that there was still another magistrate in the neighborhood and that they would go to him. In about twenty minutes and after climbing fences and jumping ditches, we, captors and captive, stood before his door; but it was after the same manner as before—he was not at home. By this time the day had worn away to one or two o'clock, and my captors evidently began to feel somewhat impatient of the loss of time. We were about a mile and a quarter from the tavern. As we set out on our return, they began to parley. Finding it was difficult for me to get over fences with my hands tied, they untied me and said, "Now John," that being the name they had given me, "if you have run away from any one, it would be much better for you to tell us!" But I continued to affirm that I was free. I knew, however, that my situation was very critical, owing to the shortness of the distance I must be from home. My advertisement might overtake me at any moment.

On our way back to the tavern, we passed through a small skirt of wood, where I resolved to make an effort to escape again. One of my captors was walking on either side of me: I made a sudden turn, and with my left arm swept the legs of one of my captors from under him. I left him nearly standing on his head and took to my heels. As soon as they could recover, they both took after me. We had to mount a fence. This I did most successfully and made across an open field towards another wood. One of my captors, being a long-legged man, was in advance of the other and consequently neared me. We had a hill to rise, and during the ascent he gained on me. Once more I thought of self-defense. I am trying to escape peaceably, but this man is determined that I shall not.

My case was now desperate, and I took this desperate thought: "I will run him a little farther from his coadjutor. I will then suddenly catch a stone and wound him in the breast." This was my fixed purpose. . . . I had arrived near the point on the top of the hill, where I expected to do the act, when to my surprise and dismay I saw the other side of the hill was not only all ploughed up, but we came suddenly upon a man ploughing, who as suddenly left his plough and cut off my flight by seizing me by the collar. At the same moment my pursuer seized my arms behind. Here I was again in a sad fix. By this time the other pursuer had come up. I was most savagely thrown down on the ploughed ground with my face downward. The ploughman placed his knee upon my shoulders, one of my captors put his upon my legs, while the other tied my arms behind me. I was then dragged up and marched off with kicks, punches, and imprecations.

We got to the tavern at three o'clock. Here they again cooled down and made an appeal to me to make a disclosure. I saw that my attempt to escape strengthened their belief that I was a fugitive. I said to them, "If you will not put me in jail, I will now tell you where I am from." They promised. "Well," said I, "a few weeks ago, I was sold from the eastern shore to a slave trader who had a large gang and set out for Georgia, but when he got to a town in Virginia, he was taken sick and died with the smallpox. Several of his gang also died with it, so that the people in the town became alarmed and did not wish the gang to remain among them. No one claimed us or wished to have anything to do with us. I left the rest, and thought I would go somewhere and get work."

When I said this, it was evidently believed by those who were present, and, notwithstanding the unkind feeling that had existed, there was a murmur of approbation. At the same time, I perceived that a panic began to seize some, at the idea that I was one of a smallpox gang. Several who had clustered near me moved off to a respectful distance. One or two left the barroom and murmured, "better let the smallpox nigger go."

I was then asked what was the name of the slave trader. Without premeditation, I said, "John Henderson."

"John Henderson!" said one of my captors. "I knew him. I took up a yaller boy for him about two years ago and got fifty dollars. He passed out with a gang about that time, and the boy ran away from him at Frederickstown. What kind of a man was he?"

At a venture, I gave a description of him. "Yes," said he, "that is the man." By this time, all the gossipers had cleared the coast. Our friend, "Jake Shouster," had also gone back to his bench to finish his custom work, after having "lost nearly the whole day, trotting about with a nigger tied," as I heard his wife say as she called him home to his dinner. I was now left alone with the man who first called to me in the morning. In a sober manner, he made this proposal to me: "John, I have a brother living in Risterstown, four miles off, who keeps a tavern. I think you had better go and live with him till we see what will turn up.

He wants an ostler." I at once assented to this. "Well," said he, "take something to eat, and I will go with you."

Although I had so completely frustrated their designs for the moment, I knew that it would by no means answer for me to go into that town, where there were prisons, handbills, newspapers, and travelers. My intention was to start with him, but not to enter the town alive.

HENRY "BOX" BROWN

The life of Henry Brown began near Richmond, Virginia. Separated from his family and subject to cruel overseers, he was repeatedly cheated of money and property by white men. Embittered, yet longing for freedom, he conceived the amazing idea of escaping slavery by Adams Express. He had himself packed in a box three feet long and two and a half feet deep and was shipped by freight from Richmond to Philadelphia. He was closed up in this box for twenty-seven hours and nearly suffocated. The shipment was received by The Philadelphia Vigilance Committee, an abolitionist group. *The Narrative of Henry "Box" Brown, Written by Himself* (which we use here) was published in 1851.

Shipped to Freedom

I was born about forty-five miles from the city of Richmond, in Louisa County, in the year 1815. I entered the world a slave—in the midst of a country whose most honored writings declare that all men have a right to liberty, but had imprinted upon my body no mark which could be made to signify that my destiny was to be that of a bondman. Neither was there any angel that stood by, at the hour of my birth, to hand my body over, by the authority of heaven, to be the property of a fellow-man. No—I was a slave because my countrymen had made it lawful, in utter contempt of the declared will of heaven, for the strong to lay hold of the weak and to buy and to sell them as marketable goods. Thus was I born a slave. Tyrants—remorseless, destitute of religion and every principle of humanity—stood by the couch of my mother, and as I entered into the world, before I had done anything to forfeit my right to liberty, and while my soul was yet undefiled by the commission of actual sin, stretched forth their bloody arms and branded me with the mark of bondage. By such means I became their own property. Yes, they robbed me of myself before I could know the nature of their wicked arts, and ever afterwards—until I forcibly wrenched myself from their hands—did they retain their stolen property.

My father and mother, of course, were then slaves. Now, both of them are enjoying such a measure of liberty, as the law affords to those who have made recompense to the tyrant for the right of property he holds in his fellowman. It was not my fortune to be long under my mother's care, but I still possess a vivid recollection of her affectionate oversight. Such lessons as the following she would frequently give me. She would take me upon her knee and, pointing to the forest trees which were then being stripped of their foliage by the winds of autumn, would say to me, "My son, as yonder leaves are stripped from off the trees of the forest, so are the children of the slaves swept away from them by the hands of cruel tyrants." Her voice would tremble and she would seem almost choked with her deep emotion, while the tears would find their way down her saddened cheeks. On those occasions, she fondly pressed me to her heaving bosom, as if to save me from so dreaded a calamity, or to feast on the enjoyments of maternal feeling while she yet retained possession of her child. I was then young, but I well recollect the sadness of her countenance and the mournful sacredness of her words as they impressed themselves upon my youthful mind —never to be forgotten.

Mothers of the North! As you gaze upon the fair forms of your idolized little ones, just pause for a moment; how would you feel if you knew that at any time the will of a tyrant, who neither could nor would sympathize with your domestic feelings, might separate them for ever from your embrace, not to be laid in the silent grave "where the wicked cease from troubling and where the weary are at rest," but to live under the dominion of tyrants and avaricious men, whose cold hearts cannot sympathize with your feelings, but who will mock at any manifestation of tenderness and scourge them to satisfy the cruelty of their own disposition. Such is the condition of hundreds of thousands of mothers in the southern states of America.

My mother used to instruct me in the principles of morality, according to her own notion of what was good and pure. But I had no means of acquiring proper conception of religion in a state of slavery, where all those who professed to be followers of Jesus Christ evinced more of the disposition of demons than of men. It is really a matter of wonder to me now, considering the character of my position, that I did not imbibe a strong and lasting hatred of every thing pertaining to the religion of Christ. My lessons in morality were of the most simple kind. I was told not to steal, not to tell lies, and to behave myself in a becoming manner towards everybody. My mother, although a slave, took great delight in watching the result of her moral training in the character of my brother and myself, whilst—whether successful or unsuccessful in the formation of superior habits in us it is not for me to say—there was sown for her a blissful remembrance in the minds of her children, which will be cherished, both by the bond and the free, as long as life shall last.

As a specimen of the religious knowledge of the slave, I may here state what were my impressions in regard to my master: assuring the reader that I am not joking but stating what were the opinions of all the slaves' children on my master's plantation, so that some judgment may be formed of the care which was taken of our religious instruction. I really believed my old master was Almighty God and that the young master was Jesus Christ! The reason of this error seems to have been that we were taught to believe thunder to be the voice of God, and when it was about to thunder my old master would approach us, if we were in the yard, and say, all you children run into the house now, for it is going to thunder. And after the thunderstorm was over he would approach us smilingly and say "What a fine shower we have had," and, bidding us look at the flowers, would observe how prettily they appeared. We children, seeing this so frequently, could not avoid the idea that it was he that thundered and made the rain to fall in order to make his flowers look beautiful, and I was nearly eight years of age before I got rid of this childish superstition. Our master was uncommonly kind (for even a slaveholder may be kind), and as he moved about in his dignity he seemed like a god to us. Notwithstanding his kindness, although he knew very well what superstitious notions we formed of him, he never made the least attempt to correct our erroneous impression, but rather seemed pleased with the reverential feelings which we entertained towards him. All the young slaves called his son Saviour, and the manner in which I was undeceived was as follows: One Sabbath after preaching time my mother told my father of a woman who wished to join the church. She had told the preacher that she had been baptized by one of the slaves at night—a practice which is quite common. After they went from their work to the minister, he asked her if she believed that our Saviour came into the world and had died for the sins of men? And she said "yes." I was listening anxiously to the conversation, and when my mother had finished, I asked her if my young master was not the Saviour whom the woman said was dead? She said he was not, but it was our Saviour in heaven. I then asked her if there was a Saviour there, too, and she told me that young master was not our Saviour—which astonished me very much. I then asked her if old master was not he? To which she replied he was not, and began to instruct me more fully in reference to the God of Heaven. After this, I believed there was a God who ruled the world, although previously I did not entertain the least idea of any such being. However dangerous my former notions were, they were not at all out of keeping with the blasphemous teachings of the hellish system of slavery.

One of my sisters became anxious to have her soul converted and for this purpose had the hair cut from her head, because it is a notion which prevails amongst the slaves, that unless the hair be cut the soul cannot be converted. My mother reproved her for this and told her that she must pray to God who dwelled in heaven and who, only, could convert her soul, and said if she wished to renounce the sins of the world she should recollect that it was not by outside show, such as the cutting of the hair, that God measured the worthiness or unworthiness of his servants. "Only ask of God," she said, "with an humble heart, forsaking your sins in obedience to his divine commandment, and whatever mercy is most fitting for your condition he will graciously bestow."

While still a lad my principal employment was waiting upon my master and mistress and at intervals taking lessons in the various kinds of work which was carried on on the plantation. I often there—where the hot sun sent forth its scorching rays upon my tender head—looked forward with dismay to the time when I, like my fellow slaves, should be driven by the taskmaster's cruel lash to separate myself from my parents and all my present associates, to toil without reward and to suffer cruelties as yet unknown. The slave has always the harrowing idea before him—however kindly he may be treated for the time being—that the auctioneer may soon set him up for public sale and knock him down as the property of the person who, whether man or demon, would pay his master the greatest number of dollars for his body.

My brother and I were in the habit of carrying grain to the mill a few times in the year, which was the means of furnishing us with some information respecting other slaves. Otherwise, we would have known nothing whatever of what was going on anywhere in the world, excepting on our master's plantation. The mill was situated in Yausinville County at a distance of about twenty miles from our residence and belonged to one Colonel Ambler. On these occasions we used to acquire some little knowledge of what was going on around us, and we neglected no opportunity of making ourselves acquainted with the condition of other slaves.

On one occasion, while waiting for grain, we entered a house in the neighborhood and, while resting ourselves there, saw a number of for-lorn looking beings pass the door. As they passed we noticed they gazed earnestly upon us. Afterwards, about fifty did the very same, and we heard some of them remarking that we had shoes, vests, and hats. We felt a desire to talk with them, and, accordingly, after receiving some bread and meat from the mistress of the house, we followed those abject beings to their quarters and saw such a sight as we had never witnessed before, as we had always lived on our master's plantation and this was the first of our journeys to the mill. These slaves were dressed in shirts made of coarse bagging such as coffee sacks are made from and some kind of light substance for pantaloons, and this was all their clothing! They had no shoes, hats, vests, or coats, and when my brother spoke of their poor clothing they said they had never before seen colored persons dressed as we were. They looked very hungry, and we divided our bread and meat among them. They said they had never had any meat given them by their master. My brother put various questions to them, such as: Did they have wives? Did they go to church? etc. They said they had wives but were obliged to marry persons who worked on the same plantation, as the master would not allow them to take wives from other plantations. Consequently, they were all related to each other, and the master obliged them to marry their relatives or to remain single. My brother asked one of them to show him his sisters. He said he could not distinguish them from the rest as they were all his sisters. Although the slaves themselves entertain considerable respect for the law of mar-riage as a moral principle and are exceedingly well pleased when they can obtain the services of a minister in the performance of the cere-mony, yet the law recognizes no right in slaves to marry at all. The rela-tion of husband and wife, parent and child, only exists by the toleration of their master, who may insult the slave's wife or violate her person at any moment, and there is no law to punish him for what he has done. Now this not only may be as I have said, but it actually is the case to an alarming extent. It is my candid opinion that one of the strongest mo-tives that operates upon the slaveholders in inducing them to maintain their iron grasp upon the unfortunate slaves is because it gives them such unlimited control over the person of their female slaves. The greater part of slaveholders are licentious men, and the most respect-able and kind masters keep some of these slaves as mistresses. It is for their pecuniary interest to do so, as their progeny is equal to so many dollars and cents in their pockets, instead of being a source of expense to them as would be the case if their slaves were free. It is a horrible idea, but it is no less true, that no slave husband has any certainty whatever of being able to retain his wife a single hour. Neither has any wife any more certainty of her husband. Their fondest affection may be utterly disregarded, and their devoted attachment cruelly ignored at any moment a brutal slaveholder may think fit.

The slaves on Colonel Ambler's plantation were never allowed to attend church, but were left to manage their religious affairs in their own way. An old slave whom they called John decided on their religious profession and would baptize the approved parties during the silent watches of the night, while their master was asleep. We might have got information on many things from these slaves of Colonel Ambler, but, while we were thus engaged, we perceived the overseer directing his steps towards us like a bear for its prey. We had, however, time to ask one of them if they were ever whipped. To which he replied that not a day passed over their heads without some of them being brutally punished, "and" said he, "we shall have to suffer for this talk with you. It was but this morning," he continued, "that many of us were severely whipped for having been baptized the night before!" After we left them, we heard the screams of these poor creatures while they were suffering under the blows of the hard treatment received from the overseer for the crime, as we supposed, of talking with us. We felt thankful that we were excepted from such treatment, but we had no certainty that we should not, ere long, be placed in a similar position.

On returning to the mill, we met a young man, a relation of the owner of this plantation, who for some time had been eyeing us very attentively. He at length asked us if we had ever been whipped, and when I told him we had not, he replied, "Well, neither of you will ever be of any value." He expressed a good deal of surprise that we were allowed to wear hats and shoes, supposing that slaves had no business to wear such clothing as their master wore. We had carried our fishing lines with us and requested the privilege of fishing in his stream, which he roughly denied us, saying, "We do not allow niggers to fish." Nothing daunted, however, by the rebuff, my brother went to another place where, without asking permission of any one, he succeeded in obtaining a plentiful supply of fish. On returning, the young slaveholder seemed to be displeased at our success, but, knowing that we caught them in a stream which was not under his control, he said nothing. He knew that our master was a rich slaveholder, and probably he guessed from our appearance that we were favorites of his. Perhaps he was somewhat induced from that consideration to let us alone; at any rate, he did not molest us any more.

We afterwards carried our corn to a mill belonging to a Mr. Bullock, only about ten miles distant from our plantation. This man was very kind to us. If we were late at night he would take us into his house, give us beds to sleep upon, and take charge of our horses. He would even carry our grain himself into the mill, and he always furnished us in the morning with a good breakfast. We were rather astonished, for some time, that this man was so kind to us—and, in this respect, so different from the other miller—until we learned that he was not a slaveholder. This miller allowed us to catch as many fish as we chose, and even furnished us with fishing implements when we had none or only very imperfect ones of our own.

While at this mill we became acquainted with a colored man from a northern part of the country, and, as our desire was strong to learn how our brethren fared in other places, we questioned him respecting his treatment. He complained much of his hard fate: he said he had a wife and one child and begged for some of our fish to carry to his wife, which we gladly gave him. He told us he had just sent a few hickory nuts to market for which he had received thirty-six cents, and that he had given the money to his wife, to furnish her with some little articles of comfort.

On our return from their place one time, we met with a colored man and woman, who were very cross to each other. We inquired as to the cause of their disagreement and the man told us that the woman had such a tongue—that some of them had taken a sheep because they did not get enough to eat and this woman, after eating of it, went and told their master, and they had all received a severe whipping. This man enjoined upon his slaves never to steal from him again, but to steal as much as they chose from any other person. If they took care to do it in such a manner as the owner could not catch them in the act, nor be able to swear to the property after they had fetched it, he would shield them from punishment provided they would give him a share of the meat. Not long after this, the slaves, availing themselves of their master's protection, stole a pig from a neighboring plantation and, according to their agreement, furnished their master with his share. The owner of the missing animal, however, having heard something to make him suspect what had become of his property, came rushing into the house of the man who had just eaten of the stolen food and in a very excited manner demanded reparation from him for the beast which his slaves had stolen. The villain, rising from the table where he had just been eating of the stolen property, said, "my servants know no more about your stolen hog than I do," which indeed was perfectly true; and the loser of the swine went away without saying any more.

Although the master of this slave with whom we were talking had told him that it was no sin to steal from others, my brother took good care to let him know, before we separated, that it was as much a sin in the sight of God to steal from the one as the other. "Oh," said the master, "niggers has nothing to do with God." And, indeed, the whole feature of slavery is so utterly inconsistent with the principles of religion, reason, and humanity that it is no wonder that the very mention of the word God grates upon the ear as if it typified the degeneracy of this hellish system.

> Turn! greater Ruler of the skies!
> Turn from their sins thy searching eyes;
> Nor let the offenses of their hand,
> Within thy book recorded stand.
> There's not a sparrow or a worm
> O'erlooked in thy decrees,
> Thou raisest monarchs to a throne—
> They sink with equal ease.
> May Christ's example, all divine,
> To us a model prove!
> Like his, O God! our hearts incline,
> Our enemies to love!

My master's son, Charles, at one time, became impressed with the evils of slavery and put his notion into practical effect by emancipating about forty of his slaves and paying their expenses to a free state. Our old master, about this time, being unable to attend to all his affairs himself, employed an overseer whose disposition was so cruel as to make many of the slaves run away. I fancy the neighbors began to clamor about our master's mild treatment to his slaves, for which reason he was induced to employ an overseer. The change in our treatment was so great, and so much for the worse, that we could not help lamenting that the master had adopted such a change. There is no telling what might have been the result of this new method amongst slaves, so unused to the lash as we were, if, in the midst of the experiment, our old master had not been called upon to go the way of all the earth. As he was about to expire he sent for my mother and me to come to his bedside. We ran with beating hearts and highly elated feelings, not doubting, in the least, but that he was about to confer upon us the boon of freedom—for we had both expected that we should be set free when master died—but imagine our deep disappointment when the old man called me to his side and said, "Henry, you will make a good ploughboy, or a good gardener; now you must be an honest boy and never tell an untruth.

"I have given you to my son William, and you must obey him." Thus the old gentleman deceived us by his former kind treatment and raised expectations in our youthful minds which were doomed to be overthrown. He went to stand before the great Jehovah to give an account of the deeds done in the body, and we, disappointed in our expectations, were left to mourn, not so much our master's death, as our galling bondage. If there is anything which tends to buoy up the spirit of the slave, under the pressure of his severe toils, more than another, it is the hope of future freedom: by this his heart is cheered and his soul is lighted up in the midst of the fearful scenes of agony and suffering which he has to endure. Occasionally, as some event approaches from which he can calculate on a relaxation of his sufferings, his hope burns with a bright blaze; but most generally the mind of the slave is filled with gloomy apprehension of a still harder fate. I have known many slaves to labor unusually hard with the view of obtaining the price of their own redemption, who, after they had paid for themselves over and over again, were—by the unprincipled tyranny and fiendish mockery of moral principle in which their barbarous masters delight to indulge— still refused what they had so fully paid for and what they so ardently desired. Indeed, a great many masters hold out to their slaves the object of purchasing their own freedom—in order to induce them to labor more—without at the same time entertaining the slightest idea of ever fulfilling their promise.

On the death of my old master, his property was inherited by four sons, whose names were: Stronn, Charles, John, and William Barret. As a result, the human as well as every other kind of property came to be divided equally amongst these four sons, which division—as it separated me from my father and mother, my sister and brother, with whom I had hitherto been allowed to live—was the most severe trial to my feelings which I had ever endured. I was then only fifteen years of age, but it is as present in my mind as if but yesterday's sun had shone upon the dreadful exhibition. My mother was separated from her youngest child, and it was not till after she had begged most piteously for its restoration that she was allowed to give it one farewell embrace before she had to let it go for ever. This kind of torture is a thousand fold more cruel and barbarous than the use of the lash that lacerates the back. The gashes which the whip or the cow skin makes may heal, and the place that was marked in a little while may cease to exhibit the signs of what it had endured, but the pangs that lacerate the soul in consequence of the forcible disruption of parent and the dearest family ties only grow deeper and more piercing as memory fetches from a greater distance the horrid acts by which they have been produced. And there is no doubt but that under the weighty infirmities of declining life and the increasing force and vividness with which the mind retains the memoranda of the agonies of former years—which form so great a part of memory's possessions in the minds of most slaves—thousands are annually hurried off from off the stage of life itself.

Mother, my sister Jane, and I fell into the hands of William Barret. My sister Mary and her children went another way; Edward, another; and John and Lewis and my sister Robinnet another. William Barret took my sister Martha for his "keep Miss." It is a difficult thing to divide all the slaves on a plantation. No person wishes for all children, or all old people—while both old, young, and middle aged have to be divided. But the tyrant slaveholder regards not the social or domestic feelings of the slave and makes his division according to the *moneyed* value they possess, without giving the slightest consideration to the domestic or social ties by which the individuals are bound to each other. Indeed, their common expression is that "niggers have no feelings."

My father and mother were left on the plantation; but I was taken to the city of Richmond, to work in a tobacco manufactory owned by my old master's son, William, who had received a special charge from his father to take good care of me, and which charge my new master endeavored to perform. He told me if I would behave well he would take good care of me and give me money to spend; he talked so kindly to me that I determined I would exert myself to the utmost to please him and do just as he wished me in every respect. He furnished me with a new suit of clothes, and gave me money to buy things to send to my mother. One day I overheard him telling the overseer that *his father had raised me*—that I was a smart boy and that he must never whip me. I tried exceedingly hard to perform what I thought was my duty and escaped the lash almost entirely, although I often thought the overseer would have liked to have given me a whipping, but my master's orders, which he dared not altogether to set aside, were my defense. Under these circumstances my lot was comparatively easy.

Our overseer at that time was a colored man, whose name was Wilson Gregory. He was generally considered a shrewd and sensible man, especially to be a man of color, and, after the orders which my master gave him concerning me, he used to treat me very kindly indeed and gave me board and lodgings in his own house. Gregory acted as bookkeeper also to my master and was much in favor with the merchants of the city and all who knew him. He instructed me how to judge of the qualities of tobacco, and, with the view of making me a more proficient judge of that article, he advised me to learn to chew and to smoke which I therefore did.

About eighteen months after I came to the city of Richmond, an extraordinary occurrence took place which caused great excitement all over the town. I did not know then precisely what was the cause of this excitement, for I could get no satisfactory information from my master. He only said that some of the slaves had plotted to kill their owners. I have since learned that it was the famous Nat Turner's insurrection. Many slaves were whipped, hung, and cut down with the swords in the streets, and some that were found away from their quarters after dark were shot. The whole city was in the utmost excitement, and the whites seemed terrified beyond measure, so true is it that the "wicked flee when no man pursueth." Great numbers of slaves were loaded with irons; some were "half-hung" as it was termed: that is, they were suspended from some tree with a rope about their necks, so adjusted as not quite to strangle them, and then they were pelted by men and boys with rotten eggs. This half-hanging is a refined species of punishment peculiar to slaves. This insurrection took place some distance from the city and was the occasion of the enacting of that law by which more than five slaves were forbidden to meet together unless they were at work, and also of that, for the silencing all colored preachers. One of that class in our city refused to obey the impious mandate and, in consequence of his refusal, was severely whipped. His religion was, however, found to be too deeply rooted for him to be silenced by any mere power of man and, consequently, no efforts could avail to extort from his lips a promise that he would cease to proclaim the glad tidings of the gospel to his enslaved and perishing fellowmen.

I had now been about two years in Richmond City, and not having, during that time, seen, and very seldom heard from, my mother, my feelings were very much tried by the separation which I had thus to endure. I missed severely her welcome smile when I returned from my daily task. No one seemed at that time to sympathize with me, and I began to feel, indeed, that I really was alone in the world. Worst of all, I could console myself with no hope, not even the most distant, that I should ever see my beloved parents again.

About this time, Wilson Gregory, who was our overseer, died. His place was supplied by a man named Stephen Bennet, who had a wooden leg. He used to creep up behind the slaves to hear what they had to talk about in his absence; but his wooden leg generally betrayed him by coming into contact with something which would make a noise, and that would call the attention of the slaves to what he was about. He was a very mean man in all his ways and was very much disliked by the slaves. He used to whip them, often, in a shameful manner. On one occasion I saw him take a slave, whose name was Pinkney, and make him take off his shirt; he then tied his hands and gave him one hundred lashes on his bare back; and all this because he lacked three pounds of his task, which was valued at six cents. I saw him do many other things which were equally cruel, but it would be useless to multiply instances here, as no rational being doubts that slavery, even in its mildest forms, is a hard and cruel fate. Yet with all his barbarities and cruelties this man was generally reckoned a very sensible man on religious subjects, and he used to be frequently talking about things of that sort, but sometimes he spoke with very great levity indeed. He used to say that if he died and went to hell, he had enough of sense to fool the Devil and get out. He did take his departure at last, to that bower from which, whence borne, no traveler returns, and whether well or ill prepared for the change, I will not say.

Bennet was followed as overseer by one Henry Bedman, and he was the best that we had. He neither used the whip nor cheated the hands of what little they had to receive, and I am confident that he had more work done by equal numbers of hands than had been done under any overseer either before or since his appointment to office. He possessed a much greater influence by his kindness than any overseer did by his lash. He was altogether a very good man, was very fond of sacred music, and used to ask me and some of the other slaves, who were working in the same room, to sing for him—something "smart" as he used to say, which we were generally as well pleased to do as he was to ask us. It was not our fate however to enjoy his kindness long. He, too, very soon died, and his death was looked upon as a misfortune by all who had been slaves under him.

[Henry Brown tried, unsuccessfully, to buy his wife and children. Cheated by his master out of the purchase money, he learned that his family had been sold to a slave trader.]

While I was thus musing, I received a message, that if I wished to see my wife and children and bid them the last farewell, I could do so by taking my stand on the street where they were all to pass on their way for North Carolina. I quickly availed myself of this information and placed myself by the side of a street. Soon I had the melancholy satisfaction of witnessing the approach of a gang of slaves, amounting to three hundred and fifty in number, marching under the direction of a Methodist minister, by whom they were purchased, and amongst which slaves were my wife and children. I stood in the midst of many who, like myself, were mourning the loss of friends and relations and had come there to obtain one parting look at those whose company they, but a short time before, had imagined they should always enjoy; but who were, without any regard to their own wills, now driven by the tyrant's voice and the smart of the whip on their way to another scene of toil and, to them, another land of sorrow in a far off southern country. These beings were marched with ropes about their necks and staples on their arms. Although in that respect the scene was no very novel one to me, yet the peculiarity of my own circumstances made it assume the appearance of unusual horror. This train of beings was accompanied by a number of wagons loaded with little children of many different families, which as they appeared rent the air with their shrieks and cries and vain endeavors to resist the separation which was thus forced upon them and the cords with which they were thus bound; but what should I now see in the very foremost wagon but a little child looking towards me and pitifully calling, "father! father!" This was my eldest child, and I was obliged to look upon it for the last time that I would, perhaps, ever see it again in life. If it had been going to the grave and this gloomy procession had been about to return its body to the dust from whence it sprang, whence its soul had taken its departure for the land of spirits, my grief would have been nothing in comparison to what I then felt. For then I could have reflected that its sufferings were over and that it

would never again require nor look for a father's care; but it went with
all those tender feelings riven, by which it was endeared to a father's
love. It still had to live subject to the deprivation of paternal care and to
the chains and wrongs of slavery and yet be dead to the pleasure of a father from whose heart the impression of its early innocence and love
will never be effaced. Thus passed my child from my presence—my
own child. I loved it with all the fondness of a father; but things were so
ordered that I could only say farewell and leave it to pass in its chains
while I looked for the approach of another gang in which my wife was
also loaded with chains. My eye soon caught her precious face—but
gracious heavens! that glance of agony may God spare me from ever
again enduring! My wife, under the influence of her feelings, jumped
aside; I seized hold of her hand while my mind felt unutterable things
and my tongue was only able to say, we shall meet in heaven! I went
with her for about four miles hand in hand, but both our hearts were so
overpowered with feeling that we could say nothing, and when at last
we were obliged to part, the look of mutual love which we exchanged
was all the token which we could give each other that we should yet
meet in heaven.

I had for a long while been a member of the choir in the Affeviar
church in Richmond, but, after the severe family affliction to which I
have just alluded in the last chapter and the knowledge that these
cruelties were perpetrated by ministers and church members, I began
strongly to suspect the Christianity of the slaveholding church members
and hesitated much about maintaining my connection with them. The
suspicion of those slavedealing Christians was the means of keeping me
absent from all their churches from the time that my wife and children
were torn from me until Christmas day in the year 1838; and I would
not have gone then, but, being a leading member of the choir, I yielded
to the entreaties of my associates to assist at a concert of sacred music
which was to be got up for the benefit of the church. My friend, Dr.
Smith, who was the conductor of the underground railway, was also a
member of the choir, and, when I had consented to attend, he assisted
me in selecting twenty-four pieces to be sung on the occasion.

On the day appointed for our concert, I went along with Dr. Smith.
The singing commenced at half-past three o'clock, p.m. When we had
sung about ten pieces and were engaged in singing the following verse,

> Again the day returns of holy rest,
> Which, when he made the world, Jehovah blest;

> When, like his own, he bade our labors cease,
> And all be piety, and all be peace,

the members were rather astonished at Dr. Smith, who stood on my right hand, suddenly closing his book and sinking down upon his seat, his eyes being at the same time filled with tears. Several of them began to inquire what was the matter with him, but he did not tell them. I guessed what it was and afterwards found out that I had judged of the circumstances correctly. Dr. Smith's feelings were overcome with a sense of doing wrongly in singing for the purpose of obtaining money to assist those who were buying and selling their fellowmen. He thought at that moment to be reproved by Almighty God for lending his aid to the cause of slaveholding religion; and it was under this impression that he closed his book and formed the resolution which he still acts upon, of never singing again or taking part in the services of a proslavery church. He is now in New England publicly advocating the cause of emancipation.

After we had sung several other pieces we commenced the anthem, which ran thus:

> Vital spark of heavenly flame,
> Quit, O quit the mortal frame.

These words awakened in me feelings in which the sting of former sufferings was still sticking fast—stimulated by the example of Dr. Smith, whose feelings I read so correctly. I too made up my mind that I would be no longer guilty of assisting those bloody dealers in the bodies and souls of men; and ever since that time I have steadfastly kept my resolution.

I now began to get weary of my bonds and earnestly panted after liberty. I felt convinced that I should be acting in accordance with the will of God if I could snap in sunder those bonds by which I was held body and soul as the property of a fellow man. I looked forward to the good time which every day I more and more firmly believed would yet come: when I should walk the face of the earth in full possession of all that freedom that the finger of God had so clearly written on the constitutions of man and which was common to the human race, but of which, by the cruel hand of tyranny, I, and millions of my fellowmen, had been robbed.

I was well acquainted with a storekeeper in the city of Richmond, from whom I used to purchase my provisions. Having formed a favorable opinion of his integrity, one day, in the course of a little conversation with him, I said to him if I were free I would be able to do business such as he was doing. He then told me that my occupation (a tobacconist) was a moneymaking one, and if I were free I had no need to change for another. I then told him my circumstances in regard to my master, having to pay him 25 dollars per month, and yet he refused to assist me in saving my wife from being sold and taken away to the South, where I should never see her again, and even refused to allow me to go and see her until my hours of labor were over. I told him this took place about five months ago and I had been meditating my escape from slavery since, and asked him, as no person was near us, if he could give me any information about how I should proceed. I told him I had a little money and if he would assist me I would pay him for so doing. The man asked me if I was not afraid to speak that way to him. I said no, for I imagined he believed that every man had a right to liberty. He said I was quite right and asked me how much money I would give him if he would assist me to get away. I told him that I had 166 dollars and that I would give him the half; so we ultimately agreed that I should have his service in the attempt for 86 dollars. Now I only wanted to fix upon a plan. He told me of several plans by which others had managed to effect their escape, but none of them exactly suited my taste. I then left him to think over what would be best to be done, and, in the mean time, went to consult my friend, Dr. Smith, on the subject. I mentioned the plans which the storekeeper had suggested, and, as he did not approve either of them very much, I still looked for some plan which would be more certain and more safe; but I was determined that come what may, I should have my freedom or die in the attempt.

One day, while I was at work and my thoughts were eagerly feasting upon the idea of freedom, I felt my soul called out to Heaven to breathe a prayer to Almighty God. I prayed fervently that he who seeth in secret and knew the inmost desires of my heart would lend me his aid in bursting my fetters asunder and in restoring me to the possession of those rights of which men had robbed me; when, suddenly, the idea flashed across my mind of shutting myself *up in a box*, and getting myself conveyed as dry goods to a free state.

Being now satisfied that this was the plan for me, I went to my friend Dr. Smith and, having acquainted him with it, we agreed to have it put at once into execution—not, however, without calculating the chances of danger with which it was attended. But, buoyed up by the prospect of freedom and increased hatred to slavery, I was willing to dare even death itself rather than endure any longer the clanking of those galling chains. It being still necessary to have the assistance of the storekeeper, to see that the box was kept in its right position on its passage, I then went to let him know my intention. He said, although he was willing to serve me in any way he could, he did not think I could live in a box for so long a time as would be necessary to convey me to Philadelphia. But as I had already made up my mind, he consented to accompany me and keep the box upright all the way.

My next object was to procure a box. With the assistance of a carpenter that was very soon accomplished and taken to the place where the packing was to be performed. In the mean time, the storekeeper had written to a friend in Philadelphia; but as no answer had arrived, we resolved to carry out our purpose as best we could. It was deemed necessary that I should get permission to be absent from my work for a few days, in order to keep down suspicion until I had once fairly started on the road to liberty. As I had then a gathered finger, I thought that would form a very good excuse for obtaining leave of absence; but when I showed it to one overseer, Mr. Allen, he told me it was not so bad as to prevent me from working. So, with a view of making it bad enough, I got Dr. Smith to procure for me some oil of vitriol in order to drop a little of this on it. In my hurry I dropped rather much and made it worse than there was any occasion for. In fact, it was very soon eaten in to the bone, and, on presenting it again to Mr. Allen, I obtained the permission required, with the advice that I should go home and get a poultice of flaxmeal on it and keep it well poulticed until it got better. I took him instantly at his word and went off directly to the storekeeper, who had by this time received an answer from his friend in Philadelphia and had obtained permission to address the box to him, this friend in that city, arranging to call for it as soon as it should arrive. There being no time to be lost, the storekeeper, Dr. Smith, and I agreed to meet next morning at four o'clock in order to get the box ready for the express train.

The box which I had procured was three feet one inch long, two feet six inches high, and two feet wide. On the morning of the 29th day of March, 1839, I went into the box—having previously bored three gimlet holes for air opposite my face and having provided myself with a bladder of water, both for the purpose of quenching my thirst and for wetting my face should I feel getting faint. I took the gimlet also with me, in order that I might bore more holes if I found that I had not sufficient air. Being thus equipped for the battle of liberty, my friends nailed down the lid and had me conveyed to the Express Office, which was about a mile distant from the place where I was packed. I had no sooner arrived at the office than I was turned heels up, while some person nailed something on the end of the box. I was then put upon a wagon and driven off to the depot with my head down. I had no sooner arrived at the depot than the man who drove the wagon tumbled me roughly into the baggage car, where, however, I happened to fall on my right side.

The next place we arrived at was Potomac Creek, where the baggage had to be removed from the cars to be put on board the steamer, where I was again placed with my head down and in this dreadful position had to remain nearly an hour and a half, which, from the sufferings I had thus to endure, seemed like an age to me; but I was forgetting the battle for liberty and I was resolved to conquer or die. I felt my eyes swelling as if they would burst from their sockets, and the veins on my temples were dreadfully distended with pressure of blood upon my head. In this position I attempted to lift my hand to my face but I had no power to move it; I felt a cold sweat coming over me which seemed to be a warning that death was about to terminate my earthly miseries; but as I feared even that less than slavery, I resolved to submit to the will of God and, under the influence of that impression, I lifted up my soul in prayer to God, who alone was able to deliver me. My cry was soon heard, for I could hear a man saying to another that he had traveled a long way and had been standing there two hours and he would like to get to sit down. Perceiving my box, standing on end, he threw it down and then the two sat upon it. I was thus relieved from a state of agony which may be more easily imagined than described. I could now listen to the men talking and heard one of them asking the other what he supposed *the box contained.* His companion replied he guessed it was "the mail." I too thought it was a mail, but not such a mail as he supposed it to be.

The next place at which we arrived was the city of Washington, where I was taken from the steamboat and again placed upon a wagon and carried to the depot right side up with care. But when the driver arrived at the depot, I heard him call for some person to help take the box off the wagon and some one answered him to the effect that he might throw it off. But, says the driver, "it is marked 'this side up with care.'"

So if I throw it off I might break something." The other answers him that it did not matter if he broke all that was in it; the railway company was able enough to pay for it. No sooner were these words spoken than I began to tumble from the wagon, and, falling on the end where my head was, I could hear my neck give a crack, as if it had been snapped asunder, and I was knocked completely insensible. The first thing I heard after that was some person saying, "there is no room for the box, it will have to remain and be sent through tomorrow with the luggage train." But the Lord had not quite forsaken me, for in answer to my earnest prayer He so ordered affairs that I should not be left behind, and I now heard a man say that the box had come with the express and it must be sent on. I was then tumbled into the car with my head downwards again; but the car had not proceeded far before, more luggage having to be taken in, my box got shifted about and so happened to turn upon its right side; and in this position I remained till I got to Philadelphia, of our arrival in which place I was informed by hearing some person say, "We are in port and at Philadelphia." My heart then leaped for joy, and I wondered if any person knew that such a box was there.

Here it may be proper to observe that the man who had promised to accompany my box failed to do what he promised; but, to prevent it remaining long at the station after its arrival, he sent a telegraphic message to his friend, and I was only twenty-seven hours in the box, though traveling a distance of three hundred and fifty miles.

I was now placed in the depot amongst the other luggage, where I lay till 7:00 p.m., at which time a wagon drove up and I heard a person inquire for such a box as that in which I was. I was then placed on a wagon and conveyed to the house where my friend in Richmond had arranged I should be received. A number of persons soon collected round the box after it was taken into the house, but as I did not know what was going on I kept myself quiet. I heard a man say "let us rap upon the box and see if he is alive," and immediately a rap ensued and a voice said, tremblingly, "Is all right within?" To which I replied, "all right." The joy of the friends was very great. When they heard that I was alive they soon managed to break open the box, and then came my resurrection from the grave of slavery. I rose a free man; but I was too weak, by reason of long confinement in that box, to be able to stand, so I immediately swooned away. After my recovery from the swoon the first thing which arrested my attention was the presence of a number of friends, every one seeming more anxious than another to have an opportunity of rendering me their assistance and of bidding me a hearty welcome to the possession of my natural rights. I had risen as it were from the dead.

I was then taken by the hand and welcomed to the houses of the following friends: Mr. J. Miller, Mr. McKim, Mr. and Mrs. Motte, Mr. and Mrs. Davis, and many others, by all of whom I was treated in the kindest manner possible. But it was thought proper that I should not remain long in Philadelphia, so arrangements were made for me to proceed to Massachusetts, where, by the assistance of a few antislavery friends, I was enabled shortly after to arrive. I went to New York, where I became acquainted with Mr. H. Long and Mr. Eli Smith, who were very kind to me the whole time I remained there. My next journey was to New Bedford, where I remained some weeks under the care of Mr. H. Ricketson—my finger being still bad from the effects of the oil of vitriol with which I dressed it before I left Richmond. While I was here I heard of a great antislavery meeting which was to take place in Boston and, being anxious to identify myself with that public movement, I proceeded there and had the pleasure of meeting the hearty sympathy of thousands to whom I related the story of my escape. I have since attended large meetings in different towns in the states of Maine, New Hampshire, Vermont, Connecticut, Rhode Island, Pennsylvania, and New York; in all of which places I have found many friends and have endeavored, according to the best of my abilities, to advocate the cause of emancipation of the slave: with what success I will not pretend to say—but with a daily increasing confidence in the humanity and justice of my cause and in the assurance of the approbation of Almighty God.

I have composed the following song in commemoration of my feat in the box:

AIR: "UNCLE NED."

I

Here you see a man by the name of Henry Brown,
Ran away from the South to the North;
Which he would not have done but they stole all his rights,
But they'll never do the like again.

> CHORUS: Brown laid down the shovel and the hoe,
> Down in the box he did go;
> No more slave work for Henry Box Brown,
> In the box *by express* he did go.

II

Then the orders they were given, and the cars did start away,
Roll along—roll along—roll along,
Down to the landing, where the steamboat lay.
To bear the baggage off to the north.

CHORUS

III

When they packed the baggage on, they turned him on his head,
There poor Brown liked to have died;
There were passengers on board who wished to sit down,
And they turned the box down on its side.

CHORUS

IV

When they got to the cars they threw the box off,
And down upon his head he did fall,
Then he heard his neck crack, and he thought it was broke,
But they never threw him off any more.

CHORUS

V

When they got to Philadelphia they said he was in port,
And Brown then began to feel glad,
He was taken on the wagon to his final destination,
And left, "this side up with care."

CHORUS

VI

The friends gathered round and asked if all was right,
As down on the box they did rap,
Brown answered them, saying, "yes, all is right!"
He was then set free from his pain.

CHORUS

SOLOMON NORTHUP

A free black man in New York, Solomon Northup was lured to Washington, D.C. by two "circus managers" who promised him a job. There he was kidnapped in 1841 and sold into slavery on a Louisiana plantation. A fiddler, a carpenter, and a valuable slave, he worked on farms producing cotton and sugar. But he never gave up the hope of liberty. It was twelve years before Northup could, with the help of lawyers, prove that he had been kidnapped and secure his rights as a citizen. His narrative is one of the most interesting antebellum documents, for Northup was a keen observer of the southern scene and an intelligent, brave man. The account of his life, *Twelve Years a Slave, The Narrative of Solomon Northup,* from which this section comes, was published in 1853.

Kidnapped into Bondage

One morning, towards the latter part of the month of March 1841, having at that time no particular business to engage my attention, I was walking about the village of Saratoga Springs, thinking to myself where I might obtain some present employment until the busy season should arrive. Anne, as was her usual custom, had gone over to Sandy Hill, a distance of some twenty miles, to take charge of the culinary department at Sherrill's Coffee House during the session of the court. Elizabeth, I think, had accompanied her. Margaret and Alonzo were with their aunt at Saratoga.

On the corner of Congress street and Broadway, near the tavern then, and for aught I know to the contrary still, kept by Mr. Moon, I was met by two gentlemen of respectable appearance, both of whom were entirely unknown to me. I have the impression that they were introduced to me by some one of my acquaintances—who, I have in vain endeavored to recall—with the remark that I was an expert player on the violin.

At any rate, they immediately entered into conversation on that subject, making numerous inquiries touching my proficiency in that respect. My responses being to all appearances satisfactory, they proposed to engage my services for a short period, stating that I was just such a person as their business required. Their names, as they afterwards gave them to me, were Merrill Brown and Abram Hamilton, though whether these were their true appellations, I have strong reasons to doubt. The former was a man apparently forty years of age, somewhat short and thickset, with a countenance indicating shrewdness and intelligence. He wore a black frock coat and black hat and said he resided either at Rochester or at Syracuse. The latter was a young man of fair complexion and light eyes and, I should judge, had not passed the age of twenty-five. He was tall and slender, dressed in a snuff-colored coat, with a glossy hat and vest of elegant pattern. His whole apparel was in the extreme of fashion. His appearance was somewhat effeminate but prepossessing, and there was about him an easy air that showed he had mingled with the world. They were connected, as they informed me, with a circus company then in the city of Washington. They said that they were on their way thither to rejoin it, having left it for a short time to make an excursion northward for the purpose of seeing the country, paying their expenses by an occasional exhibition. They also remarked that they had found much difficulty in procuring music for their entertainments and that if I would accompany them as far as New York, they would give me one dollar for each day's services and three dollars in addition for every night I played at their performances, besides sufficient to pay the expenses of my return from New York to Saratoga.

I at once accepted the tempting offer, both for the reward it promised and from a desire to visit the metropolis. They were anxious to leave immediately. Thinking my absence would be brief, I did not deem it necessary to write to Anne whither I had gone. In fact, I supposed that my return, perhaps, would be as soon as hers. So taking a change of linen and my violin, I was ready to depart. The carriage was brought round—a covered one, drawn by a pair of noble bays, altogether forming an elegant establishment. Their baggage, consisting of three large trunks, was fastened on the rack. Mounting to the driver's seat, while they took their places in the rear, I drove away from Saratoga on the road to Albany elated with my new position and happy as I had ever been on any day in all my life.

We passed through Ballston, and striking the ridge road, as it is called if my memory correctly serves me, followed it direct to Albany. We reached that city before dark and stopped at a hotel southward from the museum.

This night I had an opportunity of witnessing one of their performances—the only one during the whole period I was with them. Hamilton was stationed at the door, I formed the orchestra, while Brown provided the entertainment. It consisted in throwing balls, dancing on the rope, frying pancakes in a hat, causing invisible pigs to squeal and other like feats of ventriloquism and legerdemain. The audience was extraordinarily sparse and not of the selectest character at that. Hamilton's report of the proceeds presented but a "beggarly account of empty boxes."

Early next morning we renewed our journey. The burden of their conversation now was the expression of an anxiety to reach the circus without delay. They hurried forward, without again stopping to exhibit, and in due course of time we reached New York, taking lodgings at a house on the west side of the city in a street running from Broadway to the river. I supposed my journey was at an end and expected in a day or two at least to return to my friends and family at Saratoga. Brown and Hamilton, however, began to importune me to continue with them to Washington. They alleged that immediately on their arrival, now that the summer season was approaching, the circus would set out for the North. They promised me a situation and high wages if I would accompany them. They expatiated at large on the advantages that would result to me, and such were the flattering representations they made, that I finally concluded to accept the offer.

The next morning they suggested that, inasmuch as we were about entering a slave state, it would be well, before leaving New York, to procure free papers. The idea struck me as a prudent one, though I think it would scarcely have occurred to me, had they not proposed it. We proceeded at once to what I understood to be the Custom House. They made oath to certain facts showing I was a free man. A paper was drawn up and handed us, with the direction to take it to the clerk's office. We did so, and the clerk having added something to it, for which he was paid six shillings, we returned again to the Custom House. Some further formalities were gone through with before it was completed, when, paying the officer two dollars, I placed the papers in my pocket and started with my two friends to our hotel. I thought at the time, I must confess, that the papers were scarcely worth the cost of obtaining them—the apprehension of danger to my personal safety never having suggested itself to me in the remotest manner. The clerk to whom we were directed, I remember, made a memorandum in a large book, which, I presume, is in the office yet. A reference to the entries during the latter part of March, or first of April 1841, I have no doubt will satisfy the incredulous, at least so far as this particular transaction is concerned.

With the evidence of freedom in my possession, the next day after our arrival in New York we crossed the ferry to Jersey City and took the road to Philadelphia. Here we remained one night, continuing our journey towards Baltimore early in the morning. In due time, we arrived in the latter city and stopped at a hotel near the railroad depot, either kept by a Mr. Rathbone or known as the Rathbone House. All the way from New York their anxiety to reach the circus seemed to grow more and more intense. We left the carriage at Baltimore and, entering the cars, proceeded to Washington, at which place we arrived just at nightfall the evening previous to the funeral of General Harrison and stopped at Gadsby's Hotel on Pennsylvania Avenue.

After supper they called me to their apartments and paid me forty-three dollars, a sum greater than my wages amounted to, which act of generosity was in consequence, they said, of their not having exhibited as often during our trip from Saratoga as they had given me to anticipate. They, moreover, informed me that it had been the intention of the circus company to leave Washington the next morning, but that on account of the funeral they had concluded to remain another day. They were then, as they had been from the time of our first meeting, extremely kind. No opportunity was omitted of addressing me in the language of approbation. On the other hand, I was certainly much prepossessed in their favor. I gave them my confidence without reserve and would freely have trusted them to almost any extent. Their constant conversation and manner towards me, their foresight in suggesting the idea of free papers and a hundred other little acts, unnecessary to be repeated, all indicated that they were friends indeed, sincerely solicitous for my welfare. I know not but they were. I know not but they were innocent of the great wickedness of which I now believe them guilty. Whether they were accessory to my misfortunes—subtle and inhuman monsters in the shape of men—designedly luring me away from home and family and liberty for the sake of gold—those who read these pages will have the same means of determining as myself. If they were innocent, my sudden disappearance must have been unaccountable indeed; but revolving in my mind all the attending circumstances, I never yet could indulge towards them so charitable a supposition.

After receiving the money from them, of which they appeared to have an abundance, they advised me not to go into the streets that night, inasmuch as I was unacquainted with the customs of the city. Promising to remember their advice, I left them together and soon after was shown by a colored servant to a sleeping room on the ground floor in the back part of the hotel. I laid down to rest, thinking of home and wife and children and the long distance that stretched between us, until I fell asleep. But no good angel of pity, bidding me to fly, came to my bedside. No voice of mercy forewarned me in my dreams of the trials that were just at hand.

The next day there was a great pageant in Washington. The roar of cannon and the tolling of bells filled the air, while many houses were shrouded with crape and the streets were black with people. As the day advanced, the procession made its appearance, coming slowly through the Avenue, carriage after carriage in long succession, while thousands upon thousands followed on foot—all moving to the sound of melancholy music. They were bearing the dead body of Harrison to the grave.

From early in the morning, I was constantly in the company of Hamilton and Brown. They were the only persons I knew in Washington. We stood together as the funeral pomp passed by. I remember distinctly how the window glass would break and rattle to the ground after each report of the cannon they were firing in the burial ground. We went to the Capitol and walked a long time about the grounds. In the afternoon they strolled towards the President's House, all the time keeping me near to them and pointing out various places of interest. As yet, I had seen nothing of the circus. In fact, I had thought of it but little, if at all, amidst the excitement of the day.

My friends, several times during the afternoon, entered drinking saloons and called for liquor. They were by no means in the habit, however, so far as I knew them, of indulging to excess. On these occasions, after serving themselves, they would pour out a glass and hand it to me. I did not become intoxicated, as may be inferred from what subsequently occurred. Towards evening, and soon after partaking of one of these potations, I began to experience most unpleasant sensations. I felt extremely ill. My head commenced aching—a dull, heavy pain inexpressibly disagreeable. At the supper table I was without appetite; the sight and flavor of food was nauseous. About dark the same servant conducted me to the room I had occupied the previous night. Brown and Hamilton advised me to retire, commiserating me kindly and expressing hopes that I would be better in the morning. Divesting myself of coat and boots merely, I threw myself upon the bed. It was impossible to sleep. The pain in my head continued to increase until it became almost unbearable. In a short time I became thirsty. My lips were parched. I could think of nothing but water—of lakes and flowing rivers, of brooks where I had stooped to drink, and of the dripping bucket, rising with its cool and overflowing nectar, from the bottom of the well. Towards midnight, as near as I could judge, I arose, unable longer to bear such intensity of thirst. I was a stranger in the house and knew nothing of its apartments. There was no one up that I could observe. Groping about at random, I knew not where, I found the way at last to a kitchen in the basement. Two or three colored servants were moving through it, one of whom, a woman, gave me two glasses of water. It afforded momentary relief, but by the time I had reached my room again, the same burning desire of drink, the same tormenting thirst had again returned. It was even more torturing than before, as was also the wild pain in my head, if such a thing could be. I was in sore distress—in most excruciating agony! I seemed to stand on the brink of madness! The memory of that night of horrible suffering will follow me to the grave.

In the course of an hour or more after my return from the kitchen, I was conscious of some one entering my room. There seemed to be several—a mingling of various voices—but how many or who they were I cannot tell. Whether Brown and Hamilton were among them is a mere matter of conjecture. I only remember, with any degree of distinctness, that I was told it was necessary to go to a physician and procure medicine and that, pulling on my boots, without coat or hat, I followed them through a long passageway, or alley, into the open street. It ran out at right angles from Pennsylvania Avenue. On the opposite side there was a light burning in a window. My impression is there were then three persons with me, but it is altogether indefinite and vague and like the memory of a painful dream. Going towards the light, which I imagined proceeded from a physician's office and which seemed to recede as I advanced, is the last glimmering recollection I can now recall. From that moment I was insensible. How long I remained in that condition—whether only that night or many days and nights—I do not know; but when consciousness returned, I found myself alone, in utter darkness, and in chains.

The pain in my head had subsided in a measure, but I was very faint and weak. I was sitting upon a low bench made of rough boards and without coat or hat. I was handcuffed. Around my ankles also were a pair of heavy fetters. One end of a chain was fastened to a large ring in the floor, the other to the fetters on my ankles. I tried in vain to stand upon my feet. Waking from such a painful trance, it was some time before I could collect my thoughts. Where was I? What was the meaning of these chains? Where were Brown and Hamilton? What had I done to deserve imprisonment in such a dungeon? I could not comprehend. There was a blank of some indefinite period, preceding my awakening in that lonely place, the events of which the utmost stretch of memory was unable to recall. I listened intently for some sign or sound of life, but nothing broke the oppressive silence save the clinking of my chains whenever I chanced to move. I spoke aloud, but the sound of my voice startled me. I felt of my pockets, so far as the fetters would allow—far enough, indeed, to ascertain that I had not only been robbed of liberty, but that my money and free papers were also gone! Then did the idea begin to break upon my mind, at first dim and confused, that I had been kidnapped. But that I thought was incredible. There must have been some misapprehension—some unfortunate mistake. It could not be that a free citizen of New York, who had wronged no man nor violated any law, should be dealt with thus inhumanly. The more I contemplated my situation, however, the more I became confirmed in my suspicions. It was a desolate thought, indeed. I felt there was no trust or mercy in unfeeling man and, commending myself to the God of the oppressed, bowed my head upon my fettered hands and wept most bitterly.

Some three hours elapsed, during which time I remained seated on the low bench, absorbed in painful meditations. At length I heard the crowing of a cock and soon a distant rumbling sound, as of carriages hurrying through the streets, came to my ears and I knew that it was day. No ray of light, however, penetrated my prison. Finally, I heard footsteps immediately overhead, as of someone walking to and fro. It occurred to me then that I must be in an underground apartment, and the damp, mouldy odors of the place confirmed the supposition. The noise above continued for at least an hour, when, at last, I heard footsteps approaching from without. A key rattled in the lock—a strong door swung back upon its hinges, admitting a flood of light, and two men entered and stood before me. One of them was a large, powerful man, forty years of age, perhaps, with dark, chestnut-colored hair slightly interspersed with gray. His face was full, his complexion flush, his features grossly coarse, expressive of nothing but cruelty and cunning. He was about five-feet ten-inches tall, of full habit, and, without prejudice I must be allowed to say, was a man whose whole appearance was sinister and repugnant. His name was James H. Burch (as I learned afterwards), a well-known slave dealer in Washington, and then, or lately, connected in business, as a partner, with Theophilus Freeman of New Orleans. The person who accompanied him was a simple lackey, named Ebenezer Radburn, who acted merely in the capacity of turnkey. Both of these men still live in Washington, or did at the time of my return through that city from slavery in January last.

The light admitted through the open door enabled me to observe the room in which I was confined. It was about twelve feet square—the walls of solid masonry. The floor was of heavy plank. There was one small window, crossed with great iron bars, with a securely fastened outside shutter.

An ironbound door led into an adjoining cell, or vault, wholly destitute of windows or any means of admitting light. The furniture of the room in which I was, consisted of the wooden bench on which I sat, an old-fashioned, dirty box stove. Beside these, in neither cell was there bed, nor blanket, nor any other thing whatever. The door, through which Burch and Radburn entered, led through a small passage, up a flight of steps into a yard, surrounded by a brick wall ten or twelve feet high, immediately in rear of a building of the same width as itself. The yard extended rearward from the house about thirty feet. In one part of the wall there was a strongly-ironed door, opening into a narrow, covered passage, leading along one side of the house into the street. The doom of the colored man upon whom the door leading out of that narrow passage closed was sealed. The top of the wall supported one end of a roof, which ascended inwards, forming a kind of open shed. Underneath the roof there was a crazy loft all round, where slaves, if so disposed, might sleep at night or in inclement weather seek shelter from the storm. It was like a farmer's barnyard in most respects, save it was so constructed that the outside world could never see the human cattle that were herded there.

The building to which the yard was attached was two stories high, fronting on one of the public streets of Washington. Its outside presented only the appearance of a quiet private residence. A stranger looking at it would never have dreamed of its execrable uses. Strange as it may seem, within plain sight of this same house, looking down from its commanding height upon it, was the Capitol. The voices of patriotic representatives boasting of freedom and equality and the rattling of the poor slave's chains almost comingled. A slave pen within the very shadow of the Capitol!

Such is a correct description as it was in 1841 of Williams' slave pen in Washington, in one of the cellars of which I found myself so unaccountably confined.

"Well, my boy, how do you feel now?" said Burch as he entered through the open door. I replied that I was sick and inquired the cause of my imprisonment. He answered that I was his slave—that he had bought me and that he was about to send me to New-Orleans. I asserted, aloud and boldly, that I was a free man—a resident of Saratoga, where I had a wife and children who were also free, and that my name was Northup. I complained bitterly of the strange treatment I had received and threatened, upon my liberation, to have satisfaction for the wrong. He denied that I was free and, with an emphatic oath, declared that I came from Georgia. Again and again I asserted I was no man's slave and insisted upon his taking off my chains at once. He endeavored to hush me, as if he feared my voice would be overheard. But I would not be silent and denounced the authors of my imprisonment, whoever they might be, as unmitigated villains. Finding he could not quiet me, he flew into a towering passion. With blasphemous oaths, he called me a black liar, a runaway from Georgia, and every other profane and vulgar epithet that the most indecent fancy could conceive.

During this time Radburn was standing silently by. His business was to oversee this human, or rather inhuman, stable—receiving slaves, feeding and whipping them, at the rate of two shillings a head per day. Turning to him, Burch ordered the paddle and cat-o'-nine-tails to be brought in. He disappeared and in a few moments returned with these instruments of torture. The paddle, as it is termed in slave-beating parlance, or at least the one with which I first became acquainted and of which I now speak, was a piece of hardwood board, eighteen or twenty inches long, molded to the shape of an old-fashioned pudding stick or ordinary oar. The flattened portion, which was about the size in circumference of two open hands, was bored with a small auger in numerous places. The cat was a large rope of many strands—the strands unraveled and a knot tied at the extremity of each.

As soon as these formidable whips appeared, I was seized by both of them and roughly divested of my clothing. My feet, as has been stated, were fastened to the floor. Drawing me over the bench, face downwards, Radburn placed his heavy foot upon the fetters between my wrists, holding them painfully to the floor. With the paddle, Burch commenced beating me. Blow after blow was inflicted upon my naked body. When his unrelenting arm grew tired, he stopped and asked if I still insisted I was a free man. I did insist upon it, and then the blows were renewed, faster and more energetically, if possible, than before. When again tired, he would repeat the same question and, receiving the same answer, continue his cruel labor. All this time, the devil incarnate was uttering most fiendish oaths. At length the paddle broke, leaving the useless handle in his hand. Still I would not yield. All his brutal blows could not force from my lips the foul lie that I was a slave. Casting madly on the floor the handle of the broken paddle, he seized the rope. This was far more painful than the other. I struggled with all my power, but it was in vain. I prayed for mercy, but my prayer was only answered with imprecations and with stripes. I thought I must die beneath the lashes of the accursed brute. Even now the flesh crawls upon my bones, as I recall the scene. I was all on fire. My sufferings I can compare to nothing else than the burning agonies of hell!

At last I became silent to his repeated questions. I would make no reply. In fact, I was becoming almost unable to speak. Still he plied the lash without stint upon my poor body, until it seemed that the lacerated flesh was stripped from my bones at every stroke. A man with a particle of mercy in his soul would not have beaten even a dog so cruelly. At length, Radburn said that it was useless to whip me any more—that I would be sore enough. Thereupon, Burch desisted, saying, with an admonitory shake of his fist in my face and hissing the words through his firm-set teeth, that if ever I dared to utter again that I was entitled to my freedom, that I had been kidnaped, or anything whatever of the kind, the castigation I had just received was nothing in comparison with what would follow. He swore that he would either conquer or kill me. With these consolatory words, the fetters were taken from my wrists, my feet still remaining fastened to the ring. The shutter of the little barred window, which had been opened, was again closed, and going out, locking the great door behind them, I was left in darkness as before.

In an hour, perhaps two, my heart leaped to my throat as the key rattled in the door again. I, who had been so lonely and who had longed so ardently to see some one (I cared not who), now shuddered at the thought of man's approach. A human face was fearful to me, especially a white one. Radburn entered, bringing with him, on a tin plate, a piece of shriveled fried pork, a slice of bread, and a cup of water. He asked me how I felt and remarked that I had received a pretty severe flogging. He remonstrated with me against the propriety of asserting my freedom. In rather a patronizing and confidential manner, he gave it to me as his advice that the less I said on that subject the better it would be for me. The man evidently endeavored to appear kind—whether touched at the sight of my sad condition or with the view of silencing, on my part, any further expression of my rights, it is not necessary now to conjecture. He unlocked the fetters from my ankles, opened the shutters of the little window, and departed, leaving me again alone.

By this time I had become stiff and sore; my body was covered with blisters and it was with great pain and difficulty that I could move. From the window I could observe nothing but the roof resting on the adjacent wall. At night I laid down upon the damp, hard floor, without any pillow or covering whatever. Punctually, twice a day, Radburn came in with his pork and bread and water. I had but little appetite, though I was tormented with continual thirst. My wounds would not permit me to remain but a few minutes in any one position; so, sitting, or standing, or moving slowly round, I passed the days and nights. I was heartsick and discouraged. Thoughts of my family, of my wife and children, continually occupied my mind. When sleep overpowered me I dreamed of them—dreamed I was again in Saratoga, that I could see their faces and hear their voices calling me. Awakening from the pleasant phantasms of sleep to the bitter realities around me, I could but groan and weep. Still my spirit was not broken. I indulged the anticipation of escape, and that speedily. It was impossible, I reasoned, that men could be so unjust as to detain me as a slave when the truth of my case was known. Burch, ascertaining I was no runaway from Georgia, would certainly let me go. Though suspicions of Brown and Hamilton were not infrequent, I could not reconcile myself to the idea that they were instrumental in my imprisonment. Surely they would seek me out —they would deliver me from thraldom. Alas! I had not then learned the measure of "man's inhumanity to man," nor to what limitless extent of wickedness he will go for the love of gain.

In the course of several days the outer door was thrown open, allowing me the liberty of the yard. There I found three slaves—one of them a lad of ten years, the others young men of about twenty and twenty-five. I was not long in forming an acquaintance and learning their names and the particulars of their history.

The eldest was a colored man named Clemens Ray. He had lived in Washington, had driven a hack, and worked in a livery stable there for a long time. He was very intelligent and fully comprehended his situation.

The thought of going south overwhelmed him with grief. Burch had purchased him a few days before and had placed him there until such time as he was ready to send him to the New Orleans market. From him I learned for the first time that I was in Williams' Slave Pen, a place I had never heard of previously. He described to me the uses for which it was designed. I repeated to him the particulars of my unhappy story, but he could only give me the consolation of his sympathy. He also advised me to be silent henceforth on the subject of my freedom, for, knowing the character of Burch, he assured me that it would only be attended with renewed whipping. The next eldest was named John Williams. He was raised in Virginia, not far from Washington. Burch had taken him in payment of a debt, and he constantly entertained the hope that his master would redeem him—a hope that was subsequently realized. The lad was a sprightly child, who answered to the name of Randall. Most of the time he was playing about the yard, but occasionally would cry, calling for his mother and wondering when she would come. His mother's absence seemed to be the great and only grief in his little heart. He was too young to realize his condition, and when the memory of his mother was not in his mind, he amused us with his pleasant pranks.

At night, Ray, Williams, and the boy slept in the loft of the shed, while I was locked in the cell. Finally we were each provided with blankets such as are used upon horses—the only bedding I was allowed to have for twelve years afterwards. Ray and Williams asked me many questions about New York: how colored people were treated there; how they could have homes and families of their own, with none to disturb and oppress them; and Ray, especially, sighed continually for freedom. Such conversations, however, were not in the hearing of Burch or the keeper Radburn. Aspirations such as these would have brought down the lash upon our backs.

It is necessary in this narrative, in order to present a full and truthful statement of all the principal events in the history of my life and to portray the institution of slavery as I have seen and known it, to speak of well-known places and of many persons who are yet living. I am, and always was, an entire stranger in Washington and its vicinity—aside from Burch and Radburn, knowing no man there, except as I have heard of them through my enslaved companions. What I am about to say, if false, can be easily contradicted.

I remained in Williams' slave pen about two weeks. The night previ-

ous to my departure a woman was brought in weeping bitterly and leading by the hand a little child. They were Randall's mother and half sister. On meeting them he was overjoyed: clinging to her dress, kissing
the child, and exhibiting every demonstration of delight. The mother
also clasped him in her arms, embraced him tenderly, and gazed at him
fondly through her tears, calling him by many an endearing name.

Emily, the child, was seven or eight years old, of light complexion,
and with a face of admirable beauty. Her hair fell in curls around her
neck, while the style and richness of her dress and the neatness of her
whole appearance indicated she had been brought up in the midst of
wealth. She was a sweet child indeed. The woman also was arrayed in
silk, with rings upon her fingers and golden ornaments suspended from
her ears. Her air and manners, the correctness and propriety of her language—all showed, evidently, that she had sometime stood above the
common level of a slave. She seemed to be amazed at finding herself in
such a place as that. It was plainly a sudden and unexpected turn of fortune that had brought her there. Filling the air with her complainings,
she was hustled, with the children and myself, into the cell. Language
can convey but an inadequate impression of the lamentations to which
she gave incessant utterance. Throwing herself upon the floor and encir-
cling the children in her arms, she poured forth such touching words as
only maternal love and kindness can suggest. They nestled closely to
her, as if *there only* was there any safety or protection. At last they
slept, their heads resting upon her lap. While they slumbered, she
smoothed the hair back from their little foreheads and talked to them all
night long. She called them her darlings—her sweet babes—poor innocent things that knew not the misery they were destined to endure.
Soon they would have no mother to comfort them—they would be
taken from her. What would become of them? Oh! she could not live
away from her little Emmy and her dear boy. They had always been
good children and had such loving ways. It would break her heart, God
knew, she said, if they were taken from her, and yet she knew they
meant to sell them, and maybe they would be separated and could
never see each other any more. It was enough to melt a heart of stone to
listen to the pitiful expressions of that desolate and distracted mother.

[Northup was then sold to a planter in Louisiana.]

Edwin Epps, of whom much will be said during the remainder of
this history, is a large, portly, heavy-bodied man with light hair, high

cheek bones, and a Roman nose of extraordinary dimensions. He has blue eyes, a fair complexion, and is, as I should say, full six-feet high. He has the sharp, inquisitive expression of a jockey. His manners are repulsive and coarse and his language gives speedy and unequivocal evidence that he has never enjoyed the advantages of an education. He has the faculty of saying most provoking things, in that respect even excelling old Peter Tanner. At the time I came into his possession, Edwin Epps was fond of the bottle, his "sprees" sometimes extending over the space of two whole weeks. Latterly, however, he had reformed his habits and, when I left him, was as strict a specimen of temperance as could be found on Bayou Bœuf. When "in his cups," Master Epps was a roistering, blustering, noisy fellow, whose chief delight was in dancing with his "niggers" or lashing them about the yard with his long whip just for the pleasure of hearing them screech and scream as the great welts were planted on their backs. When sober, he was silent, reserved, and cunning, not beating us indiscriminately, as in his drunken moments, but sending the end of his rawhide to some tender spot of a lagging slave, with a sly dexterity peculiar to himself.

He had been a driver and overseer in his younger years, but at this time was in possession of a plantation on Bayou Huff Power, two and a half miles from Holmesville, eighteen from Marksville, and twelve from Cheneyville. It belonged to Joseph B. Roberts, his wife's uncle, and was leased by Epps. His principal business was raising cotton. Inasmuch as some may read this book who have never seen a cotton field, a description of the manner of its culture may not be out of place.

The ground is prepared by throwing up beds or ridges with the plough—back-furrowing, it is called. Oxen and mules, the latter almost exclusively, are used in ploughing. The women as frequently as the men perform this labor: feeding, currying, and taking care of their teams, and in all respects doing the field and stable work precisely as do the ploughboys of the North.

The beds, or ridges, are six feet wide—that is, from water furrow to water furrow. A plough drawn by one mule is then run along the top of the ridge or center of the bed, making the drill, into which a girl usually drops the seed, which she carries in a bag hung round her neck. Behind her comes a mule and harrow, covering up the seed; so that two mules, three slaves, a plough, and a harrow are employed in planting a row of cotton. This is done in the months of March and April. Corn is planted in February. When there are no cold rains, the cotton usually makes its appearance in a week. In the course of eight or ten days afterwards the first hoeing is commenced. This is performed in part, also, by the aid of the plough and mule. The plough passes as near as possible to the cotton on both sides, throwing the furrow from it. Slaves follow with their hoes, cutting up the grass and cotton, leaving hills two and a half feet apart. This is called scraping cotton. In two weeks more commences the second hoeing. This time the furrow is thrown towards the cotton. Only one stalk, the largest, is now left standing in each hill. In another fortnight it is hoed the third time, throwing the furrow towards the cotton in the same manner as before and killing all the grass between the rows. About the first of July, when it is a foot high or thereabouts, it is hoed the fourth and last time. Now the whole space between the rows is ploughed, leaving a deep water furrow in the center. During all these hoeings the overseer or driver follows the slaves on horseback with a whip, such as has been described. The fastest hoer takes the lead row. He is usually about a rod in advance of his companions. If one of them passes him, he is whipped. If one falls behind or is a moment idle, he is whipped. In fact, the lash is flying from morning until night, the whole day long. The hoeing season thus continues from April until July, a field having no sooner been finished once, than it is commenced again.

In the latter part of August begins the cotton picking season. At this time each slave is presented with a sack. A strap is fastened to it, which goes over the neck, holding the mouth of the sack breast high, while the bottom reaches nearly to the ground. Each one is also presented with a large basket that will hold about two barrels. This is to put the cotton in when the sack is filled. The baskets are carried to the field and placed at the beginning of the rows.

When a new hand, one unaccustomed to the business, is sent for the first time into the field, he is whipped up smartly and made for that day to pick as fast as he can possibly. At night it is weighed, so that his capability in cotton picking is known. He must bring in the same weight each night following. If it falls short, it is considered evidence that he has been laggard and a greater or less number of lashes is the penalty.

An ordinary day's work is two hundred pounds. A slave who is accustomed to picking is punished if he or she brings in a less quantity than that. There is a great difference among them as regards this kind of labor. Some of them seem to have a natural knack, or quickness, which enables them to pick with great celerity and with both hands, while others, with whatever practice or industry, are utterly unable to come up to the ordinary standard. Such hands are taken from the cotton field and employed in other business. Patsey, of whom I shall have more to say, was known as the most remarkable cotton picker on Bayou Bœuf. She picked with both hands and with such surprising rapidity that five hundred pounds a day was not unusual for her.

Each one is tasked, therefore, according to his picking abilities: none, however, to come short of two hundred weight. I, being unskillful always in that business, would have satisfied my master by bringing in the latter quantity, while, on the other hand, Patsey would surely have been beaten if she failed to produce twice as much.

The cotton grows from five to seven feet high, each stalk having a great many branches shooting out in all directions and lapping each other above the water furrow.

There are few sights more pleasant to the eye than a wide cotton field when it is in the bloom. It presents an appearance of purity, like an immaculate expanse of light new-fallen snow.

Sometimes the slave picks down one side of a row and back upon the other, but more usually, there is one on either side, gathering all that has blossomed, leaving the unopened bolls for a succeeding picking. When the sack is filled, it is emptied into the basket and trodden down. It is necessary to be extremely careful the first time going through the field, in order not to break the branches off the stalks. The cotton will not bloom upon a broken branch. Epps never failed to inflict the severest chastisement on the unlucky servant who, either carelessly or unavoidably, was guilty in the least degree in this respect.

The hands are required to be in the cotton field as soon as it is light in the morning, and, with the exception of ten or fifteen minutes that is given them at noon to swallow their allowance of cold bacon, they are not permitted to be a moment idle until it is too dark to see; and when the moon is full, they often times labor till the middle of the night. They do not dare to stop even at dinner time, nor return to the quarters, however late it be, until the order to halt is given by the driver.

The day's work over in the field, the baskets are "toted," or in other words carried, to the gin-house, where the cotton is weighed. No matter how fatigued and weary he may be—no matter how much he longs for sleep and rest—a slave never approaches the gin-house with his basket of cotton but with fear. If it falls short in weight, if he has not performed the full task appointed him, he knows that he must suffer. And if he has exceeded it by ten or twenty pounds, in all probability his master will measure the next day's task accordingly. So, whether he has too little or too much, his approach to the gin-house is always with fear and trembling. Most frequently they have too little, and therefore they are not anxious to leave the field. After weighing follow the whippings. Then the baskets are carried to the cotton house and their contents stored away like hay, all hands being sent in to tramp it down. If the cotton is not dry, instead of taking it to the gin-house at once, it is laid upon platforms, two feet high and some three times as wide, covered with boards or plank, with narrow walks running between them.

This done, the labor of the day is not yet ended, by any means. Each one must then attend to his respective chores. One feeds the mules, another the swine, another cuts the wood and so forth; besides, the packing is all done by candle light. Finally, at a late hour, they reach the quarters, sleepy and overcome with the long day's toil. Then a fire must be kindled in the cabin, the corn ground in the small handmill, and supper (and dinner for the next day in the field) prepared. All that is allowed them is corn and bacon, which is given out at the corncrib and smokehouse every Sunday morning. Each one receives, as his weekly allowance, three and a half pounds of bacon and corn enough to make a peck of meal. That is all—no tea, coffee, sugar, and, with the exception of a very scanty sprinkling now and then, no salt. I can say, from a ten years' residence with Master Epps, that no slave of his is ever likely to suffer from the gout, superinduced by excessive high living. Master Epps' hogs were fed on *shelled* corn—it was thrown out to his "niggers" in the ear. The former, he thought, would fatten faster by shelling and soaking it in the water—the latter, perhaps, if treated in the same manner, might grow too fat to labor. Master Epps was a shrewd calculator and knew how to manage his own animals, drunk or sober.

The corn mill stands in the yard beneath a shelter. It is like a common coffee mill, the hopper holding about six quarts. There was one privilege which Master Epps granted freely to every slave he had. They might grind their corn nightly in such small quantities as their daily wants required, or they might grind the whole week's allowance at one time, on Sundays, just as they preferred. A very generous man was Master Epps!

I kept my corn in a small wooden box, the meal in a gourd—and, by the way, the gourd is one of the most convenient and necessary utensils on a plantation. Besides supplying the place of all kinds of crockery in a slave cabin, it is used for carrying water to the fields. Another, also, contains the dinner. It dispenses with the necessity of pails, dippers, basins, and such tin and wooden superfluities altogether.

When the corn is ground and fire is made, the bacon is taken down from the nail on which it hangs, a slice cut off and thrown upon the coals to broil. The majority of slaves have no knife, much less a fork. They cut their bacon with the ax at the woodpile. The corn meal is mixed with a little water, placed in the fire, and baked. When it is "done brown," the ashes are scraped off, and being placed upon a chip, which answers for a table, the tenant of the slave hut is ready to sit down upon the ground to supper. By this time it is usually midnight. The same fear of punishment with which they approach the gin-house, possesses them again on lying down to get a snatch of rest. It is the fear of oversleeping in the morning. Such an offense would certainly be attended with not less than twenty lashes. With a prayer that he may be on his feet and wide awake at the first sound of the horn, he sinks to his slumbers nightly.

The softest couches in the world are not to be found in the log mansion of the slave. The one whereon I reclined year after year was a plank twelve inches wide and ten feet long. My pillow was a stick of wood. The bedding was a coarse blanket, and not a rag or shred beside. Moss might be used, were it not that it directly breeds a swarm of fleas.

The cabin is constructed of logs, without floor or window. The latter is altogether unnecessary, the crevices between the logs admitting sufficient light. In stormy weather the rain drives through them, rendering it comfortless and extremely disagreeable. The rude door hangs on great wooden hinges. In one end is constructed an awkward fireplace.

An hour before daylight the horn is blown. Then the slaves arise, prepare their breakfast, fill a gourd with water, in another deposit their dinner of cold bacon and corn cake, and hurry to the field again. It is an offense invariably followed by a flogging to be found at the quarters after daybreak. Then the fears and labors of another day begin, and until its close there is no such thing as rest. He fears he will be caught lagging through the day; he fears to approach the gin-house with his basket-load of cotton at night; he fears, when he lies down, that he will oversleep himself in the morning. Such is a true, faithful, unexaggerated picture and description of the slave's daily life, during the time of cotton-picking, on the shores of Bayou Bœuf.

In the month of January, generally, the fourth and last picking is completed. Then commences the harvesting of corn. This is considered a secondary crop and receives far less attention than the cotton. It is planted, as already mentioned, in February. Corn is grown in that region for the purpose of fattening hogs and feeding slaves, very little, if any, being sent to market. It is the white variety, the ear of great size and the stalk growing to the height of eight, and oftentimes ten, feet. In August the leaves are stripped off, dried in the sun, bound in small bundles, and stored away as provender for the mules and oxen. After this the slaves go through the field turning down the ear for the purpose of keeping the rains from penetrating to the grain. It is left in this condition until after cotton-picking is over, whether earlier or later. Then the ears are separated from the stalks and deposited in the corncrib with the husks on; otherwise, stripped of the husks, the weevil would destroy it. The stalks are left standing in the field.

The Carolina, or sweet potato, is also grown in that region to some extent. They are not fed, however, to hogs or cattle and are considered but of small importance. They are preserved by placing them upon the surface of the ground, with a slight covering of earth or cornstalks. There is not a cellar on Bayou Bœuf. The ground is so low it would fill with water. Potatoes are worth from two to three "bits," or shillings, a barrel. Corn, except when there is an unusual scarcity, can be purchased at the same rate.

As soon as the cotton and corn crops are secured, the stalks are pulled up, thrown into piles, and burned. The ploughs are started at the same time, throwing up the beds again, preparatory to another planting. The soil in the parishes of Rapides and Avoyelles, and throughout the whole country so far as my observation extended, is of exceeding richness and fertility. It is a kind of marl, of a brown or reddish color. It does not require those invigorating composts necessary to more barren lands, and on the same field the same crop is grown for many successive years.

Ploughing, planting, picking cotton, gathering the corn, and pulling and burning stalks occupies the whole of the four seasons of the year. Drawing and cutting wood, pressing cotton, fattening and killing hogs are but incidental labors.

In the month of September or October, the hogs are run out of the swamps by dogs and confined in pens. On a cold morning, generally about New Year's day, they are slaughtered. Each carcass is cut into six parts and piled one above the other in salt, upon large tables in the smoke-house. In this condition it remains a fortnight, when it is hung up and a fire built and continued more than half the time during the remainder of the year. This thorough smoking is necessary to prevent the bacon from becoming infested with worms. In so warm a climate it is difficult to preserve it, and very many times myself and my companions have received our weekly allowance of three pounds and a half when it was full of these disgusting vermin.

Although the swamps are overrun with cattle, they are never made the source of profit to any considerable extent. The planter cuts his mark upon the ear or brands his initials upon the side and turns them into the swamps to roam unrestricted within their almost limitless confines. They are the Spanish breed, small and spike-horned. I have known of droves being taken from Bayou Bœuf, but it is of very rare occurrence. The value of the best cows is about five dollars each. Two quarts at one milking would be considered an unusual large quantity. They furnish little tallow, and that of a soft, inferior quality. Notwithstanding the great number of cows that throng the swamps, the planters are indebted to the North for their cheese and butter, which is purchased in the New Orleans market. Salted beef is not an article of food either in the great house or in the cabin.

Master Epps was accustomed to attend shooting matches for the purpose of obtaining what fresh beef he required. These sports occurred weekly at the neighboring village of Holmesville. Fat beef are driven thither and shot at, a stipulated price being demanded for the privilege. The lucky marksman divides the flesh among his fellows, and in this manner the attending planters are supplied.

The great number of tame and untamed cattle that swarm the woods and swamps of Bayou Bœuf most probably suggested that appellation to the French, inasmuch as the term, translated, signifies the creek or river of the wild ox.

Garden products, such as cabbages, turnips and the like, are cultivated for the use of the master and his family. They have greens and vegetables at all times and seasons of the year. "The grass withereth and the flower fadeth" before the desolating winds of autumn in the chill northern latitudes, but perpetual verdure overspreads the hot lowlands and flowers bloom in the heart of winter in the region of Bayou Bœuf.

There are no meadows appropriated to the cultivation of the grasses. The leaves of the corn supply a sufficiency of food for the laboring cattle, while the rest provide for themselves all the year in the ever-growing pasture.

There are many other peculiarities of climate, habit, custom, and of the manner of living and laboring at the South, but the foregoing, it is supposed, will give the reader an insight and general idea of life on a cotton plantation in Louisiana.

JOHN THOMPSON

John Thompson's earliest memory was the sale of his sister and his mother's pleas to keep her. Another sister of his was whipped for refusing to submit to her master's passions. A licentious man, this slaveowner was the father of many of his own slaves. John Thompson was a bold and resourceful man, however, who refused to be whipped. He brought his master to terms by running off to the woods and "striking" until his demands were met. He learned to read while still a slave and was inspired to free himself by the teaching of Methodist and Baptist preachers. The passages reproduced here show his brave and determined love of liberty. A sailor after he escaped from bondage, he was impressed by the symbolic and literary possibilities of the sea. Had he been an educated man, he might have been another Herman Melville. *The Life of John Thompson, A Fugitive Slave*, written and published by himself, was printed in Worcester in 1856.

God's Judgment on the Master

I met Mr. B. returning, he having been there waiting for me. He, being a "holy man," did not swear directly, but said, "Confound you, where have you been?" accompanying the question by a blow from a four-foot stick across my head.

I tried to explain the reason of my delay, but he would not listen and continued beating me. At last I caught hold of the stick, wrenched it from his hands, struck him over the head, and knocked him down, after which I choked him until he was as black as I am. When I let him up, he ran for his gun; but when he returned I had fled to parts unknown to him. I kept away about two weeks, staying in the woods during the day and coming to the quarters at night for something to eat.

Mr. Barber, however, needing my services, as it was a very busy time, told the slaves, if they saw me, to tell me to come home and that he would not whip me. This was to me a very welcome message, for I was tired of my life in the woods, and I immediately returned home. I went to work, as usual, thinking all was right, but soon found myself very much mistaken.

I worked about three weeks, during which I accomplished six weeks labor. One day, while busily engaged hoeing up new ground, I saw two men coming towards me, whom I soon recognized as constables, both of whom I well knew. Upon approaching near me, the constable for our district said, "John, you must come with me."

I dropped my hoe and followed him. When I reached the house, I found poor David standing bound like a sheep dumb before its shearers. We were put up stairs to await Mr. B.'s orders, who was not then ready. The rope was tied so tight around David's wrists as to stop the circulation of the blood and give him excruciating pain. He begged to have the rope loosened, but the officer having him in charge would not gratify him. The other constable, however, soon came and relieved him.

Mr. Barber being ready, we set off for the magistrate's office, which was about three miles from our house. David and I were tied together, his left being tied to my right hand. On the way the constable said to me, "John, I always thought you was a good Negro; what have you been doing? You ought to behave so well as not to need whipping."

I replied, "I have done nothing wrong, and if I am whipped, it shall be the last time on that farm."

"What will you do?" asked Mr. Barber. "Run away," I answered. "When we are done with you, you will not be able to run far," said he. "Well sir, if you whip me so that I am unable to walk, I can do you no good; but if I can walk, I will take the balance of the year to myself and go home to my mistress, at Christmas."

He did not relish this kind of talk, for he did not wish to pay my wages and not have my service, so he told me to shut my head or he would break it. Of course I said no more.

We soon arrived at the dreaded place and were left seated in the piazza awaiting our trial, a constable being present to watch us. I asked him for a drink of water, when he said, "Would you not like a glass of brandy?" a drink very acceptable on such occasions. I replied in the affirmative, upon which he brought out a half-pint tumbler nearly full, of which I drank the whole. This roused my courage and I felt brave. My expected punishment was not half as much dreaded as before.

The court being ready, we were brought before his honor, Justice Barber, uncle to my master. David was first tried, declared guilty, and sentenced to have thirty-nine lashes well laid upon his bare back.

My case was next in order, but Mr. Barber, instead of preferring any charge against me, told the judge he would forgive me this time, as he thought I would do better in future. Upon this the old man, raising his spectacles and looking at me, said, "Do you think you can behave so as not to have to be brought before me again?" "Yes sir," I answered quickly. "Well sir," he said, "go home to your work, and if you are brought before me again, I will order the skin all taken from your back!"

The rope was taken off my hands, and I was told to go in peace and sin no more. I waited to see the fate of poor David. He was taken to the whipping post, strung up until his toes scarce touched the ground, his back stripped and whipped until the blood flowed in streams to the ground. When he was taken down he staggered like a drunken man. We returned together, talking over the matter on the way. He said, "O, I wish I could die! I am whipped for no fault of my own. I wish I had killed him and been hung at once; I should have been better off." I felt sorry for him.

I determined then, if he struck me again, I would kill him. I expected another attack and accordingly planned where I would conceal his body, where it would not readily be found, in case no one saw me perform the act. But God overruled. He had his destiny fixed, and no mortal could resist it, no mortal arm could stay his mighty purpose. But I must hasten to the close of the year.

Mr. Barber had a most luxuriant crop of tobacco nearly ripe and ready for the harvest. Tobacco is so delicate a plant that it will not stand the frost, and if exposed to it is thereby rendered nearly useless. Our crops had all been gathered except two fields, when, by a sudden change in the wind to the north, it became so cold as to threaten a frost, which would probably destroy the tobacco remaining in the field. Mr. Barber feared this and, notwithstanding it was the Sabbath, ordered his slaves to go and secure the remainder of the crop.

Soon all hands were in the field at work. No other farmer in the neighborhood went out; all, excepting Mr. B., being willing to trust their crops to Him who had given them, although many had larger quantities exposed. Being angry with the great Omnipotent for this threatening arrangement of his providence, Mr. Barber fell to beating his slaves on the Lord's day. But his suspected enemy did not come; his fears were groundless. The night cleared off warm and no frost came.

> God moves in a mysterious way,
> His wonders to perform;
> He plants his footsteps in the sea,
> And rides upon the storm.
> Deep and unfathomable mine
> Of never failing skill;
> He treasures up his bright design,
> And works his sovereign will.
> Ye fearful saints, fresh courage take;

The clouds ye so much dread
Are big with mercy, and shall break
With blessings on your head.

Judge not the Lord with feeble sense,
But trust him for his grace;
Behind a frowning providence
He hides a smiling face.
His purposes will ripen fast,
Unfolding every hour;
The bud may have a bitter taste,
But sweet will be the flower.
Blind unbelief is sure to err,
And scan his works in vain;
God is his own interpreter,
And he will make it plain.

We worked until midnight on Sunday and secured all the crops, as Mr. B. thought.

The manner of curing tobacco is to hang it up in the barn and put a hot fire under it, so as to cure it gradually. But the heat must be in proportion to the dampness of the tobacco.

All things being regulated, Mr. B. began to boast of the security of his great crops. The following Saturday at three o'clock, he told his slaves that they might have the remainder of that day to compensate for the previous Sabbath, when they had worked.

The same day, while preparing to go to confession as usual, one of the slaves ran in and told him that the barn was on fire! I looked from the kitchen door, saw the smoke bursting from the roof, and ran to the spot. Master got there before me and within three minutes all the slaves were upon the spot; but seeing it would be of no avail, they did not attempt to enter the barn.

Mr. Barber, moved by his usual ambition, rushed in, notwithstanding the slaves trying to persuade him of the danger and pleading with him to desist; but, blinded by the god of this world, he would not listen to their entreaties and rushed in just as the roof was ready to fall! When they beheld the awful sight, the wails of the slaves might have been heard fully two miles.

He was caught by the end of the roof only, as it fell, from which, in a minute or two, he made his escape, his clothes all on fire. He was taken to the house, but died the next Sunday week. Before he died, however, like Nebuchadnezzar of old, he acknowledged that God reigns among the kingdoms of men.

This sad event transpired in the month of October; after which nothing more worthy of note occurred while I remained in the family, which was until Christmas. After this I returned to my mistress, who gave me a note permitting me to get myself another home.

JOSIAH HENSON

Josiah Henson was an unusually faithful slave during most of his
early life in Maryland. For striking an overseer who attempted to
rape his wife, Henson's father had his ear cropped and was sold
to Alabama. But the boy, Josiah, grew up with his mother and a
relatively kind master who considered him his favorite slave. He
trusted Henson to take a group of slaves to Kentucky to escape
his creditors. On this journey Henson passed through free territory, but would not strike for freedom. He delivered the slaves to
his master's brother, who sold them, and he returned with his
own family to bondage in Maryland. On one occasion Henson's
master's son took him to New Orleans to sell him, but the slaveholder fell sick and found he needed the loyal slave. Threatened
again with sale, Henson fled with his wife and children to Canada, where he was one of the leaders of a colony of refugees from
slavery. This group established a cooperative community with a
sawmill and a school. Henson became famous as "Harriet
Beecher Stowe's Uncle Tom." He was presented to the Archbishop of Canterbury and Queen Victoria of England. The first
edition of his autobiography, dictated to Samuel Eliot, was published in Boston in 1849. The chapters below are taken from the
edition of 1858 which contains an introduction by Mrs. Stowe.

A Faithful Slave
Declines Liberty

My earliest employments were to carry buckets of water to the men at work and to hold a horseplough, used for weeding between the rows of corn. As I grew older and taller, I was entrusted with the care of master's saddle horse. Then a hoe was put into my hands, and I was soon required to do the day's work of a man; and it was not long before I could do it, at least as well as my associates in misery.

The everyday life of a slave on one of our southern plantations, however frequently it may have been described, is generally little understood at the North, and must be mentioned as a necessary illustration of the character and habits of the slave and the slaveholder, created and perpetuated by their relative position. The principal food of those upon my master's plantation consisted of cornmeal and salt herrings, to which was added in summer a little buttermilk and the few vegetables which each might raise for himself and his family on the little piece of ground (called a truck patch) which was assigned to him for the purpose.

In ordinary times we had two regular meals in a day: breakfast at twelve o'clock (after laboring from daylight) and supper when the work of the remainder of the day was over. In harvest season we had three. Our dress was of towcloth: for the children nothing but a shirt; for the older ones, in addition, a pair of pantaloons or a gown, according to the sex. Besides these, in the winter a round jacket or overcoat, a wool hat once in two or three years for the males, and a pair of coarse shoes once a year.

We lodged in log huts and on the bare ground. Wooden floors were an unknown luxury. In a single room were huddled, like cattle, ten or a dozen persons—men, women and children. All ideas of refinement and decency were, of course, out of the question. There were neither bedsteads, nor furniture of any description. Our beds were collections of straw and old rags, thrown down in the corners and boxed in with boards, a single blanket the only covering. Our favorite way of sleeping, however, was on a plank: our heads raised on an old jacket and our feet toasting before the smouldering fire. The wind whistled and the rain and snow blew in through the cracks and the damp earth soaked in the moisture till the floor was miry as a pigsty. Such were our houses. In these wretched hovels were we penned at night, and fed by day; here were the children born and the sick—neglected.

Notwithstanding this system of management, I grew to be a robust and vigorous lad. At fifteen years of age there were few who could compete with me in work or sport. I was as lively as a young buck and running over with animal spirits. I could run faster, wrestle better, and jump higher than anybody about me, and at an evening shakedown in our own or a neighbor's kitchen my feet became absolutely invisible from the rate at which they moved. All this caused my master and my fellow slaves to look upon me as a wonderfully smart fellow, and prophesy the great things I should do when I became a man. My vanity became vastly inflamed, and I fully coincided in their opinion. Julius Cæsar never aspired and plotted for the imperial crown more ambitiously than did I to out-hoe, out-reap, out-husk, out-dance, out-everything every competitor; and from all I can learn he never enjoyed his triumph half as much. One word of commendation from the petty despot who ruled over us would set me up for a month.

I have no desire to represent the life of slavery as an experience of nothing but misery. God be praised that, however hedged in by circumstances, the joyful exuberance of youth will bound at times over them all. Ours is a lighthearted race. The sternest and most covetous master cannot frighten or whip the fun out of us; certainly old Riley never did out of me. In those days I had many a merry time, and would have had, had I lived with nothing but moccasins and rattlesnakes in Okefenokee swamp. Slavery did its best to make me wretched; I feel no particular obligation to it; but nature, or the blessed God of youth and joy, was mightier than slavery. Along with memories of miry cabins, frosted feet, weary toil under the blazing sun, curses and blows, there flock in others:

of jolly Christmas times, dances before old massa's door for the first drink of eggnog, extra meat at holiday times, midnight visits to apple orchards, broiling stray chickens, and first-rate tricks to dodge work. The God who makes the pup gambol and the kitten play and the bird sing and the fish leap was the author in me of many a lighthearted hour. True it was, indeed, that the fun and freedom of Christmas, at which time my master relaxed his front, was generally followed up by a portentous back-action, under which he drove and cursed worse than ever. Still, the fun and freedom were fixed facts; we had had them and he could not help it.

Besides these pleasant memories I have others of a deeper and richer kind. I early learned to employ my spirit of adventure for the benefit of my fellow sufferers. The condition of the male slave is bad enough; but that of the female, compelled to perform unfit labor, sick, suffering, and bearing the peculiar burdens of her own sex unpitied and unaided as well as the toils which belong to the other, is one that must arouse the spirit of sympathy in every heart not dead to all feeling. The miseries which I saw many of the women suffer often oppressed me with a load of sorrow. No *white* knight, rescuing white fair ones from cruel oppression, ever felt the throbbing of a chivalrous heart more intensely than I, a *black* knight, did, in running down a chicken in an out-of-the-way place to hide till dark and then carry to some poor overworked black fair one to whom it was at once food, luxury, and medicine. No Scotch borderer, levying blackmail or sweeping off a drove of cattle, ever felt more assured of the justice of his act than I of mine in driving a mile or two into the woods a pig or a sheep and slaughtering it for the good of those whom Riley was starving. I felt good, moral, heroic. The beautiful combination of a high time and a benevolent act— the harmonious interplay of nature and grace—was absolutely entrancing. I felt then the excellency of a sentiment I have since found expressed in a hymn:

> Religion never was designed
> To make our pleasures less.

Was this wrong? I can only say in reply that, at this distance of time, my conscience does not reproach me for it. Then I esteemed it among the best of my deeds. It was my training in the luxury of doing good, in the divinity of a sympathetic heart, in the righteousness of indignation against the cruel and oppressive. There and then was my soul made conscious of its heavenly original. This, too, was all the chivalry of which my circumstances and condition in life admitted. I love the sentiment in its splendid environment of castles and tilts and gallantry, but having fallen on other times, I love it also in the homely guise of Sambo as Paladin, Dinah as outraged maiden, and old Riley as grim oppressor.

By means of the influence thus acquired, the increased amount of work thus done upon the farm, and by the detection of the knavery of the overseer, who plundered his employer for more selfish ends and through my watchfulness was caught in the act and dismissed, I was promoted to be superintendent of the farm work and managed to raise more than double the crops, with more cheerful and willing labor, than was ever seen on the estate before.

Yes, I was now practically overseer. My pride and ambition had made me master of every kind of farm work. But like all ambition its reward was increase of burdens. The crops of wheat, oats, barley, potatoes, corn, tobacco—all had to be cared for by me. I was often compelled to start at midnight with the wagon for the distant market, to drive on through mud and rain till morning, sell the produce, reach home hungry and tired, and nine times out of ten reap my sole reward in curses for not getting higher prices. My master was a fearful blasphemer. Clearly though he saw my profitableness to him, he was too much of a brute, and too great a fool through his brutality, to reward me with kindness or even decent treatment.

When I was about twenty-two years of age, I married a very efficient and, for a slave, a very well-taught girl, reputed to be pious and kind, belonging to a neighboring family, whom I first met at the religious meetings which I attended. She has borne me twelve children, eight of whom still survive and promise to be the comfort of my declining years.

Things remained in this condition for a considerable period, my occupations being to superintend the farming operations and to sell the produce in the neighboring markets of Washington and Georgetown. Many respectable people, yet living there, may possibly have some recollection of "Siah," or "Sie" (as they used to call me), as their marketman; but if they have forgotten me, I remember them with an honest satisfaction.

After passing his youth in the manner I have mentioned in a general way, and which I do not wish more particularly to describe, my master, at the age of forty-five or upwards, married a young woman of eighteen, who had some little property and more thrift. Her economy was remarkable and was certainly no addition to the comfort of the establishment. She had a younger brother, Francis, to whom Riley was appointed guardian, and who used to complain—not without reason, I am confident—of the meanness of the provision made for the household. He would often come to me, with tears in his eyes, to tell me he could not get enough to eat. I made him my friend for life by sympathizing in his emotions and satisfying his appetite, sharing with him the food I took care to provide for my own family. He is still living, and, I understand, one of the wealthiest men in Washington City.

After a time, however, continual dissipation was more than a match for domestic saving. My master fell into difficulty, and from difficulty into a lawsuit with a brother-in-law, who charged him with dishonesty in the management of property confided to him in trust. The lawsuit was protracted enough to cause his ruin of itself.

Harsh and tyrannical as my master had been, I really pitied him in his present distress. At times he was dreadfully dejected, at others crazy with drink and rage. Day after day he would ride over to Montgomery Courthouse about his business, and every day his affairs grew more desperate. He would come into my cabin to tell me how things were going, but spent the time chiefly in lamenting his misfortunes and cursing his brother-in-law. I tried to comfort him as best I could. He had confidence in my fidelity and judgment, and—partly through pride, partly through that divine spirit of love I had learned to worship in Jesus—I entered with interest into all his perplexities. The poor, drinking, furious, moaning creature was utterly incapable of managing his affairs. Shiftlessness, licentiousness and drink had complicated them as much as actual dishonesty.

One night in the month of January, long after I had fallen asleep, he came into my cabin and woke me up. I thought it strange, but for a time he said nothing and sat moodily warming himself at the fire. Then he began to groan and wring his hands. "Sick, massa?" said I. He made no reply but kept on moaning. "Can't I help you any way, massa?" I spoke tenderly, for my heart was full of compassion at his wretched appearance. At last, collecting himself, he cried, "Oh, Sie! I'm ruined, ruined, ruined!" "How so, massa?" "They've got judgment against me, and in less than two weeks every nigger I've got will be put up and sold." Then he burst into a storm of curses at his brother-in-law. I sat silent, powerless to utter a word. Pity for him and terror at the anticipation of my own family's future fate filled my heart. "And now, Sie," he continued, "there's only one way I can save anything. You can do it; won't you, won't you?" In his distress he rose and actually threw his arms around me. Misery had leveled all distinctions. "If I can do it, massa, I will. What is it?" Without replying he went on, "won't you, won't you? I raised you, Sie; I made you overseer; I know I've abused you, Sie, but I didn't mean it." Still he avoided telling me what he wanted. "Promise me you'll do it, boy." He seemed resolutely bent on having my promise first, well knowing from past experience that what I agreed to do I spared no pains to accomplish. Solicited in this way, with urgency and tears, by the man whom I had so zealously served for over thirty years and who now seemed absolutely dependent upon his slave—impelled, too, by the fear, which he skillfully wakened, that the sheriff would seize everyone who belonged to him and that all would be separated or perhaps sold to go to Georgia or Louisiana, an object of perpetual dread to the slave of the more northern states—I consented, and promised faithfully to do all I could to save him from the fate impending over him.

At last the proposition came. "I want you to run away, Sie, to your master Amos in Kentucky and take all the servants along with you." I could not have been more startled had he asked me to go to the moon. Master Amos was his brother. "Kentucky, massa? Kentucky? I don't know the way." "O, it's easy enough for a smart fellow like you to find it. I'll give you a pass and tell you just what to do." Perceiving that I hesitated, he endeavored to frighten me by again referring to the terrors of being sold to Georgia.

For two or three hours he continued to urge the undertaking, appealing to my pride, my sympathies, and my fears. At last, appalling as it seemed, I told him I would do my best. There were eighteen Negroes, besides my wife, two children and myself, to transport nearly a thousand miles, through a country about which I knew nothing, and in midwinter—for it was the month of February 1825. My master proposed to follow me in a few months and establish himself in Kentucky.

My mind once made up, I set earnestly about the needful preparations. They were few and easily made. A one-horse wagon, well stocked with oats, meal, bacon, for our own and the horse's support, was soon made ready. My pride was aroused in view of the importance of my responsibility, and heart and soul I became identified with my master's project of running off his Negroes. The second night after the scheme was formed we were under way. Fortunately for the success of the undertaking, these people had long been under my direction and were devotedly attached to me in return for the many alleviations I had afforded to their miserable condition, the comforts I had procured them, and the consideration I had always manifested for them. Under these circumstances no difficulty arose from want of submission to my authority. The dread of being separated and sold away down south, should they remain on the old estate, united them as one man and kept them patient and alert.

We started from home about eleven o'clock at night and till the following noon made no permanent halt. The men trudged on foot, the children were put into the wagon, and now and then my wife rode for a while. On we went through Alexandria, Culpeper, Fauquier, Harper's Ferry, Cumberland, over the mountains on the National Turnpike, to Wheeling. In all the taverns along the road were regular places for the droves of Negroes continually passing along under the system of the internal slave trade. In these we lodged, and our lodging constituted our only expense, for our food we carried with us. To all who asked questions I showed my master's pass, authorizing me to conduct his Negroes to Kentucky, and often was the encomium of "smart nigger" bestowed on me, to my immense gratification.

At the places where we stopped for the night, we often met Negro drivers with their droves, who were almost uniformly kept chained to prevent them from running away. The inquiry was often propounded to me by the drivers, "Whose niggers are those?" On being informed, the next inquiry usually was, "Where are they going?" "To Kentucky." "Who drives them?" "Well, I have charge of them," was my reply. "What a smart nigger!" was the usual exclamation, with an oath. "Will your master sell you? Come in and stop with us." In this way I was often invited to pass the evening with them in the barroom; their Negroes, in the meantime, lying chained in the pen, while mine were scattered around at liberty.

Arriving at Wheeling, in pursuance of the plan laid down by my master, I sold the horse and wagon and purchased a large boat, called in that region a yawl. Our mode of locomotion was now decidedly more agreeable than tramping along day after day at the rate we had kept up ever since leaving home. Very little labor at the oars was necessary. The tide floated us steadily along, and we had ample leisure to sleep and recruit our strength.

A new and unexpected trouble now assailed me. On passing along the Ohio shore, we were repeatedly told by persons conversing with us that we were no longer slaves but free men, if we chose to be so. At Cincinnati, especially, crowds of colored people gathered round us and insisted on our remaining with them. They told us we were fools to think of going on and surrendering ourselves up to a new owner, that now we could be our own masters and put ourselves out of all reach of pursuit. I saw the people under me were getting much excited. Divided counsels and signs of insubordination began to manifest themselves. I began, too, to feel my own resolution giving way. Freedom had ever been an object of my ambition, though no other means of obtaining it had occurred to me but purchasing myself. I had never dreamed of running away. I had a sentiment of honor on the subject. The duties of the slave to his master as appointed over him in the Lord, I had ever heard urged by ministers and religious men. It seemed like outright stealing. And now I felt the Devil was getting the upper hand of me. Strange as all this may seem, I really felt it then. Entrancing as the idea was that the coast was clear for a run for freedom, that I might liberate my companions, carry off my wife and children, and some day own a house and land and be no longer despised and abused—still my notions of right were against it. I had promised my master to take his property to Kentucky and deposit it with his brother Amos. Pride, too, came in to confirm me. I had undertaken a great thing; my vanity had been flattered all along the road by hearing myself praised; I thought it would be a feather in my cap to carry it through thoroughly; and had often painted the scene in my imagination of the final surrender of my charge to master Amos and the immense admiration and respect with which he would regard me.

Under the influence of these impressions and seeing that the allurements of the crowd were producing a manifest effect, I sternly assumed the captain and ordered the boat to be pushed off into the stream. A shower of curses followed me from the shore; but the Negroes under me, accustomed to obey and, alas! too degraded and ignorant of the advantages of liberty to know what they were forfeiting, offered no resistance to my command.

Often since that day has my soul been pierced with bitter anguish at the thought of having been thus instrumental in consigning to the infernal bondage of slavery so many of my fellow beings. I have wrestled in prayer with God for forgiveness. Having experienced myself the sweetness of liberty and knowing too well the after misery of numbers of many of them, my infatuation has seemed to me the unpardonable sin. But I console myself with the thought that I acted according to my best light, though the light that was in me was darkness. Those were my days of ignorance. I knew not the glory of free manhood. I knew not that the title deed of the slaveowner is robbery and outrage.

What advantages I may have personally lost by thus throwing away an opportunity of obtaining freedom, I know not; but the perception of my own strength of character, the feeling of integrity, the sentiment of high honor I thus gained by obedience to what I believed right—these advantages I do know and prize. He that is faithful over a little, will alone be faithful over much. Before God, I tried to do my best, and the error of judgment lies at the door of the degrading system under which I had been nurtured.

[Henson rationalizes his failure to free himself and the other slaves while they were in Ohio by saying he had been taught to obey his master and could not betray a trust. Later he felt "bitter anguish" over the decision. Upon his arrival in Kentucky all the slaves except Henson and his family were sold. Henson returned to Maryland. Now a Methodist preacher, he held religious meetings and collected money. He then attempted to buy his freedom from his master who tricked him out of his purchase money.]

Before I left Ohio and set my face towards Montgomery County, I was master of two hundred and seventy-five dollars, besides my horse and clothes. Proud of my success, I enjoyed the thought of showing myself once more in the place where I had been known simply as "Riley's head nigger"; and it was with no little satisfaction that about Christmas I rode up to the old house.

My master gave me a boisterous reception and expressed great delight at seeing me. "Why, what in the devil have you been doing, Sie? You've turned into a regular black gentleman." My horse and dress sorely puzzled him, and I soon saw it began to irritate him. The clothes I wore were certainly better than his. And already the workings of that tyrannical hate with which the coarse and brutal, who have no inherent superiority, ever regard the least sign of equality in their dependents were visible in his manner. His face seemed to say, "I'll take the gentleman out of you pretty soon." I gave him such an account of my preaching as, while it was consistent with the truth and explained my appearance, did not betray to him my principal purpose. He soon asked to see my pass, and when he found it authorized me to return to Kentucky, handed it to his wife and desired her to put it into his desk. The maneuver was cool and startling. I heard the old prison gate clang and the bolt shoot into the socket once more. But I said nothing, and resolved to maneuver also.

After putting my horse in the stable, I retired to the kitchen, where my master told me I was to sleep for the night. O, how different from my accommodations in the free states, for the last three months, was the crowded room, with its dirt floor, and filth, and stench! I looked around me with a sensation of disgust. The Negroes present were strangers to me, being slaves that Mrs. Riley had brought to her husband. "Fool that I was to come back!" I found my mother had died during my absence, and every tie which had ever connected me with the place was broken. The idea of lying down with my nice clothes in this nasty sty was insufferable. Full of gloomy reflections at my loneliness and the poverty-stricken aspect of the whole farm, I sat down, and while my companions were snoring in unconsciousness, I kept awake thinking how I should escape from the accursed spot. I knew of but one friend to whom I could appeal: "Master Frank," the brother of Riley's wife, before mentioned, who was now of age and had established himself in business in Washington. I knew he would take an interest in me, for I had done much to lighten his sorrows when he was an abused and harshly-treated boy in the house. I resolved to go to him, and as soon as I thought it time to start, I saddled my horse and rode up to the house. It was early in the morning and my master had already gone to the tavern on his usual business, when Mrs. Riley came out to look at my horse and equipments. "Where are you going, 'Siah?" was the natural question. I replied, "I am going to Washington, mistress, to see Mr. Frank, and I must take my pass with me, if you please." "O, everybody knows you here; you won't need your pass." "But I can't go to Washington without it. I may be met by some surly stranger who will stop me and plague me, if he can't do anything worse." "Well, I'll get it for you," she answered; and glad was I to see her return with it in her hand, and to have her give it to me, while she little imagined its importance to my plan.

My reception by Master Frank was all I expected, as kind and hearty as possible. He was delighted at my appearance, and I immediately told him all my plans and hopes. He entered cordially into them and expressed, as he felt, I doubt not, a strong sympathy for me. I found that he thoroughly detested Riley, whom he charged with having defrauded him of a large proportion of his property which he had held as guardian, though, as he was not at warfare with him, he readily agreed to negotiate for my freedom and bring him to the most favorable terms. Accordingly, in a few days he rode over to the house and had a long conversation with him on the subject of my emancipation. He disclosed to him the facts that I had got some money and my pass, and urged that I was a smart fellow, who was bent upon getting his freedom and had served the family faithfully for many years; that I had really paid for myself a hundred times over, in the increased amount of produce I had raised by my skill and influence; and that if he did not take care and accept a fair offer when I made it to him, he would find some day that I had the means to do without his help, and that he would see neither me nor my money; that with my horse and my pass I was pretty independent of him already, and he had better make up his mind to do what was really inevitable, and do it with a good grace. By such arguments as these, Mr. Frank not only induced him to think of the thing, but before long brought him to an actual bargain by which he agreed to give me my manumission papers for four hundred and fifty dollars, of which three hundred and fifty dollars were to be in cash and the remainder in my note. My money and my horse enabled me to pay the cash at once, and thus my great hope seemed in a fair way of being realized.

Some time was spent in the negotiation of this affair, and it was not until the ninth of March, 1829, that I received my manumission papers in due form of law. I prepared to start at once on my return to Kentucky. On the tenth, as I was getting ready in the morning for my journey, my master accosted me in the most friendly manner and entered into conversation with me about my plans. He asked me what I was going to do with my certificate of freedom; whether I was going to show it if questioned on the road. I told him, "Yes." "You'll be a fool if you do," he rejoined. "Some slavetrader will get hold of it and tear it up, and the first thing you know, you'll be thrown into prison, sold for your jail fees, and be in his possession before any of your friends can help you. Don't show it at all. Your pass is enough. Let me enclose your papers for you under cover to my brother. Nobody will dare to break a seal, for that is a state-prison matter, and when you arrive in Kentucky you will have it with you all safe and sound."

For this friendly advice, as I thought it, I felt extremely grateful. Secure in my happiness, I cherished no suspicion of others. I accordingly permitted him to enclose my precious papers in an envelope composed of several wrappers. After he had sealed it with three seals and directed it to his brother in Davies County, Kentucky, in my care, I carefully stowed it in my carpet bag. Leaving immediately for Wheeling, to which place I was obliged to travel on foot, I there took boat and in due time reached my destination. I was arrested repeatedly on the way; but by insisting always on being carried before a magistrate, I succeeded in escaping all serious impediments by means of my pass, which was quite regular and could not be set aside by any responsible authority.

The boat which took me down from Louisville landed me about dark, and my walk of five miles brought me to the plantation at bedtime. I went directly to my own cabin and found my wife and little ones well. Of course we had enough to communicate to each other. I soon found that I had something to learn as well as to tell. Letters had reached the "great house"—as the master's was always called—long before I arrived, telling them what I had been doing. The children of the family had eagerly communicated the good news to my wife—how I had been preaching, and raising money, and making a bargain for my freedom. It was not long before Charlotte began to question me, with much excitement, about how I raised the money. She evidently thought I had stolen it. Her opinion of my powers as a preacher was not exalted enough to permit her to believe I had gained it as I really did. It was the old story of the prophet without honor in his own place. I contrived however to quiet her fears on this score. "But how are you going to raise enough to pay the remainder of the thousand dollars?" "What thousand dollars?" "The thousand dollars you were to give for your freedom." O, how those words smote me! At once I suspected treachery. Again and again I questioned her as to what she had heard. She persisted in repeating the same story as to the substance of my master's letters. Master Amos said I had paid three hundred and fifty dollars down and when I had made up six hundred and fifty more I was to have my free papers. I now began to perceive the trick that had been played upon me and to see the management by which Riley had contrived that the only evidence of my freedom should be kept from every eye but that of his brother Amos, who was requested to retain it until I had made up the balance I was reported to have agreed to pay. Indignation is a faint word to express my deep sense of such villainy. I was alternately beside myself with rage and paralyzed with despair. My dream of bliss was over. What could I do to set myself right? The only witness to the truth, Master Frank, was a thousand miles away. I could neither write to him or get any one else to write. Every man about me who could write was a slaveholder. I dared not go before a magistrate with my papers, for fear I should be seized and sold down the river before anything could be done. I felt that every man's hand would be against me. "My God! my God! why hast thou forsaken me?" was my bitter cry. One thing only seemed clear. My papers must never be surrendered to Master Amos. I told my wife I had not seen them since I left Louisville. They might be in my bag, or they might be lost. At all events I did not wish to look myself. If she found them there, and hid them away, out of my knowledge, it would be the best disposition to make of them.

The next morning, at the blowing of the horn, I went out to find Master Amos. I found him sitting on a stile, and as I drew near enough for him to recognize me, he shouted out a hearty welcome in his usual chaste style. "Why, halloa, Sie! is that you? Got back, eh! Why, you old son of a bitch, I'm glad to see you! Drot your blood, drot your blood, why, you're a regular black gentleman!" And he surveyed my dress with an appreciative grin. "Well, boy, how's your master? Isaac says you want to be free. Want to be free, eh! I think your master treats you pretty hard, though. Six hundred and fifty dollars don't come so easy in old Kentuck. How does he ever expect you to raise all that. It's too much, boy; it's too much." In the conversation that followed, I found my wife was right. Riley had no idea of letting me off and supposed I could contrive to raise six hundred and fifty as easily as one hundred dollars.

Master Amos soon asked me if I had not a paper for him. I told him I had had one, but the last I saw of it was at Louisville, and now it was not in my bag and I did not know what had become of it. He sent me back to the landing to see if it had been dropped on the way. Of course I did not find it. He made, however, little stir about it, for he had intentions of his own to keep me working for him and regarded the whole as a trick of his brother's to get money out of me. All he said about the loss was, "Well, boy, bad luck happens to everybody, sometimes."

. All this was very smooth and pleasant to a man who was in a frenzy of grief at the base and apparently irremediable trick that had been played upon him. I had supposed that I should now be free to start out and gain the other hundred dollars which would discharge my obligation to my master. But I soon saw that I was to begin again with my old labors. It was useless to give expression to my feelings, and I went about my work with as quiet a mind as I could, resolved to trust in God and never despair.

Things went on in this way about a year. From time to time Master Amos joked me about the six hundred and fifty dollars and said his brother kept writing to know why I did not send something. It was "diamond cut diamond" with the two brothers. Mr. Amos had no desire to play into the hands of Mr. Isaac. He was glad enough to secure my services to take care of his stock and his people.

One day my master suddenly informed me that his son Amos, a young man about twenty-one years of age, was going down the river to New Orleans with a flat-boat loaded with produce and that I was to go with him. He was to start the next day and I was to accompany him and help him dispose of his cargo to the best advantage.

This intimation was enough. Though it was not distinctly stated, yet I well knew what was intended, and my heart sunk within me at the near prospect of this fatal blight to all my long-cherished hopes. There was no alternative but death itself, and I thought that there was hope as long as there was life and I would not despair even yet. The expectation of my fate, however, produced the degree of misery nearest to that of despair; and it is in vain for me to attempt to describe the wretchedness I experienced as I made ready to go on board the flatboat. I had little preparation to make, to be sure, and there was but one thing that seemed to me important. I asked my wife to sew up my manumission paper securely in a piece of cloth and to sew that again round my person. I thought that having possession of it might be the means of saving me yet, and I would not neglect anything that offered the smallest chance of escape from the frightful servitude that threatened me.

The immediate cause of this movement on the part of Master Amos I never fully understood. It grew out of a frequent exchange of letters, which had been kept up between him and his brother in Maryland. Whether as a compromise between their rival claims it was agreed to sell me and divide the proceeds, or that Master Amos, in fear of my running away, had resolved to turn me into riches without wings, for his own profit, I never knew. The fact of his intention, however, was clear enough, and God knows it was a fearful blow.

My wife and children accompanied me to the landing, where I bade them an adieu which might be for life and then stepped into the boat, which I found manned by three white men who had been hired for the trip. Mr. Amos and myself were the only other persons on board. The load consisted of beef cattle, pigs, poultry, corn, whisky, and other articles from the farm and from some of the neighboring estates that were to be sold as we dropped down the river—wherever they could be disposed of to the greatest advantage. It was a common trading voyage to New Orleans in which I was embarked, the interest of which consisted not in the incidents that occurred, not in storms or shipwreck or external disaster of any sort, but in the storm of passions contending within me and the imminent risk of the shipwreck of my soul, which was impending over me nearly the whole period of the voyage. One circumstance, only, I will mention, illustrating, as other events in my life have often done, the counsel of the Savior, "He that will be chief among you, let him be your servant."

We were, of course, all bound to take our trick at the helm in turn, sometimes under direction of the captain and sometimes on our own responsibility, as he could not be always awake. In the daytime there was less difficulty than at night, when it required someone who knew the river to avoid sandbars and snags, and the captain was the only person on board who had this knowledge. But whether by day or by night, as I was the only Negro in the boat, I was made to stand at least three tricks (white men are very fond of such tricks) to any other person's one; so that, from being much with the captain and frequently thrown upon my own exertions, I learned the art of steering and managing the boat far better than the rest. I watched the maneuvers necessary to shoot by a sawyer, to land on a bank, or avoid a snag or a steamboat, in the rapid current of the Mississippi, till I could do it as well as the captain. After a while he was attacked by a disease of the eyes; they became very much inflamed and swollen. He was soon rendered totally blind and unable to perform his share of duty. This disorder is not an infrequent consequence of exposure to the light of the sun, doubled in intensity as it is by the reflection from the river. I was the person who could best take his place, and I was in fact master of the boat from that time till our arrival at New Orleans.

After the captain became blind, we were obliged to lie by at night, as none of the rest of us had been down the river before, and it was necessary to keep watch all night to prevent depredations by the Negroes on shore, who used frequently to attack such boats as ours for the sake of the provisions on board.

On our way down the river we stopped at Vicksburg, and I got permission to visit a plantation a few miles from the town, where some of my old companions whom I had brought from Kentucky were living. It was the saddest visit I ever made. Four years in an unhealthy climate and under a hard master had done the ordinary work of twenty. Their cheeks were literally caved in with starvation and disease and their bodies infested with vermin. No hell could equal the misery they described as their daily portion. Toiling half naked in malarious marshes, under a burning, maddening sun, and poisoned by swarms of mosquitoes and black gnats, they looked forward to death as their only deliverance. Some of them fairly cried at seeing me there and at thought of the fate which they felt awaited me. Their worst fears of being sold down South had been more than realized. I went away sick at heart, and to this day the sight of that wretched group haunts me.

WILLIAM AND ELLEN CRAFT

William Craft, a slave in Macon, Georgia, escaped with his near-white wife (who was also a slave) by a daring ruse. His wife disguised herself as a "gentleman," while William, a full black, accompanied her as her body servant. Together they traveled north in public coaches and trains, staying at the best hotels until they reached Philadelphia. Craft, a cabinet maker, had saved the money for the trip by hiring himself out for wages. In the section of their autobiography reprinted here, they record conversations with white Southerners whom they met in transit. William Craft refers to Ellen as "my master." In New England the two spoke before antislavery audiences who marveled that a woman as white as Ellen could be held a slave. William, described as "a noble specimen of a man," was said to resemble Cinques, the hero of the *Amistad* mutiny. Like Cinques, William was prepared to resist attempts to recapture him. "I had made up my mind to kill or be killed, before I would be taken," he said. The Crafts went to Canada and finally, with the help of friends, settled in England. The excerpt below comes from William and Ellen Craft's autobiography *Running a Thousand Miles for Freedom: or The Escape of William and Ellen Craft from Slavery* published in London in 1860.

Flight with Dignity

My master's first impression, after seeing Mr. Cray, was that he was there for the purpose of securing him. However, my master thought it was not wise to give any information respecting himself, and, for fear that Mr. Cray might draw him into conversation and recognize his voice, my master resolved to feign deafness as the only means of self-defense.

After a little while, Mr. Cray said to my master, "It is a very fine morning, sir." The latter took no notice, but kept looking out of the window. Mr. Cray soon repeated this remark, in a little louder tone, but my master remained as before. This indifference attracted the attention of the passengers near, one of whom laughed out. This, I suppose, annoyed the old gentleman, so he said, "I will make him hear," and in a loud tone of voice repeated, "It is a very fine morning, sir."

My master turned his head and with a polite bow said, "Yes," and commenced looking out of the window again.

One of the gentlemen remarked that it was a very great deprivation to be deaf. "Yes," replied Mr. Cray, "and I shall not trouble that fellow any more." This enabled my master to breathe a little easier and to feel that Mr. Cray was not his pursuer after all.

The gentlemen then turned the conversation upon the three great topics of discussion in first-class circles in Georgia, namely, niggers, cotton, and the abolitionists.

My master had often heard of abolitionists, but in such a connection as to cause him to think that they were a fearful kind of wild animal. But he was highly delighted to learn, from the gentlemen's conversation, that the abolitionists were persons who were opposed to oppression and therefore, in his opinion, not the lowest but the very highest of God's creatures.

Without the slightest objection on my master's part, the gentlemen left the carriage at Gordon for Milledgeville (the capital of the State).

We arrived at Savannah early in the evening and got into an omnibus, which stopped at the hotel for the passengers to take tea. I stepped into the house and brought my master something on a tray to the omnibus, which took us in due time to the steamer, which was bound for Charleston, South Carolina.

Soon after going on board, my master turned in. As the captain and some of the passengers seemed to think this strange and also questioned me respecting him, my master thought I had better get out the flannels and opodeldoc which we had prepared for the rheumatism, warm them quickly by the stove in the gentleman's saloon, and bring them to his berth. We did this as an excuse for my master's retiring to bed so early.

While at the stove one of the passengers said to me, "Buck, what have you got there?" "Opodeldoc, sir," I replied. "I should think it's opo*devil*," said a lanky swell, who was leaning back in a chair with his heels upon the back of another and chewing tobacco as if for a wager, "It stinks enough to kill or cure twenty men. Away with it, or I reckon I will throw it overboard!"

It was by this time warm enough, so I took it to my master's berth, remained there a little while, and then went on deck and asked the steward where I was to sleep. He said there was no place provided for colored passengers, whether slave or free. So I paced the deck till a late hour, then mounted some cotton bags in a warm place near the funnel, sat there till morning, and then went and assisted my master to get ready for breakfast.

He was seated at the right hand of the captain, who, together with all the passengers, inquired very kindly after his health. As my master had one hand in a sling, it was my duty to carve his food. But when I went out the captain said, "You have a very attentive boy, sir; but you had better watch him like a hawk when you get on to the North. He seems all very well here, but he may act quite differently there. I know several gentlemen who have lost their valuable niggers among them d-----d cutthroat abolitionists."

Before my master could speak, a rough slavedealer, who was sitting opposite, with both elbows on the table, and with a large piece of broiled fowl in his fingers, shook his head with emphasis and, in a deep Yankee tone, forced through his crowded mouth the words, "Sound doctrine, captain, very sound." He then dropped the chicken into the plate, leant back, placed his thumbs in the armholes of his fancy waistcoat, and continued: "I would not take a nigger to the North under no consideration. I have had a deal to do with niggers in my time, but I never saw one who ever had his heel upon free soil that was worth a d--n." "Now stranger," addressing my master, "if you have made up your mind to sell that ere nigger, I am your man; just mention your price, and if it isn't out of the way, I will pay for him on this board with hard silver dollars." This hard-featured, bristly-bearded, wire-headed, red-eyed monster, staring at my master as the serpent did at Eve, said, "What do you say, stranger?" He replied, "I don't wish to sell, sir; I cannot get on well without him."

"You will have to get on without him if you take him to the North," continued this man. "For I can tell ye, stranger, as a friend. I am an older cove than you, I have seen lots of this ere world, and I reckon I have had more dealings with niggers than any man living or dead. I was once employed by General Wade Hampton, for ten years, in doing nothing but breaking 'em in, and everybody knows that the General would not have a man that didn't understand his business. So I tell ye, stranger, again, you had better sell, and let me take him down to Orleans. He will do you no good if you take him across Mason's and Dixon's line. He is a keen nigger, and I can see from the cut of his eye that he is certain to run away." My master said, "I think not, sir; I have great confidence in his fidelity." "*Fidevil,*" indignantly said the dealer, as his fist came down upon the edge of the saucer and upset a cup of hot coffee in a gentleman's lap. (As the scalded man jumped up the trader quietly said, "Don't disturb yourself, neighbor; accidents will happen in the best of families.") "It always makes me mad to hear a man talking about fidelity in niggers. There isn't a d----d one on 'em who wouldn't cut sticks, if he had half a chance."

The gentleman said my master could obtain the very best advice in Philadelphia. Which turned out to be quite correct, though he did not receive it from physicians but from kind abolitionists who understood his case much better. The gentleman also said, "I reckon your master's father hasn't any more such faithful and smart boys as you." "O, yes, sir, he has," I replied, "lots on 'em." Which was literally true. This seemed all he wished to know. He thanked me, gave me a ten-cent piece, and requested me to be attentive to my good master. I promised that I would do so and have ever since endeavored to keep my pledge. During the gentleman's absence, the ladies and my master had a little cosy chat. But on his return, he said, "You seem to be very much afflicted, sir." "Yes, sir," replied the gentleman in the poultices. "What seems to be the matter with you, sir, may I be allowed to ask?" "Inflammatory rheumatism, sir." "Oh! that is very bad, sir," said the kind gentleman: "I can sympathize with you, for I know from bitter experience what the rheumatism is." If he did, he knew a good deal more than Mr. Johnson.

The gentleman thought my master would feel better if he would lie down and rest himself, and as he was anxious to avoid conversation, he at once acted upon this suggestion. The ladies politely rose, took their extra shawls, and made a nice pillow for the invalid's head. My master wore a fashionable cloth cloak, which they took and covered him comfortably on the couch. After he had been lying a little while the ladies, I suppose, thought he was asleep. So one of them gave a long sigh and said, in a quiet fascinating tone, "Papa, he seems to be a very nice young gentleman." But before papa could speak, the other lady quickly said, "Oh! dear me, I never felt so much for a gentleman in my life!" To use an American expression, "they fell in love with the wrong chap."

After my master had been lying a little while he got up. The gentleman assisted him in getting on his cloak, the ladies took their shawls, and soon all were seated. They then insisted upon Mr. Johnson taking some of their refreshments, which of course he did, out of courtesy to the ladies. All went on enjoying themselves until they reached Richmond, where the ladies and their father left the train. But before doing so, the good old Virginian gentleman, who appeared to be much pleased with my master, presented him with a recipe, which he said was a perfect cure for the inflammatory rheumatism. The invalid not being able to read it, and fearing he should hold it upside down in pretending to do so, thanked the donor kindly and placed it in his waistcoat pocket. My master's new friend also gave him his card and requested that the next time he traveled that way to do him the kindness to call, adding, "I shall be pleased to see you and so will my daughters." Mr. Johnson expressed his gratitude for the proffered hospitality and said he should feel glad to call on his return. I have not the slightest doubt that he will fulfill the promise whenever that return takes place. After changing trains we went on a little beyond Fredericksburg and took a steamer to Washington.

At Richmond, a stout elderly lady, whose whole demeanor indicated that she belonged (as Mrs. Stowe's Aunt Chloe expresses it) to one of the "firstest families," stepped into the carriage and took a seat near my master. Seeing me passing quickly along the platform, she sprang up as if taken by a fit and exclaimed, "Bless my soul! There goes my nigger, Ned!"

My master said, "No, that is my boy."

The lady paid no attention to this; she poked her head out of the window and bawled to me, "You Ned, come to me, sir, you runaway rascal!"

On my looking round she drew her head in and said to my master, "I beg your pardon, sir, I was sure it was my nigger; I never in my life saw two black pigs more alike than your boy and my Ned."

After the disappointed lady had resumed her seat and the train had moved off, she closed her eyes, slightly raised her hands, and in a sanctified tone said to my master, "Oh! I hope, sir, your boy will not turn out to be so worthless as my Ned has. Oh! I was as kind to him as if he had been my own son. Oh! sir, it grieves me very much to think that after all I did for him, he should go off without having any cause whatever."

"When did he leave you?" asked Mr. Johnson.

"About eighteen months ago, and I have never seen hair or hide of him since."

"Did he have a wife?" inquired a very respectable-looking young gentleman, who was sitting near my master and opposite to the lady.

"No, sir, not when he left, though he did have one a little before that. She was very unlike him; she was as good and as faithful a nigger as any one need wish to have. But, poor thing! She became so ill that she was unable to do much work, so I thought it would be best to sell her, to go to New Orleans where the climate is nice and warm."

"I suppose she was very glad to go South for the restoration of her health?" said the gentleman.

"No, she was not," replied the lady. "For niggers never know what is best for them. She took on a great deal about leaving Ned and the little nigger; but, as she was so weakly, I let her go."

"Was she good-looking?" asked the young passenger, who was evidently not of the same opinion as the talkative lady and therefore wished her to tell all she knew.

"Yes, she was very handsome and much whiter than I am and therefore will have no trouble in getting another husband. I am sure I wish her well. I asked the speculator who bought her to sell her to a good master. Poor thing! She has my prayers, and I know she prays for me. She was a good Christian and always used to pray for my soul. It was through her earliest prayers," continued the lady, "that I was first led to seek forgiveness of my sins, before I was converted at the great camp meeting."

This caused the lady to snuffle and to draw from her pocket a richly embroidered handkerchief and apply it to the corner of her eyes. But my master could not see that it was at all soiled.

The silence which prevailed for a few moments was broken by the gentleman's saying, "As your 'July' was such a very good girl and had served you so faithfully before she lost her health, don't you think it would have been better to have emancipated her?"

"No, indeed I do not!" scornfully exclaimed the lady, as she impatiently crammed the fine handkerchief into a little workbag. "I have not patience with people who set niggers at liberty. It is the very worst thing you can do for them. My dear husband just before he died willed all his niggers free. But I and all our friends knew very well that he was too good a man to have ever thought of doing such an unkind and foolish thing, had he been in his right mind, and, therefore, we had the will altered as it should have been in the first place."

"Did you mean, madam," asked my master, "that willing the slaves free was unjust to yourself, or unkind to them?"

"I mean that it was decidedly unkind to the servants themselves. It always seems to me such a cruel thing to turn niggers loose to shift for themselves, when there are so many good masters to take care of them. As for myself," continued the considerate lady, "I thank the Lord my dear husband left me and my son well provided for. Therefore I care nothing for the niggers on my own account, for they are a great deal more trouble than they are worth. I sometimes wish that there was not one of them in the world, for the ungrateful wretches are always running away. I have lost no less than ten since my poor husband died. It's ruinous, sir!"

"But as you are well provided for, I suppose you do not feel the loss very much," said the passenger.

"I don't feel it at all," haughtily continued the good soul; "but that is no reason why property should be squandered. If my son and myself had the money for those valuable niggers, just see what a great deal of good we could do for the poor and in sending missionaries abroad to the poor heathen, who have never heard the name of our blessed Redeemer. My dear son, who is a good Christian minister, has advised me not to worry and send my soul to hell for the sake of niggers, but to sell every blessed one of them for what they will fetch and go and live in peace with him in New York. This I have concluded to do. I have just been to Richmond and made arrangements with my agent to make clean work of the forty that are left."

"Your son being a good Christian minister," said the gentleman, "it's strange he did not advise you to let the poor Negroes have their liberty and go North."

"It's not at all strange, sir; it's not at all strange. My son knows what's best for the niggers. He has always told me that they were much better off than the free niggers in the North. In fact, I don't believe there are any white laboring people in the world who are as well off as the slaves."

"You are quite mistaken, madam," said the young man. "For instance, my own widowed mother, before she died, emancipated all her slaves and sent them to Ohio where they are getting along well. I saw several of them last summer myself."

"Well," replied the lady, "freedom may do for your ma's niggers, but it will never do for mine; and, plague them, they shall never have it; that is the word, with the bark on it."

"If freedom will not do for your slaves," replied the passenger, "I have no doubt your Ned and the other nine Negroes will find out their mistake and return to their old home."

"Blast them!" exclaimed the old lady, with great emphasis. "If I ever get them, I will cook their infernal hash and tan their accursed black hides well for them! God forgive me," added the old soul, "the niggers will make me lose all my religion!"

By this time the lady had reached her destination. The gentleman got out at the next station beyond. As soon as she was gone, the young Southerner said to my master, "What a d----d shame it is for that old whining hypocritical humbug to cheat the poor Negroes out of their liberty! If she has religion, may the Devil prevent me from ever being converted!"

For the purpose of somewhat disguising myself, I bought and wore a very good second-hand white beaver, an article which I had never indulged in before. So just before we arrived at Washington, an uncouth planter, who had been watching me very closely, said to my master, "I reckon, stranger, you are *'spiling'* that ere nigger of yourn by letting him wear such a devilish fine hat. Just look at the quality on it; the President couldn't wear a better. I should just like to go and kick it overboard." His friend touched him and said, "Don't speak so to a gentleman." "Why not?" exclaimed the fellow. He grated his short teeth, which appeared to be nearly worn away by the incessant chewing of tobacco, and said, "It always makes me itch all over, from head to toe, to get hold of every d----d nigger I see dressed like a white man. Washington is run away with *spiled* and free niggers. If I had my way I would sell every d----d rascal of 'em way down South, where the devil would be whipped out on 'em."

This man's fierce manner made my master feel rather nervous, and therefore he thought the less he said the better, so he walked off without making any reply. In a few minutes we were landed at Washington, where we took a conveyance and hurried off to the train for Baltimore.

We left our cottage on Wednesday morning, the 21st of December, 1848, and arrived at Baltimore, Saturday evening, the 24th (Christmas Eve). Baltimore was the last slave port of any note at which we stopped.

On arriving there we felt more anxious than ever, because we knew not what that last dark night would bring forth. It is true we were near the goal, but our poor hearts were still as if tossed at sea, and, as there was another great and dangerous bar to pass, we were afraid our liberties would be wrecked and, like the ill-fated *Royal Charter*, go down forever just off the place we longed to reach.

They are particularly watchful at Baltimore to prevent slaves from escaping into Pennsylvania, which is a Free State. After I had seen my master into one of the best carriages and was just about to step into mine, an officer, a full-blooded Yankee of the lower order, saw me. He came quickly up and, tapping me on the shoulder, said in his unmistakable native twang, together with no little display of his authority, "Where are you going, boy?" "To Philadelphia, sir," I humbly replied. "Well, what are you going there for?" "I am traveling with my master, who is in the next carriage, sir." "Well, I calculate you had better get him out, and be mighty quick about it, because the train will soon be starting. It is against my rules to let any man take a slave past here unless he can satisfy them in the office that he has a right to take him along."

The officer then passed on and left me standing upon the platform, with my anxious heart apparently palpitating in the throat. At first I scarcely knew which way to turn. But it soon occurred to me that the good God, who had been with us thus far, would not forsake us at the eleventh hour. So with renewed hope I stepped into my master's carriage to inform him of the difficulty. I found him sitting at the farther end, quite alone. As soon as he looked up and saw me, he smiled. I also tried to wear a cheerful countenance in order to break the shock of the sad news. I knew what made him smile. He was aware that if we were fortunate we should reach our destination at five o'clock the next morning. This made it the more painful to communicate what the officer had said, but as there was no time to lose, I went up to him and asked him how he felt. He said, "Much better," and that he thanked God we were getting on so nicely. I then said we were not getting on quite so well as we had anticipated. He anxiously and quickly asked what was the matter. I told him. He started as if struck by lightning and exclaimed, "Good Heavens! William, is it possible that we are, after all, doomed to hopeless bondage?" I could say nothing; my heart was too full to speak, for at first I did not know what to do. However, we knew it would never do to turn back to the "City of Destruction," like Bunyan's *Mistrust* and *Timorous*, because they saw lions in the narrow way after ascending the hill Difficulty, but press on, like noble *Christian* and *Hopeful*, to the great city in which dwelt a few "shining ones." So, after a few moments, I did all I could to encourage my companion and we stepped out and made for the office. How or where my master obtained sufficient courage to face the tyrants who had power to blast all we held dear, heaven only knows! Queen Elizabeth could not have been more terror-stricken, on being forced to land at the traitors' gate leading to the Tower, than we were on entering that office. We felt that our very existence was at stake, and that we must either sink or swim. But, as God was our present and mighty helper in this as well as in all former trials, we were able to keep our heads up and press forwards.

On entering the room we found the principal man, to whom my master said, "Do you wish to see me, sir?" "Yes," said this eagle-eyed officer. He added, "It is against our rules, sir, to allow any person to take a slave out of Baltimore into Philadelphia, unless he can satisfy us that he has a right to take him along." "Why is that?" asked my master, with more firmness than could be expected. "Because, sir," continued he, in a voice and manner that almost chilled our blood, "if we should suffer any gentleman to take a slave past here into Philadelphia, and should the gentleman with whom the slave might be traveling turn out not to be his rightful owner, and should the proper master come and prove that his slave escaped on our road, we shall have him to pay for, and therefore we cannot let any slave pass here without receiving security to show, and to satisfy us, that it is all right."

This conversation attracted the attention of the large number of bustling passengers. After the officer had finished, a few of them said, "Chit, chit, chit"—not because they thought we were slaves endeavoring to escape, but merely because they thought my master was a slaveholder and invalid gentleman, and therefore it was wrong to detain him. The officer, observing that the passengers sympathized with my master, asked him if he was not acquainted with some gentleman in Baltimore that he could get to endorse for him, to show that I was his property and that he had a right to take me off. He said, "No," and added, "I bought tickets in Charleston to pass us through to Philadelphia, and therefore you have no right to detain us here." "Well, sir," said the man, indignantly, "right or no right, we shan't let you go." These sharp words fell upon our anxious hearts like the crack of doom and made us feel that hope only smiles to deceive.

For a few moments perfect silence prevailed. My master looked at me, and I at him, but neither of us dared to speak a word, for fear of making some blunder that would tend to our detection. We knew that the officers had power to throw us into prison, and if they had done so we must have been detected and driven back, like the vilest felons, to a life of slavery, which we dreaded far more than sudden death.

We felt as though we had come into deep waters and were about to be overwhelmed, and that the slightest mistake would clip asunder the last brittle thread of hope by which we were suspended and let us down for ever into the dark and horrible pit of misery and degradation from which we were straining every nerve to escape. While our hearts were crying lustily unto Him who is ever ready and able to save, the conductor of the train that we had just left stepped in. The officer asked if we came by the train with him from Washington. He said we did and left the room. Just then the bell rang for the train to leave, and had it been the sudden shock of an earthquake it could not have given us a greater thrill. The sound of the bell caused every eye to flash with apparent interest and to be more steadily fixed upon us than before. But, as God would have it, the officer all at once thrust his fingers through his hair and in a state of great agitation said, "I really don't know what to do; I calculate it is all right." He then told the clerk to run and tell the conductor to "let this gentleman and slave pass"—adding, "As he is not well, it is a pity to stop him here. We will let him go." My master thanked him and stepped out and hobbled across the platform as quickly as possible. I tumbled him unceremoniously into one of the best carriages and leaped into mine just as the train was gliding off towards our happy destination.

We thought of this plan about four days before we left Macon, and as we had our daily employment to attend to, we only saw each other at night. So we sat up the four long nights talking over the plan and making preparations.

We had also been four days on the journey, and as we traveled night and day, we got but very limited opportunities for sleeping. I believe nothing in the world could have kept us awake so long but the intense excitement produced by the fear of being retaken on the one hand and the bright anticipation of liberty on the other.

We left Baltimore about eight o'clock in the evening, and not being aware of a stopping-place of any consequence between there and Philadelphia, and also knowing that if we were fortunate we should be in the latter place early the next morning, I thought I might indulge in a few minutes' sleep in the car; but I, like Bunyan's Christian in the arbor, went to sleep at the wrong time and took too long a nap. So, when the train reached Havre de Grace, all the first-class passengers had to get out of the carriages and into a ferry-boat to be ferried across the Susquehanna River and take the train on the opposite side.

HARRIET JACOBS

Harriet Jacobs was the daughter of a valued slave carpenter and
grew up to become a house servant. An intelligent and attractive
girl, she was the object of her master's lust and her mistress's jealousy and spite. Her life story is a valuable source for such delicate
relationships in a slaveholding family. Harriet describes many of
the cruelties of the slave system: a runaway slave who was
crushed between the screws of the cotton gin as punishment; the
flogging, intimidation, and lynching of Negroes after the Nat
Turner rebellion; and other outrages. She escaped slavery by
stowing away on a ship bound for a northern port. Her life story,
told under the pseudonym, Linda Brent, was edited by Lydia
Maria Child. The book, from which the following section comes,
is entitled *Incidents in the Life of a Slave Girl*, published in Boston in 1861.

The Auction Block Ends
a Childhood Dream

I was born a slave; but I never knew it till six years of happy childhood had passed away. My father was a carpenter and considered so intelligent and skillful in his trade that, when buildings out of the common line were to be erected, he was sent for from long distances to be head workman. On condition of paying his mistress two hundred dollars a year and supporting himself, he was allowed to work at his trade and manage his own affairs. His strongest wish was to purchase his children; but, though he several times offered his hard earnings for that purpose, he never succeeded. In complexion my parents were a light shade of brownish yellow and were termed mulattoes. They lived together in a comfortable home, and, though we were all slaves, I was so fondly shielded that I never dreamed I was a piece of merchandise, trusted to them for safe keeping and liable to be demanded of them at any moment. I had one brother, William, who was two years younger than myself—a bright, affectionate child. I had also a great treasure in my maternal grandmother, who was a remarkable woman in many respects. She was the daughter of a planter in South Carolina, who, at his death, left her mother and his three children free, with money to go to St. Augustine, where they had relatives. It was during the Revolutionary War, and they were captured on their passage, carried back, and sold to different purchasers. Such was the story my grandmother used to tell me; but I do not remember all the particulars. She was a little girl when she was captured and sold to the keeper of a large hotel. I have often heard her tell how hard she fared during childhood. But as she grew older she evinced so much intelligence, and was so faithful, that her master and mistress could not help seeing it was for their interest to take care of such a valuable piece of property. She became an indispensable personage in the household, officiating in all capacities from cook and wet nurse to seamstress. She was much praised for her cooking, and her nice crackers became so famous in the neighborhood that many people were desirous of obtaining them. In consequence of numerous requests of this kind, she asked permission of her mistress to bake crackers at night, after all the household work was done; and she obtained leave to do it, provided she would clothe herself and her children from the profits. Upon these terms, after working hard all day for her mistress, she began her midnight bakings, assisted by her two oldest children. The business proved profitable, and each year she laid by a little, which was saved for a fund to purchase her children. Her master died and the property was divided among his heirs. The widow had her dower in the hotel, which she continued to keep open. My grandmother remained in her service as a slave, but her children were divided among her master's children. As she had five, Benjamin, the youngest one, was sold in order that each heir might have an equal portion of dollars and cents. There was so little difference in our ages that he seemed more like my brother than my uncle. He was a bright, handsome lad, nearly white; for he inherited the complexion my grandmother had derived from Anglo-Saxon ancestors. Though only ten years old, seven hundred and twenty dollars were paid for him. His sale was a terrible blow to my grandmother; but she was naturally hopeful, and she went to work with renewed energy, trusting in time to be able to purchase some of her children. She had laid up three hundred dollars, which her mistress one day begged as a loan, promising to pay her soon. The reader probably knows that no promise or writing given to a slave is legally binding; for according to southern laws, a slave, *being* property, can *hold* no property. When my grandmother lent her hard earnings to her mistress, she trusted solely to her honor. The honor of a slaveholder to a slave!

To this good grandmother I was indebted for many comforts. My brother Willie and I often received portions of the crackers, cakes, and preserves she made to sell; and after we ceased to be children we were indebted to her for many more important services.

Such were the unusually fortunate circumstances of my early childhood. When I was six years old, my mother died; and then, for the first time, I learned, by the talk around me, that I was a slave. My mother's mistress was the daughter of my grandmother's mistress. She was the foster sister of my mother; they were both nourished at my grandmother's breast. In fact, my mother had been weaned at three months old, that the babe of the mistress might obtain sufficient food. They played together as children, and, when they became women, my mother was a most faithful servant to her whiter foster sister. On her deathbed her mistress promised that her children should never suffer for any thing, and during her lifetime she kept her word. They all spoke kindly of my dead mother, who had been a slave merely in name, but in nature was noble and womanly. I grieved for her, and my young mind was troubled with the thought who would now take care of me and my little brother. I was told that my home was now to be with her mistress, and I found it a happy one. No toilsome or disagreeable duties were imposed upon me. My mistress was so kind to me that I was always glad to do her bidding and proud to labor for her as much as my young years would permit. I would sit by her side for hours sewing diligently, with a heart as free from care as that of any freeborn white child. When she thought I was tired, she would send me out to run and jump, and away I bounded to gather berries or flowers to decorate her room. Those were happy days—too happy to last. The slave child had no thought for the morrow, but there came that blight, which too surely waits on every human being born to be a chattel.

When I was nearly twelve years old, my kind mistress sickened and died. As I saw the cheek grow paler and the eye more glassy, how earnestly I prayed in my heart that she might live! I loved her; for she had been almost like a mother to me. My prayers were not answered. She died, and they buried her in the little churchyard, where, day after day, my tears fell upon her grave.

I was sent to spend a week with my grandmother. I was now old enough to begin to think of the future, and again and again I asked myself what they would do with me. I felt sure I should never find another mistress so kind as the one who was gone. She had promised my dying mother that her children should never suffer for anything; and when I remembered that, and recalled her many proofs of attachment to me, I could not help having some hopes that she had left me free. My friends were almost certain it would be so. They thought she would be sure to do it, on account of my mother's love and faithful service. But, alas! we all know that the memory of a faithful slave does not avail much to save her children from the auction block.

After a brief period of suspense, the will of my mistress was read, and we learned that she had bequeathed me to her sister's daughter, a child five years old. So vanished our hopes. My mistress had taught me the precepts of God's Word: "Thou shalt love thy neighbor as thyself." "Whatsoever ye would that men should do unto you, do ye even so unto them." But I was her slave, and I suppose she did not recognize me as her neighbor. I would give much to blot out from my memory that one great wrong. As a child, I loved my mistress; and, looking back on the happy days I spent with her, I try to think with less bitterness of this act of injustice. While I was with her, she taught me to read and spell, and for this privilege, which so rarely falls to the lot of a slave, I bless her memory.

She possessed but few slaves, and at her death those were all distributed among her relatives. Five of them were my grandmother's children, and had shared the same milk that nourished her mother's children. Notwithstanding my grandmother's long and faithful service to her owners, not one of her children escaped the auction block. These God-breathing machines are no more, in the sight of their masters, than the cotton they plant or the horses they tend.

ISRAEL CAMPBELL

While a slave Israel Campbell lived near Nashville, Tennessee. His master was a tavern keeper. Later he was compelled to work as a field hand picking cotton in Mississippi. Driven and whipped as a slave, he resisted his oppressors. After repeated attempts, he finally escaped from slavery, crossing the Ohio River to Illinois and thence to Canada. A slave preacher, he became a minister of the gospel. His life story, part of which is reprinted here, is entitled *Bond and Free: or Yearnings for Freedom from my Green Brier House*, published in Philadelphia in 1861.

Melons, Pumpkins and Cotton

The next day after my whipping, Mr. Crookesty came to me in the field where I was working and said, "Israel, I tell you what I will do; I have bought you, and you have caused me to give you a severe whipping for running away; this I do not wish to have to do any more. Now, if you will be a good boy and not run away any more, I will take you to wait on the house and let you be hostler at the stable; then you can have a chance of making some money, and I will give you enough to eat and wear."

"Sir," I replied, "I will do the very best I can."

So he took me to the house, and all of us had plenty to eat and wear, and never did he have occasion to whip me again. The place where he lived was an old town, about one hundred and ten miles from Nashville and twenty-five miles from the mouth of the Cumberland River, by the name of Centreville, and master was said to keep the best tavern in that part of Kentucky. After I had lived here a little over two years, master took a notion to go to Mississippi. He advertised and sold everything except his slaves. He then purchased a large flatboat and, after we had all embarked, we rowed down the Ohio and Mississippi rivers. In going down the rivers we often met large steamboats which would terribly frighten old mistress. All the way she was praying and crying. Among the boys there was one who was her favorite, named King, and when she saw one of the boats coming, she would cry to King to pull with all his might and see her out of danger, as she was sure they would kill them.

One day, while rowing down the Mississippi, there came blenching and blowing down the river a large steamer, with an Indian painted on the side, named Tecumseh. This so frightened old mistress that it threw her into hysterics. In fact, so completely did this voyage affect old mistress that by the time we reached Vicksburg she died. For this event the slaves did not feel sorry, for she had treated them very meanly.

Old master Crookesty did not commence operations here immediately, but hired all his slaves except one woman, who he kept to take care of his children. He hired me to a gentleman by the name of Mr. Bellfer, who had a large cotton farm. Here I entered on a new life, that of the plantation system. That is, every one had to be up with the blowing of the horn and be in the field by daylight. Every Sunday each one had their rations dealt out to them: three pounds of meat and one peck of corn for the week, which they had to grind and cook for themselves.

When cotton-picking time came, they talked of giving every one a stated task and told me I would have to pick a hundred pounds a day. I tried it for three days, but could not get over ninety pounds; but they put it down one hundred, and the Monday morning following they gave each one their task and told them that if they did not pick the amount they would have as many lashes as there were pounds short. I tried it and took my basket up to be weighed at noon. The overseer noticed that I was going to fall short of my number of pounds and exclaimed, to hurry me up, "Jatherous, jatherous, by the holy and just God, Israel, you will have to buy the rabbit agin night," meaning that I would get a whipping.

The overseer was an Irishman by birth, and was a singular old fellow. He kept a slate with each hand's name on it and would put each draft of cotton down as they brought it in. At night his voice could be heard at its loudest pitch, "All ye's, all ye's gather up your baskets and away to the cottonhouse." So we would gather up the baskets and go to the cottonhouse. As I was going I espied Mr. Bellfer coming to the cottonhouse with the lantern, bullwhip, and rope to tie the delinquents. I knew that my task was short, and that I would get as many lashes as my task was wanting pounds. I could not brave the settlement, so as the others went up I set my basket down and slipped behind the house and went into the woods. I remained there until I thought all the white people had retired; then I took my sack, which I used for picking cotton, and went into the sweet potato patch and digged some potatoes, which I took into the cook's house to roast. Hardly had I them covered, before Mr. Bellfer made his appearance at the door, and exclaimed, "Well Israel, is that you?"

"Yes, sir," I replied.

"Well, I will settle with you now," adding an oath for emphasis.

The overseer was not in the house, but was in the slave quarters, he having a fine black woman for a wife, he not having as much prejudice against color as many of our northern brethren. Mr. Bellfer aroused him, and soon after he made his appearance,

"So you have him, have you, Doctor; by the holy and just God, he will buy the rabbit now."

They ordered me to cross my hands, and they fastened them and led me out into the yard. There was no whipping ground there, so while Mr. Bellfer held me, the overseer prepared the stakes to which to tie me while they were whipping me. Finding they were going to give me a hard whipping, I commenced begging and pleading that if they would only forgive me that time I would do better in future. But they were deaf to my cries. Mrs. Bellfer coming to the door at that time, I entreated her to plead for me, told her I would do better, and that I was sorry for what I had done.

Mistress Betsy had great influence with her husband, and, seeing that I was not as hardened as many of the other slaves, she stopped him and inquired into my case. The Doctor told her that I had not picked my task and had commenced running away.

Mistress Betsy then asked the Doctor not to whip me this time, for she was sure I would try and do better. But he told her to go away, that I had commenced running away, and if he did not break me all the niggers would do likewise.

But I kept on pleading and so awakened Mistress Betsy's feelings in my behalf that she begged the Doctor to let me off this time and offered to go my security that I would have my task hereafter and never run away any more. She asked me if I understood what she had promised.

"Yes ma'am," I replied.

Then Mr. Bellfer said, "Israel, if Mrs. Bellfer will go your security, I will let you off this time; but never expect it again." He then untied my hands, and I went into the kitchen and took my potatoes out of the fire and began to eat them.

While thus engaged I commenced revolving in my mind as to how I should make good my word and give myself a good character for promptness and energy. To pick a hundred pounds of cotton a day I knew I could not, and yet to break my word and lose my good name was equally as hard. I began thinking of some way by which I might succeed in always having my task made up. Thought I, we have a large watermelon patch near the field, and if I do not succeed in having a full quantity before the last load, I will slip one of them in the bottom of the basket. This settled, I went to sleep and dreamt my plan over.

The next morning we all started as usual to the cotton-field. All went on as usual. At eight o'clock we went to the cottonhouse and I had thirty-two pounds; after breakfast we picked until two o'clock and then I had twenty-eight pounds. The overseer, who could tell very near how much each one ought to average, said, "Jatherous, jatherous, Israel, by the holy and just God you will buy the rabbit agin night."

"The fast racehorse runs the fastest the last round," says I to myself, and off I went to the field and picked hard until dark. Then the overseer's voice could be heard, "All ye's, all ye's, get up your baskets and away to the cottonhouse." During the time I was picking, I had selected a good sized melon and put it in the basket and went up to have it weighed.

I was among one of the first who put their baskets in the scales that night, and the result was announced as a hundred and five pounds for my day's work. "I knew you could reach a hundred pounds," said the Doctor.

"Hard work, sir, hard work," I replied. Thought I to myself, if you only knew how much less cotton there was, you would not look so pleased. I leapt into the cottonhouse and emptied my basket as far back as I possibly could. I succeeded this time without being caught, but I must confess I felt greatly afraid. Yet I knew that if I did not have the hundred pounds a whipping was sure, and if nothing ventured nothing would be gained, and this overbalanced my fear. I thought myself pretty smart to play such a trick upon as sharp persons as were master and the overseer.

I continued this whenever I thought my task was short and was never caught. When melons were gone I used pumpkins, and finally filled my sack with dirt and was equally successful.

It may be thought that this is exaggerated, as the melons would increase and then all would be brought to light. But when they all left the cottonhouse I would pretend to have forgotten something and go and get them out, take them into my house, and eat them.

There was another boy who was whipped nearly every day. I took pity on him and, he promising me faithfully not to expose my plan, I let him into my secret and thus saved him also. Before the season was over every one of the delinquents knew how to save their backs, and they found it much easier to pick melons and pumpkins than to have their backs cut to pieces.

But a day of reckoning was to come with master. Before the cotton was salable it had to be ginned—that is, cleaned of the seed and dirt and put up in bales of 450 pounds. It was then ready for market. As they always put down the amount picked, allowing so much for waste, they could calculate very nearly the amount it ought to make.

When the ginner had completed his work and had baled all the cotton, there were several bales short. Master accused him of stealing the cotton, but he proved to him that he had only got the ninth bale, which he was entitled to for ginning. The falling short was a mystery which was never solved.

About this time there occurred the following incident, which shows how little mercy the overseers have upon the slaves. There was a woman on the plantation named Mary, who was an extraordinary hand at picking cotton. Her task was put at a hundred and seventy-five pounds. She never had to be whipped for not getting her task, but was industrious and faithful. One day the overseer (generally they had rather see laziness and meanness), who had become uneasy under her good example, thought he would find some fault with her and whip her. Her husband seeing him, interfered. He then turned on him and, the husband resisting and trying to get out of his way, he took up his gun and deliberately fired at him. He did not kill him, but he was laid up a long time and cost master considerable to have him attended to and cured.

So ended my year on that farm.

After I had got fairly installed into my new home, Mr. Hestel came to me and said he wanted me to take charge of his hands and do just the same for him as I had done for my old master.

"Well, master," I replied, "I am willing to do the very best I can for you. What kind of a chance are you going to give for overwork?"

"Well, I am not able to do as your master did, Israel; but I will pay you for all you pick over your task and on Sundays; and when cotton-picking is over, I want you to be teamster."

"I do not wish to work on Sundays, master. All the rest I like very well," said I.

"Just as you please about that," said he.

After cotton-picking was over, Master Charles and his wife concluded they would take a trip to Tennessee to see their parents and left his younger brother to manage his business.

An insurrection broke out this year, but did not come to open riot, although many poor fellows suffered on suspicion of being concerned in raising it. The first I knew of it was this: Two white men came to my house one night after I had gone to bed and ordered me to get up immediately. I could not think, for my life, what was the matter. Before I got my clothes on, they became impatient and called for me to open the door. As I done this, one of them seized me by the collar, having a bowie knife in one hand. Uttering a horrible oath, he asked,

"What do you know about Doctor Cotton's scrape?"

"Nothing at all, sir," I replied.

"Don't you tell me a lie. Do you know Dr. Cotton? When did you see him last?"

I replied that I would not tell them a lie, that I did know Mr. Cotton, but that I had not seen him for some time. They went on asking a number of questions, wanting to know if I knew Harris' old Dave, the Negro preacher, and when I heard him preach last, and where at? I answered them satisfactorily these queries. They then wanted to know if I stayed at the meeting until the people had all dispersed?—if they talked anything about getting free and killing the white people?

I replied to them about knowing the different parties; but about the rising of the slaves I had heard nothing.

After convincing themselves that I was ignorant, they left, warning me, however, not to be caught outside our own plantation, nor talk with any strange Negroes or white men. They told me that Dr. Cotton and some other mean white men and a great many of the Negroes were laying plans to rise and kill off the white people and free the Negroes. After giving me some brandy and again warning me that if I did not heed their advice I would be shot, they left my house.

They, with other parties, went around among all the slave quarters. Many they scared so badly that they told lies of every description and suffered for it. When they thought they had succeeded in quelling the insurrection, they commenced punishing those they had caught. Some they hung, others they burned, and some of those they thought not so guilty they pulled cats backwards on their bare backs. Two of the party hung themselves in the prison.

They then got the bloodhounds and scoured the swamps and forests. When they thought their work was complete, they gave a large feast to the citizens. I was at this myself, to help wait on the table. They had a long table set in the woods, and at every man's plate was a bottle of wine, and champagne went freely. At the proper time, twelve armed men escorted Mr. Stewart (the man who first detected the plan that was being laid) to the table. Mayor Green, a wealthy farmer, was called on to address the meeting. He said,

"Friends and fellow citizens, we have the pleasure today of meeting with Mr. Stewart, who has been the means of saving the lives of our wives and children and preserving our farms from destruction. The state owes him a debt they can never repay, and I am glad to see those who are acquainted with the importance of his acts showing a just appreciation of his worth. I call upon you, gentlemen, to drink the health of Mr. Stewart, the protector of our families and firesides."

Then they all drank his health and filled the woods with their cheers. Mr. Stewart then arose and replied,

"Gentlemen and fellow citizens, I am happy to meet you here today in this time of rejoicing after we have succeeded in putting an end to the diabolical plot which was being laid. As you appointed me your leader, I have done no more than it was my duty to do and which, I am sure, every true friend to his country would have done. Thanking you for this heartfelt manifestation of your feelings, I assure you I will long hold this day in grateful, though painful, remembrance."

They then all sat down to the dinner that was prepared. After all was over, they went into the village.

I saw the place where the slaughter took place. Two large wooden forks, with a pole laid from one to the other, served for the gallows, and they told me men hung there two days and nights.

Dr. Cotton was a steam doctor, and the parties who were making arrests endeavored to get hold of every steam doctor and colored preacher they could. When once in their grasp, there was very little mercy shown them. The heads of the preachers they cut off and put on poles, and placed them along the road, where they remained until they were bleached. I saw several of their skulls in an apothecary store at

Mount Vernon the latter part of that fall. Dr. Cotton was a noble-looking man and a friend to the slave, and he died a martyr to the cause he had so much at heart—the emancipation of the slave.

This affair was known as Murrell's Insurrection, and happened, as well as I can remember, in the year 1836.

WILLIAM PARKER

On September 9, 1851, William Parker was involved in a riot at Christiana, Pennsylvania, which made his name a household word all over the land. Himself a fugitive slave, Parker had joined with other Negroes in forming an organization to protect fugitives from those who would recapture them. Well armed, Parker's men resisted slavecatchers and federal marshals acting under the Fugitive Slave Act. But in the 1851 affair at Christiana, Edward Gorsuch, a slaveholder from Maryland, was killed while attempting to seize four black men whom he claimed as his chattels. Parker and two of his band fled to Rochester and then to Canada. The state of Pennsylvania offered $1,000 reward for Parker's arrest. The Christiana riot and its aftermath cost the U.S. government $50,000. No event save John Brown's raid aroused such sectional bitterness between North and South.

William Parker was born a slave in Anne Arundel County, Maryland. Early deprived of his parents, he was cared for by a grandmother. Indignant about his slave status, and fearing daily that he would be sold to pay his master's debts, William Parker and his brothers ran away from the plantation. "I was tired of working without pay," he wrote. Having escaped to Pennsylvania, he found a job, married, and organized a vigilance group to protect fugitive slaves from kidnappers.

The selection which follows appeared in *The Atlantic Monthly* (February and March, 1866) pp. 152–167; 276–295.

Fugitives Resist Kidnapping

I was born opposite to Queen Anne, in Anne Arundel County, in the State of Maryland, on a plantation called Rowdown. My master was Major William Brogdon, one of the wealthy men of that region. He had two sons—William, a doctor, and David, who held some office at Annapolis and for some years was a member of the Legislature.

My old master died when I was very young; so I know little about him, except from statements received from my fellow-slaves or casual remarks made in my hearing from time to time by white persons. From those I conclude that he was in no way peculiar, but should be classed with those slaveholders who are not remarkable either for the severity or the indulgence they extend to their people.

My mother, who was named Louisa Simms, died when I was very young; and to my grandmother I am indebted for the very little kindness I received in my early childhood; and this kindness could only be shown me at long intervals, and in a hurried way, as I shall presently show.

Like every southern plantation of respectable extent and pretensions, our place had what is called the "Quarter," or place where the slaves of both sexes are lodged and fed. With us the Quarter was composed of a number of low buildings, with an additional building for single people and such of the children as were either orphans or had parents sold away or otherwise disposed of. This building was a hundred feet long by thirty wide, and had a large fireplace at either end, and small rooms arranged along the sides. In these rooms the children were huddled from day to day, the smaller and weaker subject to the whims and caprices of the larger and stronger. The largest children would always seize upon the warmest and best places and say to us who were smaller, "Stand back, little chap, out of my way"; and we had to stand back or get a thrashing.

When my grandmother, who was cook at the "great house," came to look after me, she always brought me a morsel privately; and at such times I was entirely free from annoyance by the older ones. But as she could visit me only once in twenty-four hours, my juvenile days enjoyed but little rest from my domineering superiors in years and strength.

When my grandmother would inquire of the others how her "little boy" was getting on, they would tell her that I was doing well, and kindly invite me to the fire to warm myself. I was afraid to complain to her of their treatment, as, for so doing, they would have beaten me after she had gone to the "great house" again. I was thus compelled to submit to their misrepresentation, as well as to their abuse and indifference, until I grew older, when, by fighting first with one and then with another, I became "too many" for them, and could have a seat at the fire as well as the best. This experience of my boyhood has since been repeated in my manhood. My rights at the fireplace were won by my child-fists; my rights as a freeman were, under God, secured by my own right arm.

Old master had seventy slaves, mostly fieldhands. My mother was a fieldhand. He finally died; but after that everything went on as usual for about six years, at the end of which time the brothers, David and William, divided the land and slaves. Then, with many others, including my brother and uncle, it fell to my lot to go with Master David, who built a house on the southeast part of the farm, and called it Nearo.

Over the hands at Nearo an overseer named Robert Brown was placed; but as he was liked by neither master nor slaves, he was soon discharged. The following circumstance led to his dismissal sooner, perhaps, than it would otherwise have happened.

While master was at Annapolis, my mistress, who was hard to please, fell out with one of the house servants and sent for Mr. Brown to come and whip her. When he came, the girl refused to be whipped, which angered Brown, and he beat her so badly that she was nearly killed before she gave up. When Master David came home and saw the girl's condition, he became very angry and turned Brown away at once.

Master David owned a colored man named Bob Wallace. He was a trusty man, and as he understood farming thoroughly, he was installed foreman in place of Brown. Everything went on very well for a while under Wallace, and the slaves were as contented as it is possible for slaves to be.

Neither of our young masters would allow his hands to be beaten or abused, as many slaveholders would; but every year they sold one or more of them—sometimes as many as six or seven at a time. One morning word was brought to the Quarter that we should not work that day, but go up to the "great house." As we were about obeying the summons, a number of strange white men rode up to the mansion. They were Negro traders. Taking alarm, I ran away to the woods with a boy of about my own age, named Levi Storax, and there we remained until the selections for the sale were made and the traders drove away. It was a serious time while they remained. Men, women, and children: all were crying, and general confusion prevailed. For years they had associated together in their rude way—the old counseling the young, recounting their experience, and sympathizing in their trials; and now, without a word of warning, and for no fault of their own, parents and children, husbands and wives, brothers and sisters were separated to meet no more on earth. A slave sale of this sort is always as solemn as a funeral, and partakes of its nature in one important particular—the meeting no more in the flesh.

Levi and I climbed a pine tree, when we got to the woods, and had this conversation together.

"Le," I said to him, "our turn will come next; let us run away, and not be sold like the rest."

"If we can only get clear this time," replied Le, "maybe they won't sell us. I will go to Master William and ask him not to do it."

"What will you get by going to Master William?" I asked him. "If we see him and ask him not to sell us, he will do as he pleases. For my part, I think the best thing is to run away to the Free States."

"But," replied Levi, "see how many start for the Free States, and are brought back and sold away down South. We could not be safe this side of Canada, and we should freeze to death before we got there."

So ended our conversation. I must have been about ten or eleven years old then; yet, young as I was, I had heard of Canada as the land far away in the North, where the runaway was safe from pursuit; but, to my imagination, it was a vast and cheerless waste of ice and snow. So the reader can readily conceive of the effect of Levi's remarks. They were a damper upon our flight for the time being.

When night came, Levi wanted to go home and see if they had sold his mother; but I did not care about going back, as I had no mother to sell. How desolate I was! No home, no protector, no mother, no attachments. As we turned our faces toward the Quarter—where we might at any moment be sold to satisfy a debt or replenish a failing purse,—I felt myself to be what I really was, a poor, friendless slave boy. Levi was equally sad. His mother was not sold, but she could afford him no protection.

To the question, "Where had we been?" we answered, "Walking around." Then followed inquiries and replies as to who were sold, who remained, and what transpired at the sale.

Said Levi, "Mother, were you sold?"

"No, child; but a good many were sold; among them, your Uncles Anthony and Dennis."

I said, "Aunt Ruthy, did they sell Uncle Sammy?"

"No, child."

"Where, then, is Uncle Sammy?"

I thought, if I could be with Uncle Sammy, maybe I would be safe. My Aunt Rachel and her two children, Jacob and Priscilla, were among the sold, who altogether comprised a large number of the servants.

The apologist for slavery at the North and the owner of his fellow man at the South have steadily denied that the separation of families, except for punishment, was perpetrated by southern masters; but my experience of slavery was that separation by sale was a part of the system. Not only was it resorted to by severe masters, but, as in my own case, by those generally regarded as mild. No punishment was so much dreaded by the refractory slave as selling. The atrocities known to be committed on plantations in the Far South, tidings of which reached the slave's ears in various ways, his utter helplessness upon the best farms and under the most humane masters and overseers, in Maryland and other northern Slave States, together with the impression that the journey was of great extent and comfortless even to a slave, all combined to make a voyage down the river or down South an era in the life of the poor slave to which he looked forward with the most intense and bitter apprehension and anxiety.

This slave sale was the first I had ever seen. The next did not occur until I was thirteen years old; but every year, during the interval, one or more poor souls were disposed of privately.

Levi, my comrade, was one of those sold in this interval. Well may the good John Wesley speak of slavery as the sum of all villainies; for no resort is too despicable, no subterfuge too vile, for its supporters. Is a slave intractable, the most wicked punishment is not too severe; is he timid, obedient, attached to his birthplace and kindred, no lie is so base that it may not be used to entrap him into a change of place or of owners. Levi was made the victim of a stratagem so peculiarly Southern, and so thoroughly the outgrowth of an institution which holds the bodies and souls of men as of no more account, for all moral purposes, than the unreasoning brutes, that I cannot refrain from relating it. He was a likely lad and, to all appearance, fully in the confidence of his master. Prompt and obedient, he seemed to some of us to enjoy high favor at the "great house." One morning he was told to take a letter to Mr. Henry Hall, an acquaintance of the family; and it being a part of his usual employment to bring and carry such missives, off he started, in blind confidence, to learn at the end of his journey that he had parted with parents, friends, and all, to find in Mr. Hall a new master. Thus, in a moment, his dearest ties were severed.

I met him about two months afterwards at the Cross-Road Meeting-House on West River; and, after mutual recognition, I said to him, "Levi, why don't you come home?"

"I am at home," said he; "I was sold by Master William to Mr. Henry Hall."

He then told me about the deception practiced upon him. I thought that a suitable opportunity to remind him of our conversation when up the pine tree, years before, and said, "You told me that if you could escape the big sale, Master William would not sell you. Now you see how it was: the big sale was over, and yet you were sold to a worse master than you had before. I told you this would be so. The next time I hear from you, you will be sold again. Master Mack will be selling me one of these days, no doubt; but if he does, he will have to do it running."

Here ended our conversation and our association, as it was not in our power to meet afterward.

The neighbors generally called Master David, Mack, which was one of his Christian names, and the slaves called him Master Mack; so the reader will understand that whenever that name occurs, Master David is meant.

After the sale of Levi, I became greatly attached to Alexander Brown, another slave. Though not permitted to learn to read and write, and kept in profound ignorance of everything save what belonged strictly to our plantation duties, we were not without crude perceptions of the dignity and independence belonging to freedom; and often, when out of hearing of the white people or certain ones among our fellow servants, Alexander and I would talk the subject over in our simple way.

Master Mack had a very likely young house servant named Ann. She was between sixteen and eighteen years old; every one praised her intelligence and industry; but these commendable characteristics did not save her. She was sold next after Levi. Master told the foreman, Bob Wallace, to go to Annapolis and take Ann with him. When Wallace told me he was going, I had a presentiment that the purpose was to sell the girl and I told him so; but, man as he was, he had no fear about it. Wallace and Ann started for the city on horseback and journeyed along pleasantly until they reached the town and were near the marketplace, when a man came up to them, took Ann off the horse without ceremony, and put her into jail. Wallace, not suspecting the maneuver, attacked the man, and came well-nigh getting into difficulty. When Wallace returned, he said to Master Mack, "Why did you not tell me that Ann was sold, and not have me fighting for her? They might have put me in jail." But his master did not appear to hear him.

Poor Uncle Henry followed Ann. His wife lived in Annapolis and belonged to a Mr. George McNear residing there. Uncle Henry went one Saturday night to see her, when Master William put him into jail for sale; and that was the last we saw or heard of him.

Alex Brown's mother followed next. After the poor woman was gone, I said to Alex, "Now that your mother has been sold, it is time that you and I studied out a plan to run away and be free." But so thoroughly had his humanity been crushed by the foul spirit of slavery, so apathetic had he—though in the vigor of youth—become from long oppression, that he would not agree to my suggestion.

"No," he said, " 'tis no use for you and I to run away. It is too far to the Free States. We could not get there. They would take us up and sell us; so we had better not go. Master Mack can't sell any more of his hands; there are no more than can carry on his farm."

"Very well," said I, "trust to that, and you will see what will come of it."

After that I said no more to him, but determined to be free. My brother Charles was of like mind; but we kept our thoughts to ourselves. How old I was then I do not know; but from what the neighbors told me, I must have been about seventeen. Slaveholders are particular to keep the pedigree and age of favorite horses and dogs, but are quite in-different about the age of their servants, until they want to purchase. Then they are careful to select young persons, though not one in twenty can tell year, month, or day. Speaking of births . . . it is the time of "corn-planting," "corn-husking," "Christmas," "New Year," "Easter," "the Fourth of July," or some similar indefinite date. My own time of birth was no more exact; so that to this day I am uncertain how old I am.

About the time of the conversation last narrated, Jefferson Dorsey, a planter near by, had a butchering. One of Dorsey's men met me, and said that they wanted more help and that Master Mack said I might go and lend a hand. Thinking that he spoke truth, I did not ask permission, but went, and stayed until noon. I soon learned, however, that the man had deceived me.

Master Mack, when told by some of the people where I was, sent my brother John after me, with the threat of a whipping. On reaching home, the women also told me that master would almost kill me. This excited me greatly, and I replied, "Master Mack is 'most done whipping me."

When I went in to see him, I saw plainly enough that his face fore-told a storm. "Boy," said he, "yoke up the oxen and haul a load of wood."

I went at once, and did the task; but, to my dismay, there he stood at the stable. I had to drive near to him; and as he evidently intended to catch me, I was all vigilance.

"When you unload that wood, come to me, sir," he said.

I made no reply, but unloaded the wood, left the oxen standing, and stole away to Dorsey's, where I staid until the next day. Then I pre-vailed upon Samuel Dorsey to go home with me. Master Mack told me to go to my work, and he would forgive me; but the next time he would pay me for "the new and the old." To work I went; but I determined not to be paid for "the new and the old."

This all occurred in the month of May. Everything went on well until June, when the long-sought-for opportunity presented itself. I had been making preparations to leave ever since Master Mack had threat-ened me; yet I did not like to go without first having a difficulty with him. Much as I disliked my condition, I was ignorant enough to think that something besides the fact that I was a slave was necessary to exonerate me from blame in running away. A cross word, a blow, a good fright, anything would do; it mattered not whence nor how it came. I told my brother Charles, who shared my confidence, to be ready; for the time was at hand when we should leave Old Maryland forever. I was only waiting for the first crooked word from my master.

A few days afterwards all hands were ordered to the fields to work; but I stayed behind, lurking about the house. I was tired of working without pay. Master Mack saw me and wanted to know why I did not go out. I answered, that it was raining, that I was tired, and did not want to work. He then picked up a stick used for an ox-gad, and said, if I did not go to work, he would whip me as sure as there was a God in heaven. Then he struck at me; but I caught the stick, and we grappled and handled each other roughly for a time, when he called for assistance. He was badly hurt. I let go my hold, bade him good-bye, and ran for the woods. As I went by the field, I beckoned to my brother, who left work and joined me at a rapid pace.

I was now at the beginning of a new and important era in my life. Although upon the threshold of manhood, I had, until the relation with my master was sundered, only dim perceptions of the responsibilities of a more independent position. I longed to cast off the chains of servitude because they chafed my free spirit, and because I had a notion that my position was founded in injustice; but it has only been since a struggle of many years, and, indeed, since I settled upon British soil, that I have realized fully the grandeur of my position as a free man.

One fact, when I was a slave, often filled me with indignation. There were many poor white lads of about my own age, belonging to families scattered around, who were as poor in personal effects as we were; and yet, though our companions (when we chose to tolerate them), they did not have to be controlled by a master, to go and come at his command, to be sold for his debts, or whenever he wanted extra pocket money. The preachers of a slave-trading gospel frequently told us, in their sermons, that we should be "good boys" and not break into master's henroost, nor steal his bacon; but they never told this to these poor white people, although they knew very well that they encouraged the slaves to steal, trafficked in stolen goods, and stole themselves.

Why this difference? I felt I was the equal of these poor whites, and naturally I concluded that we were greatly wronged and that all this talk about obedience, duty, humility, and honesty was, in the phrase of my companions, "all gammon."

But I was now on the high-road to liberty. I had broken the bonds that held me so firmly; and now, instead of fears of recapture, that before had haunted my imagination whenever I thought of running away, I felt as light as a feather and seemed to be helped onward by an irresistible force.

Some time before this, I had been able, through the instrumentality of a friend, to procure a pass, for which I paid five dollars—all the money I had saved in a long time; but as my brother determined to go with me, and as we could not both use it safely, I destroyed it.

On the day I ceased working for master, after gaining the woods, we lurked about and discussed our plans until after dark. Then we stole back to the Quarter, made up our bundles, bade some of our friends farewell, and at about nine o'clock of the night set out for Baltimore. How shall I describe my first experience of free life? Nothing can be greater than the contrast it affords to a plantation experience, under the suspicious and vigilant eye of a mercenary overseer or a watchful master. Day and night are not more unlike. The mandates of slavery are like leaden sounds, sinking with dead weight into the very soul, only to deaden and destroy. The impulse of freedom lends wings to the feet, buoys up the spirit within, and the fugitive catches glorious glimpses of light through rifts and seams in the accumulated ignorance of his years of oppression. How briskly we traveled on that eventful night and the next day!

We reached Baltimore on the following evening, between seven and eight o'clock. When we neared the city, the patrols were out, and the difficulty was to pass them unseen or unsuspected. I learned of a brick-yard at the entrance to the city; and thither we went at once, took brickdust, and threw it upon our clothes, hats, and boots, and then walked on. Whenever we met a passerby, we would brush off some of the dust and say aloud, "Boss gave us such big tasks, we would leave him. We ought to have been in a long time before." By this ruse we reached quiet quarters without arrest or suspicion.

We remained in Baltimore a week, and then set out for Pennsylvania.

We started with the brightest visions of future independence; but soon they were suddenly dimmed by one of those unpleasant incidents which annoy the fugitive at every step of his onward journey.

The first place at which we stopped to rest was a village on the old York road, called New Market. There nothing occurred to cause us alarm; so, after taking some refreshments, we proceeded towards York; but when near Logansville, we were interrupted by three white men, one of whom, a very large man, cried, "Hallo!"

I answered, "Hallo to you!"

"Which way are you travelling?" he asked.

We replied, "To Little York."

"Why are you travelling so late?"

"We are not later than you are," I answered.

"Your business must be of consequence," he said.

"It is. We want to go to York to attend to it; and if you have any business, please attend to it and don't be meddling with ours on the public highway. We have no business with you, and I am sure you have none with us."

"See here!" said he; "you are the fellows that this advertisement calls for," at the same time taking the paper out of his pocket, and reading it to us.

Sure enough, there we were, described exactly. He came closely to us, and said, "You must go back."

I replied, "If I must, I must, and you must take me."

"Oh, you need not make any big talk about it," he answered; "for I have taken back many a runaway, and I can take you. What's that you have in your hand?"

"A stick."

He put his hand into his pocket, as if to draw a pistol, and said, "Come! give up your weapons."

I said again, " 'Tis only a stick."

He then reached for it, when I stepped back and struck him a heavy blow on the arm. It fell as if broken; I think it was. Then he turned and ran, and I after him. As he ran, he would look back over his shoulder, see me coming, and then run faster and halloo with all his might. I could not catch him, and it seemed that the longer he ran, the faster he went. The other two took to their heels at the first alarm, thus illustrating the valor of the chivalry!

At last I gave up the chase. The whole neighborhood by that time was aroused, and we thought best to retrace our steps to the place whence we started. Then we took a roundabout course until we reached the railroad, along which we traveled. For a long distance there was unusual stir and commotion. Every house was lighted up; and we heard people talking and horses galloping this way and that way, with other evidences of unusual excitement. This was between one and two o'clock in the morning. We walked on a long distance before we lost the sounds; but about four o'clock the same morning, we entered York, where we remained during the day.

Once in York, we thought we should be safe, but were mistaken. A similar mistake is often made by fugitives. Not accustomed to traveling and unacquainted with the facilities for communication, they think that a few hours' walk is a long journey, and foolishly suppose that if they have few opportunities of knowledge, their masters can have none at all at such great distances. But our ideas of security were materially lessened when we met with a friend during the day who advised us to proceed farther, as we were not out of imminent danger.

According to this advice we started that night for Columbia. Going along in the dark, we heard persons following. We went very near to the fence, that they might pass without observing us. There were two, apparently in earnest conversation. The one who spoke so as to be distinctly heard we discovered to be Master Mack's brother-in-law. He remarked to his companion that they must hurry and get to the bridge before we crossed. He knew that we had not gone over yet. We were then near enough to have killed them, concealed as we were by the darkness; but we permitted them to pass unmolested, and went on to Wrightsville that night.

The next morning we arrived at Columbia before it was light—fortunately without crossing the bridge, for we were taken over in a boat. At Wrightsville we met a woman with whom we were before acquainted, and our meeting was very gratifying. We there inclined to halt for a time.

I was not used to living in town and preferred a home in the country; so to the country we decided to go. After resting for four days, we started towards Lancaster to try to procure work. I got a place about five miles from Lancaster, and then set to work in earnest.

While a slave, I was, as it were, groping in the dark, no ray of light penetrating the intense gloom surrounding me. My scanty garments felt too tight for me, my very respiration seemed to be restrained by some supernatural power. Now, free as I supposed, I felt like a bird on a pleasant May morning. Instead of the darkness of slavery, my eyes were almost blinded by the light of freedom.

Those were memorable days, and yet much of this was boyish fancy. After a few years of life in a Free State, the enthusiasm of the lad materially sobered down, and I found, by bitter experience, that to preserve my stolen liberty I must pay, unremittingly, an almost sleepless vigilance; yet to this day I have never looked back regretfully to Old Maryland, nor yearned for her fleshpots.

I have said I engaged to work; I hired my services for three months for the round sum of three dollars per month. I thought this an immense sum. Fast work was no trouble to me; for when the work was done, the money was mine. That was a great consideration. I could go out on Saturdays and Sundays, and home when I pleased, without being whipped. I thought of my fellow servants left behind, bound in the chains of slavery—and I was free! I thought that if I had the power, they should soon be as free as I was; and I formed a resolution that I would assist in liberating every one within my reach at the risk of my life, and that I would devise some plan for their entire liberation.

My brother went about fifteen miles farther on, and also got employment. I "put in" three months with my employer, "lifted" my wages, and then went to visit my brother. He lived in Bart Township, near Smyrna; and after my visit was over, I engaged to work for a Dr. Dengy, living near by. I remained with him thirteen months. I never have been better treated than by the Doctor; I liked him and the family, and they seemed to think well of me.

While living with Dr. Dengy, I had, for the first time, the great privilege of seeing that true friend of the slave, William Lloyd Garrison, who came into the neighborhood, accompanied by Frederick Douglass. They were holding antislavery meetings. I shall never forget the impression that Garrison's glowing words made upon me. I had formerly known Mr. Douglass as a slave in Maryland; I was therefore not prepared for the progress he then showed—neither for his free-spoken and manly language against slavery. I listened with the intense satisfaction that only a refugee could feel, when hearing, embodied in earnest, well-chosen, and strong speech, his own crude ideas of freedom, and his own hearty censure of the man-stealer. I believed—I knew—every word he said was true. It was the whole truth: nothing kept back, no trifling with human rights, no trading in the blood of the slave extenuated, nothing against the slaveholder said in malice. I have never listened to words from the lips of mortal man which were more acceptable to me; and although privileged since then to hear many able and good men speak on slavery, no doctrine has seemed to me so pure, so unworldly, as his. I may here say, and without offense, I trust, that, since that time, I have had a long experience of Garrisonian abolitionists and have always found them men and women with hearts in their bodies. They are, indeed and in truth, the poor slave's friend. To shelter him, to feed and clothe him, to help him on to freedom, I have ever found them ready; and I should be wanting in gratitude, if I neglected this opportunity— the only one I may ever have—to say thus much of them, and to declare for myself and for the many colored men in this free country whom I know they have aided in their journey to freedom, our humble confidence in them. Yes, the good spirit with which he is imbued constrained William Lloyd Garrison to plead for the dumb; and for his earnest pleadings all these years, I say, God bless him! By agitation, by example, by suffering, men and women of like spirit have been led to adopt his views as the great necessity and to carry them out into actions. They, too, have my heartfelt gratitude. They, like Gideon's band, though few, will yet rout the enemy slavery, make him flee his own camp, and eventually fall upon his own sword.

One day, while living at Dr. Dengy's, I was working in the barnyard, when a man came to the fence, and, looking at me intently, went away. The Doctor's son, observing him, said, "Parker, that man, from his movements, must be a slaveholder or kidnapper. This is the second time he has been looking at you. If not a kidnapper, why does he look so steadily at you and not tell his errand?"

I said, "The man must be a fool! If he should come back and not say anything to me, I shall say something to him." We then looked down the road and saw him coming again. He rode up to the same place and halted. I then went to the fence and, looking him steadily in the eye, said, "Am I your slave?"

He made no reply, but turned his horse and rode off at full speed towards the valley. We did not see him again; but that same evening word was brought that kidnappers were in the valley, and, if we were not careful, they would "hook" some of us. This caused a great excitement among the colored people of the neighborhood.

A short while prior to this, a number of us had formed an organization for mutual protection against slaveholders and kidnappers and had resolved to prevent any of our brethren being taken back into slavery, at the risk of our own lives. We collected together that evening and went down to the valley; but the kidnappers had gone. We watched for them several nights in succession, without result; for so much alarmed were the tavern keepers by our demonstration, that they refused to let them stop overnight with them. Kidnapping was so common, while I lived with the Doctor, that we were kept in constant fear. We would hear of slaveholders or kidnappers every two or three weeks; sometimes a party of white men would break into a house and take a man away, no one knew where; and, again, a whole family would be carried off. There was no power to protect them, nor prevent it. So completely roused were my feelings that I vowed to let no slaveholder take back a fugitive, if I could but get my eye on him.

One day word was sent to me that slaveholders had taken William Dorsey and had put him into Lancaster jail to await a trial. Dorsey had a wife and three or four children; but what was it to the slaveholder, if the wife and children should starve? We consulted together as to what course to take to deliver him; but no plan that was proposed could be worked. At last we separated, determining to get him away some way or other on the day of trial. His case caused great excitement. We attended the trial and eagerly watched all the movements from an outside position, and had a man to tell us how proceedings were going on within. He finally came out and said that the case would go against Dorsey. We then formed in a column at the courthouse door and when the slaveholders and Dorsey came out, we walked close to them—behind and around them—trying to separate them from him. Before we had gone far towards the jail, a slaveholder drew a pistol on Williams Hopkins, one of our party. Hopkins defied him to shoot; but he did not. Then the slaveholder drew the pistol on me, saying he would blow my black brains out if I did not go away. I doubled my fists to knock him down, but some person behind caught my hand; this started a fracas, and we got Dorsey loose; but he was so confused that he stood stock still, until they tied him again. A general fight followed. Bricks, stones, and sticks fell in showers. We fought across the road and back again, and I thought our brains would be knocked out; when the whites, who were too numerous for us, commenced making arrests. They got me fast several times, but I succeeded in getting away. One of our men was arrested and afterwards stood trial; but they did not convict him. Dorsey was put into jail, but was afterwards bought and liberated by friends.

My friends now said that I had got myself into a bad difficulty and that my arrest would follow. In this they were mistaken. I never was disturbed because of it, nor was the house at which I lodged ever searched, although the neighbors were repeatedly annoyed in that way. I distinctly remember that this was the second time that resistance had been made to their wicked deeds. Whether the kidnappers were clothed with legal authority or not, I did not care to inquire, as I never had faith in— nor respect for—the Fugitive Slave Law.

The whites of that region were generally such Negro-haters, that it was a matter of no moment to them where fugitives were carried— whether to Lancaster, Harrisburg, or elsewhere.

The insolent and overbearing conduct of the Southerners, when on such errands to Pennsylvania, forced me to my course of action. They did not hesitate to break open doors and to enter, without ceremony, the houses of colored men; and when refused admission, or when a manly and determined spirit was shown, they would present pistols and strike and knock down men and women indiscriminately.

I was sitting one evening in a friend's house, conversing about these marauding parties, when I remarked to him that a stop should be put to such "didos" and declared that the next time a slaveholder came to a house where I was, I would refuse to admit him. His wife replied, "It will make a fuss." I told her, "It is time a fuss was made." She insisted that it would cause trouble, and it was best to let them alone and have peace. Then I told her we must have trouble before we could have peace. "The first slaveholder that draws a pistol on me I shall knock down."

We were interrupted, just at this stage of the conversation, by some one rapping at the door.

"Who's there?" I asked.

"It's me! Who do you think? Open the door!" was the response, in a gruff tone.

"What do you want?" I asked.

Without replying, the man opened the door and came in, followed by two others.

The first one said, "Have you any niggers here?"

"What have we to do with your niggers?" said I.

After bandying a few words, he drew his pistol upon me. Before he could bring the weapon to bear, I seized a pair of heavy tongs and struck him a violent blow across the face and neck, which knocked him down. He lay for a few minutes senseless, but afterwards rose and walked out of the house without a word, followed by his comrades, who also said nothing to us but merely asked their leader, as they went out, if he was hurt.

The part of Lancaster County in which I lived was near Chester County. Not far away, in the latter county, lived Moses Whitson, a well-known abolitionist and member of the Society of Friends. Mr. Whitson had a colored girl living in his family, who was pounced upon by the slaveholders, a while after the Dorsey arrest. About daylight, three men went to Mr. Whitson's house and told him that the girl he had living with him was their property and that they intended to have her. Friend Whitson asked the girl if she knew any of the men and if any of them was her master. She said, "No!" One of the slaveholders said he could prove that she was his property; and then they forcibly tied her, put her into a carriage, and started for Maryland.

While the kidnappers were contending with Moses Whitson for the girl, Benjamin Whipper, a colored man, who now lives in this country, sounded the alarm that "the kidnappers were at Whitson's and were taking away his girl." The news soon reached me, and with six or seven others, I followed them. We proceeded with all speed to a place called the Gap-Hill, where we overtook them and took the girl away. Then we beat the kidnappers, and let them go. We learned afterwards that they were all wounded badly, and that two of them died in Lancaster, and the other did not get home for some time. Only one of our men was hurt, and he had only a slight injury in the hand.

Dr. Duffield and Squire Henderson, two respectable citizens of the town, were looking on during this entire engagement; and after we had stopped firing, they went up to the slaveholders, and the following conversation took place:

Squire Henderson. What's the matter?

Slaveholder. You may ask, what's the matter! Is this the way you allow your niggers to do?

Squire. Why did you not shoot them?

Slaveholder. We did shoot at them, but it did not take effect.

Squire. There's no use shooting at our niggers, for their heads are like iron pots; the balls will glance off. What were you doing?

Slaveholder. Taking our property, when the niggers jumped on us and nearly killed some of the men.

Squire. Men coming after such property ought to be killed.

Slaveholder. Do you know where we can find a doctor?

Squire. Yes; there are plenty of doctors South.

Being much disabled, and becoming enraged, they abruptly left and journeyed on until they reached McKenzie's tavern, where their wounds were dressed and their wants attended to. So strongly was McKenzie in sympathy with these demons, that he declared he would never employ another nigger, and actually discharged a faithful colored woman who had lived a long time in his employ. Dr. Lemmon, a physician on the road to Lancaster, refused to attend the slaveholders; so that by the time they got to the city, from being so long without surgical aid, their limbs were past setting, and two of them died, as before stated, while the other survived but a short time after reaching Maryland.

A large reward was offered by the Maryland authorities for the perpetrators of the flogging, but without effect.

McKenzie, the tavern keeper referred to, boasted after this that he would entertain all slaveholders who came along, and help them recapture their slaves. We were equally determined he should not, if we could prevent it. The following affliction was eventually the means, under Providence, by which he was led to adopt other views, and become a practical Abolitionist.

A band of five men stood off, one dark night, and saw with evident satisfaction the curling flames ascend above his barn, from girder to roof, and lap and lash their angry tongues in wild license, until every vestige of the building was consumed. After that mysterious occurrence, the poor fugitive had no better friend than the publican McKenzie.

Shortly after the incidents just related, I was married to Eliza Ann Elizabeth Howard, a fugitive, whose experience of slavery had been much more bitter than my own. We commenced housekeeping, renting a room from Enoch Johnson for one month. We did not like our landlord, and when the time was up left and rented a house of Isaac Walker for one year. After the year was out, we left Walker's and went to Smyrna, and there I rented a house from Samuel D. Moore for another year. After the year was out we left Smyrna also and went to Joseph Moore's to live. We lived on his place about five years.

While we were living there, several kidnappers came into the neighborhood. On one occasion, they took a colored man and started for Maryland. Seven of us set out in pursuit and, soon getting on their track, followed them to a tavern on the Westchester road, in Chester County. Learning that they were to remain for the night, I went to the door and asked for admittance. The landlord demanded to know if we were white or colored. I told him colored. He then told us to be gone, or he would blow out our brains. We walked aside a little distance and consulted about what we should do. Our men seemed to dread the undertaking; but I told them we could overcome them, and that I would go in. One of them said he would follow at the risk of his life. The other five said we would all get killed; that we were men with families; that our wives and children needed our assistance; and that they did not think we would be doing our families justice by risking our lives for one man. We two then went back to the tavern and, after rapping, were told again by the landlord to clear out, after he found that we were colored. I pretended that we wanted something to drink. He put his head out of the window and threatened again to shoot us; upon which my comrade raised his gun and would have shot him down, had I not caught his arm and persuaded him not to fire. I told the landlord that we wanted to come in and intended to come in. Then I went to the yard, got a piece of scantling, took it to the door, and, by battering with it a short time, opened it. As soon as the door flew open, a kidnapper shot at us and the ball lodged in my ankle, bringing me to the ground. But I soon rose, and my comrade then firing on them, they took to their heels. As they ran away, I heard one say, "We have killed one of them."

My companion and I then rushed into the house. We unbound the man, took him out, and started for home; but had hardly crossed the doorsill before people from the neighboring houses began to fire on us. At this juncture, our other five came up, and we all returned the compliment. Firing on both sides was kept up for ten or fifteen minutes, when the whites called for quarter, and offered to withdraw, if we would stop firing. On this assurance we started off with the man, and reached home safely.

The next day my ankle was very painful. With a knife I extracted the ball, but kept the wound secret; as long before we had learned that for our own security it was best not to let such things be generally known.

About ten o'clock of a Sabbath night, a while after the event last narrated, we were aroused by the cry of "Kidnappers! kidnappers!" and immediately someone halloed under my window, "William! William!" I put my head out and demanded his errand. He said, "Come here!"

I answered, "You must be a fool to think I am going to you at this time of the night, without knowing who you are and what you want."

He would not satisfy me, so I took my gun and went out to him. I was then informed that kidnappers had been at Allen Williams's; that they had taken Henry Williams and gone towards Maryland. I called one of our party, who dressed and proceeded to arouse our men. Two of us then started for the Nine Points, in Lancaster County, and left instructions for the other men to meet us in the valley. They did so, and we hurried on to our destination. We had not gone far before we heard some one calling, "Kidnappers! kidnappers!" Going back some distance, we found the cry came from a man who had fallen into a lime quarry. He was in a bad situation and unable to get out without assistance, and, hearing us pass, concluded we were kidnappers and raised the cry. We were delayed for a time in helping him out, and it provoked me very much, as it was important we should be in haste.

We started again for the Nine Points, but, arriving there, learned to our dismay that the kidnappers had passed an hour before. The chase was given up, but with saddened feelings. A fellow being had been dragged into hopeless bondage, and we, his comrades, held our liberty as insecurely as he had done but a few short hours before! We asked ourselves the question, "Whose turn will come next?" I was delegated to find out, if possible, who had betrayed him, which I accordingly did.

Lynch law is a code familiar to the colored people of the Slave States. It is of so diabolical a character as to be without justification, except when enforced by men of pure motives, and then only in extreme cases, as when the unpunished party has it in his power to barter away the lives and liberties of those whose confidence he possesses, and who would, by bringing him before a legal tribunal, expose themselves to the same risks that they are liable to from him. The frequent attacks from slaveholders and their tools, the peculiarity of our position, many being escaped slaves, and the secrecy attending these kidnapping exploits, all combined to make an appeal to the Lynch Code in our case excusable, if not altogether justifiable. Ourselves, our wives, our little ones were insecure, and all we had was liable to seizure. We felt that something must be done, for some one must be in our midst with whom the slaveholders had communication. I inquired around, quietly, and soon learned that Allen Williams, the very man in whose house the fugitive was, had betrayed him. This information I communicated to our men. They met at my house and talked the matter over, and, after most solemnly weighing all the facts and evidence, we resolved that he should die, and we set about executing our purpose that evening. The difficulty was, how to punish him. Some were for shooting him, but this was not feasible. I proposed another plan, which was agreed to.

Accordingly, we went to his house and asked if a man named Carter, who lived with him, was at home, as rumor said that he had betrayed Henry Williams. He denied it and said that Carter had fought for Henry with him, but the slaveholders being too strong for them, they had to give him up. He kept beyond reach, and the men apologized for intruding upon him, while I stepped up to the door and asked for a glass of water. He gave it to me and to the others. When he was giving water to one of the party, I caught him by the throat, to prevent his giving the alarm, and drew him over my head and shoulders. Then the rest beat him until we thought we heard some one coming, which caused us to flee. If we had not been interrupted, death would have been his fate. At that time I was attending a threshing-machine for George Whitson and Joseph Scarlot.

It must have been a month after the Williams affrray, that I was sitting at home one evening talking with Pinckney and Samuel Thompson about how I was getting on with my work, when I thought I heard some one call my name. I went out, but all was quiet. When I went in, Pinckney and Thompson laughed at me and said that I had become so "scary" that I could not stay in the house. But I was not satisfied. I was sure some one had called me. I said so and that I would go to Marsh Chamberlain's to see if anything was wrong. They concluded to go also, and we started.

Arriving near the house, I told Pinckney and Thompson to stop outside, and I would go in, and if anything was wrong, would càll them. When I reached the house, I saw a chair broken to pieces, and knew that something had happened. I said, "Hallo, Marsh!"

"Who is that?" said he.

And his wife said, "Parker, is that you?"

"Yes," I said.

"Oh, Parker, come here!" she called.

I called Pinckney and Thompson, and we went in. Marsh met us, and said that kidnappers had been there, had taken John Williams, and gone with him towards Buck Hill. They had then been gone about fifteen minutes. Off we started on a rapid run to save him. We ran to a stable, got out two horses, and Pinckney and I rode on. Thompson soon got the rest of our party together and followed. We were going at a pretty good gait, when Pinckney's horse stumbled and fell, fastening his rider's leg; but I did not halt. Pinckney got his horse up and caught up with me.

"You would not care," said he, "if a man were to get killed! You would not help him!"

"Not in such a case as this," I replied.

We rode on to the Maryland line, but could not overtake them. We were obliged to return, as it was near daybreak. The next day a friend of ours went to Maryland to see what had been done with Williams. He went to Dr. Savington's, and the Doctor told him that the fugitive could not live—the kidnappers had broken his skull, and otherwise beaten him very badly; his ankle, too, was out of place. In consequence of his maimed condition, his mistress refused to pay the men anything for bringing him home. That was the last we ever heard of poor John Williams; but we learned afterwards why we failed to release him on the night he was taken. The kidnappers heard us coming and went into the woods out of the way, until we had passed them.

A while before this occurrence, there lived in a town not far away from Christiana a colored man who was in the habit of decoying fugitives fresh from bondage to his house on various pretexts, and, by assuming to be their friend, getting from them the name of their master, his residence, and other needed partculars. He would then communicate with the master about his slave, tell him at what time the man would be at his house, and when he came at the appointed hour, the poor refugee would fall into the merciless clutches of his owner. Many persons, mostly young people, had disappeared mysteriously from the country, from whom nothing could be heard. At last the betrayer's connection with these transactions was clearly traced; and it was decided to force him to quit the nefarious business.

He was too wary to allow himself to be easily taken, and a resort was had to stratagem. I, with others, thought he deserved to be shot openly in his daughter's house, and was willing to take the consequences.

At last this man's outrages became so notorious that six of our most reliable men resolved to shoot him, if they had to burn him out to do it. After I had sworn the men in the usual form, we went to his barn, took two bundles of wheat straw, and, fastening them under the eaves with wisps, applied a lighted match to each. We then took our stations a few rods off, with rifles ready and in good condition: mine was a smooth-bore, with a heavy charge.

The house burned beautifully; and half an hour after it ignited the walls fell in, but no betrayer showed himself. Instead of leaving the house by the rear door (as we had expected), just before the roof fell in, he broke out the front way, rushed to his next neighbor's, and left his place without an effort to save it. We had built the fire in the rear and looked for him there; but he ran in the opposite direction, not only as if his life was in danger, but as if the spirit of his evil deeds was after him.

A short time after the events narrated in the preceding number, it was whispered about that the slaveholders intended to make an attack on my house; but, as I had often been threatened, I gave the report little attention. About the same time, however, two letters were found thrown carelessly about, as if to attract notice. These letters stated that kidnappers would be at my house on a certain night, and warned me to be on my guard. Still I did not let the matter trouble me. But it was no idle rumor. The bloodhounds were upon my track.

I was not at this time aware that in the city of Philadelphia there was a band of devoted, determined men—few in number, but strong in purpose—who were fully resolved to leave no means untried to thwart the barbarous and inhuman monsters who crawled in the gloom of midnight, like the ferocious tiger, and, stealthily springing on their unsuspecting victims, seized, bound, and hurled them into the ever open jaws of slavery. Under the pretext of enforcing the Fugitive Slave Law, the slaveholders did not hesitate to violate all other laws made for the good government and protection of society. They converted the old state of Pennsylvania, so long the hope of the fleeing bondman, wearied and heartbroken, into a common hunting ground for their human prey. But this little band of true patriots in Philadelphia united for the purpose of standing between the pursuer and the pursued, the kidnapper and his victim, and, regardless of all personal considerations, were ever on the alert, ready to sound the alarm to save their fellows from a fate far more to be dreaded than death. In this they had frequently succeeded, and many times had turned the hunter home bootless of his prey. They began their operations at the passage of the Fugitive Slave Law, and had thoroughly examined all matters connected with it, and were perfectly cognizant of the plans adopted to carry out its provisions in Pennsylvania, and, through a correspondence with reliable persons in various sections of the South, were enabled to know these hunters of men, their agents, spies, tools, and betrayers. They knew who performed this work in Richmond, Alexandria, Washington, Baltimore, Wilmington, Philadelphia, Lancaster, and Harrisburg, those principal depots of villainy, where organized bands prowled about at all times, ready to entrap the unwary fugitive.

They also discovered that this nefarious business was conducted mainly through one channel; for, spite of man's inclination to vice and crime, there are but few men, thank God, so low in the scale of humanity as to be willing to degrade themselves by doing the dirty work of four-legged bloodhounds. Yet such men, actuated by the love of gold and their own base and brutal natures, were found ready for the work. These fellows consorted with constables, police officers, aldermen, and even with learned members of the legal profession, who disgraced their respectable calling by low, contemptible arts, and were willing to clasp hands with the lowest ruffian in order to pocket the reward that was the price of blood. Every facility was offered these bad men; and whether it was night or day, it was only necessary to whisper in a certain circle that a Negro was to be caught, and horses and wagons, men and officers, spies and betrayers, were ready, at the shortest notice, armed and equipped and eager for the chase.

Thus matters stood in Philadelphia on the 9th of September, 1851, when Mr. Gorsuch and his gang of Maryland kidnappers arrived there. Their presence was soon known to the little band of true men who were called "The Special Secret Committee." They had agents faithful and true as steel; and through these agents the whereabouts and business of Gorsuch and his minions were soon discovered. They were noticed in close converse with a certain member of the Philadelphia bar, who had lost the little reputation he ever had by continual dabbling in Negro-catching, as well as by association with and support of the notorious Henry H. Kline, a professional kidnapper of the basest stamp. Having determined as to the character and object of these Marylanders, there remained to ascertain the spot selected for their deadly spring; and this required no small degree of shrewdness, resolution, and tact.

Some one's liberty was imperiled; the hunters were abroad; the time was short, and the risk imminent. The little band bent themselves to the task they were pledged to perform with zeal and devotion; and success attended their efforts. They knew that one false step would jeopardize their own liberty, and very likely their lives, and utterly destroy every prospect of carrying out their objects. They knew, too, that they were matched against the most desperate, daring, and brutal men in the kidnappers' ranks—men who, to obtain the proffered reward, would rush willingly into any enterprise, regardless alike of its character or its consequences. That this was the deepest, the most thoroughly organized and best-planned project for man-catching that had been concocted since the infamous Fugitive Slave Law had gone into operation, they also knew; and consequently this nest of hornets was approached with great care. But by walking directly into their camp, watching their plans as they were developed, and secretly testing every inch of ground on which they trod, they discovered enough to counterplot these plotters, and to spring upon them a mine which shook the whole country and put an end to man-stealing in Pennsylvania forever.

The trusty agent of this Special Committee, Mr. Samuel Williams, of Philadelphia—a man true and faithful to his race, and courageous in the highest degree—came to Christiana traveling most of the way in company with the very men whom Gorsuch had employed to drag into slavery four as good men as ever trod the earth. These Philadelphia roughs, with their Maryland associates, little dreamed that the man who sat by their side carried with him their inglorious defeat and the death-warrant of at least one of their party.

Williams listened to their conversation and marked well their faces, and, being fully satisfied by their awkward movements that they were heavily armed, managed to slip out of the cars at the village of Downington unobserved and proceed to Penningtonville, where he encountered Kline, who had started several hours in advance of the others. Kline was terribly frightened, as he knew Williams and felt that his presence was an omen of ill to his base designs. He spoke of horse thieves; but Williams replied, "I know the kind of horse thieves you are after. They are all gone; and you had better not go after them."

Kline immediately jumped into his wagon and rode away, whilst Williams crossed the country and arrived at Christiana in advance of him.

The manner in which information of Gorsuch's designs was obtained will probably ever remain a secret; and I doubt if any one outside of the little band who so masterly managed the affair knows anything of it. This was wise; and I would to God other friends had acted thus. Mr. Williams's trip to Christiana, and the many incidents connected therewith, will be found in the account of his trial; for he was subsequently arrested and thrown into the cold cells of a loathsome jail for this good act of simple Christian duty; but, resolute to the last, he publicly stated that he had been to Christiana, and, to use his own words, "I done it, and will do it again." Brave man, receive my thanks!

Of the Special Committee I can only say that they proved themselves men; and through the darkest hours of the trials that followed, they were found faithful to their trust, never for one moment deserting those who were compelled to suffer. Many, many innocent men residing in the vicinity of Christiana, the ground where the first battle was fought for liberty in Pennsylvania, were seized, torn from their families, and, like Williams, thrown into prison for long, weary months to be tried for their lives. By them this committee stood, giving them every consolation and comfort, furnishing them with clothes, and attending to their wants, giving money to themselves and families, and procuring for them the best legal counsel. This I know, and much more of which it is not wise, even now, to speak: 'tis enough to say they were friends when and where it cost something to be friends, and true brothers where brothers were needed.

After this lengthy digression, I will return, and speak of the riot and the events immediately preceding it.

The information brought by Mr. Williams spread through the vicinity like a fire in the prairies; and when I went home from my work in the evening, I found Pinckney (whom I should have said before was my brother-in-law), Abraham Johnson, Samuel Thompson, and Joshua Kite at my house, all of them excited about the rumor. I laughed at them and said it was all talk. This was the 10th of September, 1851. They stopped for the night with us, and we went to bed as usual. Before daylight, Joshua Kite rose and started for his home. Directly, he ran back to the house, burst open the door, crying, "O William! kidnappers! kidnappers!"

He said that, when he was just beyond the yard; two men crossed before him, as if to stop him, and others came up on either side. As he said this, they had reached the door. Joshua ran upstairs (we slept upstairs), and they followed him; but I met them at the landing and asked, "Who are you?"

The leader, Kline, replied, "I am the United States marshal."

I then told him to take another step, and I would break his neck.

He said again, "I am the United States marshal."

I told him I did not care for him nor the United States. At that he turned and went down stairs.

Pinckney said, as he turned to go down, "Where is the use in fighting? They will take us."

Kline heard him and said, "Yes, give up, for we can and will take you anyhow."

I told them all not to be afraid, nor to give up to any slaveholder, but to fight until death.

"Yes," said Kline, "I have heard many a Negro talk as big as you, and then have taken him; and I'll take you."

"You have not taken me yet," I replied; "and if you undertake it you will have your name recorded in history for this day's work."

Mr. Gorsuch then spoke, and said, "Come, Mr. Kline, let's go up-stairs and take them. We *can* take them. Come, follow me. I'll go up and get my property. What's in the way? The law is in my favor, and the people are in my favor."

At that he began to ascend the stair; but I said to him, "See here, old man, you can come up, but you can't go down again. Once up here, you are mine."

Kline then said, "Stop, Mr. Gorsuch. I will read the warrant, and then, I think, they will give up."

He then read the warrant, and said, "Now, you see, we are commanded to take you, dead or alive; so you may as well give up at once."

"Go up, Mr. Kline," then said Gorsuch, "you are the marshal."

Kline started, and when a little way up said, "I am coming."

I said, "Well, come on."

But he was too cowardly to show his face. He went down again and said, "You had better give up without any more fuss, for we are bound to take you anyhow. I told you before that I was the United States marshal, yet you will not give up. I'll not trouble the slaves. I will take you and make you pay for all."

"Well," I answered, "take me and make me pay for all. I'll pay for all."

Mr. Gorsuch then said, "You have my property."

To which I replied, "Go in the room down there and see if there is anything there belonging to you. There are beds and a bureau, chairs, and other things. Then go out to the barn; there you will find a cow and some hogs. See if any of them are yours."

He said, "They are not mine; I want my men. They are here, and I am bound to have them."

Thus we parleyed for a time, all because of the pusillanimity of the marshal, when he, at last, said, "I am tired waiting on you; I see you are not going to give up. Go to the barn and fetch some straw," said he to one of his men. "I will set the house on fire, and burn them up."

"Burn us up and welcome," said I. "None but a coward would say the like. You can burn us, but you can't take us; before I give up, you will see my ashes scattered on the earth."

By this time day had begun to dawn; and then my wife came to me and asked if she should blow the horn to bring friends to our assistance. I assented, and she went to the garret for the purpose. When the horn sounded from the garret window, one of the ruffians asked the others what it meant; and Kline said to me, "What do you mean by blowing that horn?"

I did not answer. It was a custom with us, when a horn was blown at an unusual hour, to proceed to the spot promptly to see what was the matter. Kline ordered his men to shoot any one they saw blowing the horn. There was a peach tree at that end of the house. Up it two of the men climbed; and when my wife went a second time to the window, they fired as soon as they heard the blast, but missed their aim. My wife then went down on her knees and—drawing her head and body below the range of the window, the horn resting on the sill—blew blast after blast while the shots poured thick and fast around her. They must have fired ten or twelve times. The house was of stone, and the windows were deep, which alone preserved her life.

They were evidently disconcerted by the blowing of the horn. Gorsuch said again, "I want my property, and I will have it."

"Old man," said I, "you look as if you belonged to some persuasion."

"Never mind," he answered, "what persuasion I belong to; I want my property."

While I was leaning out of the window, Kline fired a pistol at me, but the shot went too high; the ball broke the glass just above my head. I was talking to Gorsuch at the time. I seized a gun and aimed it at Gorsuch's breast, for he evidently had instigated Kline to fire; but Pinckney caught my arm and said, "Don't shoot." The gun went off, just grazing Gorsuch's shoulder. Another conversation then ensued between Gorsuch, Kline, and myself, when another one of the party fired at me, but missed. Dickinson Gorsuch, I then saw, was preparing to shoot; and I told him if he missed, I would show him where shooting first came from.

I asked them to consider what they would have done, had they been in our position. "I know you want to kill us," I said, "for you have shot at us time and again. We have only fired twice, although we have guns and ammunition, and could kill you all if we would, but we do not want to shed blood."

"If you do not shoot any more," then said Kline, "I will stop my men from firing."

They then ceased for a time. This was about sunrise.

Mr. Gorsuch now said, "Give up, and let me have my property. Hear what the marshal says; the marshal is your friend. He advises you to give up without more fuss, for my property I will have."

I denied that I had his property, when he replied, "You have my men."

"Am I your man?" I asked.

"No."

I then called Pinckney forward. "Is that your man?"

"No."

Abraham Johnson I called next, but Gorsuch said he was not his man.

The only plan left was to call both Pinckney and Johnson again; for had I called the others, he would have recognized them, for they were his slaves.

Abraham Johnson said, "Does such a shriveled up old slaveholder as you own such a nice, genteel young man as I am?"

At this Gorsuch took offense and charged me with dictating his language. I then told him there were but five of us, which he denied, and still insisted that I had his property. One of the party then attacked the abolitionists, affirming that, although they declared there could not be property in man, the Bible was conclusive authority in favor of property in human flesh.

"Yes," said Gorsuch, "does not the Bible say, 'Servants, obey your masters'?"

I said that it did, but the same Bible said, "Give unto your servants that which is just and equal."

At this stage of the proceedings, we went into a mutual Scripture inquiry, and bandied views in the manner of garrulous old wives.

When I spoke of duty to servants, Gorsuch said, "Do you know that?"

"Where," I asked, "do you see it in Scripture, that a man should traffic in his brother's blood?"

"Do you call a nigger my brother?" said Gorsuch.

"Yes," said I.

"William," said Samuel Thompson, "he has been a class-leader."

When Gorsuch heard that, he hung his head, but said nothing. We then all joined in singing—

> Leader, what do you say
> About the judgment day?
> I will die on the field of battle,
> Die on the field of battle,
> With glory in my soul.

Then we all began to shout, singing meantime, and shouted for a long while. Gorsuch, who was standing head bowed, said, "What are you doing now?"

Samuel Thompson replied, "Preaching a sinner's funeral sermon." "You had better give up and come down."

I then said to Gorsuch: " 'If a brother see a sword coming, and he warn not his brother, then the brother's blood is required at his hands; but if the brother see the sword coming, and warn his brother, and his brother flee not, then his brother's blood is required at his own hand.' I see the sword coming, and, old man, I warn you to flee; if you flee not, your blood be upon your own hand."

It was now about seven o'clock.

"You had better give up," said old Mr. Gorsuch after another while, "and come down, for I have come a long way this morning, and want my breakfast; for my property I will have, or I'll breakfast in hell. I will go up and get it."

He then started up stairs and came far enough to see us all plainly. We were just about to fire upon him, when Dickinson Gorsuch, who was standing on the old oven, before the door, and could see into the upstairs room through the window, jumped down and caught his father, saying, "O father, do come down! do come down! They have guns, swords, and all kinds of weapons! They'll kill you! Do come down!"

The old man turned and left. When down with him, young Gorsuch could scarce draw breath, and the father looked more like a dead than a living man, so frightened were they at their supposed danger. The old man stood some time without saying anything; at last he said, as if soliloquizing, "I want my property and I will have it."

Kline broke forth, "If you don't give up by fair means, you will have to by foul."

I told him we would not surrender on any conditions.

Young Gorsuch then said, "Don't ask them to give up, *make* them do it. We have money and can call men to take them. What is it that money won't buy?"

Then said Kline, "I am getting tired waiting on you; I see you are not going to give up." He then wrote a note and handed it to Joshua Gorsuch, saying at the same time, "Take it, and bring a hundred men from Lancaster."

As he started, I said, "See here! When you go to Lancaster, don't bring a hundred men; bring five hundred. It will take all the men in Lancaster to change our purpose or take us alive."

He stopped to confer with Kline, when Pinckney said, "We had better give up."

"You are getting afraid," said I.

"Yes," said Kline, "give up like men. The rest would give up if it were not for you."

"I am not afraid," said Pinckney; "but where is the sense in fighting against so many men, and only five of us?"

The whites, at this time, were coming from all quarters, and Kline was enrolling them as fast as they came. Their numbers alarmed Pinckney, and I told him to go and sit down; but he said, "No, I will go downstairs."

I told him, if he attempted it, I should be compelled to blow out his brains. "Don't believe that any living man can take you," I said. "Don't give up to any slaveholder."

To Abraham Johnson, who was near me, I then turned. He declared he was not afraid. "I will fight till I die," he said.

At this time, Hannah, Pinckney's wife, had become impatient of our persistent course; and my wife, who brought me her message urging us to surrender, seized a corncutter and declared she would cut off the head of the first one who should attempt to give up.

Another one of Gorsuch's slaves was coming along the highroad at this time, and I beckoned to him to go around. Pinckney saw him and soon became more inspirited. Elijah Lewis, a Quaker, also came along about this time; I beckoned to him, likewise; but he came straight on and was met by Kline, who ordered him to assist him. Lewis asked for his authority, and Kline handed him the warrant. While Lewis was reading, Castner Hanway came up, and Lewis handed the warrant to him. Lewis asked Kline what Parker said.

Kline replied, "He won't give up."

Then Lewis and Hanway both said to the marshal, "If Parker says they will not give up, you had better let them alone, for he will kill some of you. We are not going to risk our lives"; and they turned to go away.

While they were talking, I came down and stood in the doorway, my men following behind.

Old Mr. Gorsuch said, when I appeared, "They'll come out, and get away!" and he came back to the gate.

I then said to him, "You said you could and would take us. Now you have the chance."

They were a cowardly-looking set of men.

Mr. Gorsuch said, "You can't come out here."

"Why?" said I. "This is my place. I pay rent for it. I'll let you see if I can't come out."

"I don't care if you do pay rent for it," said he. "If you come out, I will give you the contents of these," presenting, at the same time, two revolvers, one in each hand.

I said, "Old man, if you don't go away, I will break your neck."

I then walked up to where he stood, his arms resting on the gate, trembling as if afflicted with palsy, and laid my hand on his shoulder, saying, "I have seen pistols before to-day."

Kline now came running up and entreated Gorsuch to come away.

"No," said the latter, "I will have my property, or go to hell."

"What do you intend to do?" said Kline to me.

"I intend to fight," said I. "I intend to try your strength."

"If you will withdraw your men," he replied, "I will withdraw mine."

I told him it was too late. "You would not withdraw when you had the chance—you shall not now."

Kline then went back to Hanway and Lewis. Gorsuch made a signal to his men, and they all fell into line. I followed his example as well as I could; but as we were not more than ten paces apart, it was difficult to do so. At this time we numbered but ten, while there were between thirty and forty of the white men.

While I was talking to Gorsuch, his son said, "Father, will you take all this from a nigger?"

I answered him by saying that I respected old age; but that if he would repeat that I should knock his teeth down his throat. At this he fired upon me, and I ran up to him and knocked the pistol out of his hand, upon which the other one fell and ran in the field.

My brother-in-law, who was standing near, then said, "I can stop him"; and with his double-barrel gun he fired.

Young Gorsuch fell, but rose and ran on again. Pinckney fired a second time, and again Gorsuch fell, but was soon up again, and, running into the cornfield, lay down in the fence corner.

I returned to my men and found Samuel Thompson talking to old Mr. Gorsuch, his master. They were both angry.

"Old man, you had better go home to Maryland," said Samuel.

"You had better give up, and come home with me," said the old man.

Thompson took Pinckney's gun from him, struck Gorsuch and brought him to his knees. Gorsuch rose and signaled to his men. Thompson then knocked him down again, and he again rose. At this time all the white men opened fire, and we rushed upon them; upon which they turned, threw down their guns, and ran away. We, being closely engaged, clubbed our rifles. We were too closely pressed to fire, but we found a good deal could be done with empty guns.

Old Mr. Gorsuch was the bravest of his party; he held on to his pistols until the last, while all the others threw away their weapons. I saw as many as three at a time fighting with him. Sometimes he was on his knees, then on his back, and again his feet would be where his head should be. He was a fine soldier and a brave man. Whenever he saw the least opportunity, he would take aim. While in close quarters with the whites, we could load and fire but two or three times. Our guns got bent and out of order. So damaged did they become, that we could shoot with but two or three of them. Samuel Thompson bent his gun on old Mr. Gorsuch so badly, that it was of no use to us.

When the white men ran, they scattered. I ran after Nathan Nelson, but could not catch him. I never saw a man run faster. Returning, I saw Joshua Gorsuch coming and Pinckney behind him. I reminded him that he would like "to take hold of a nigger," told him that now was his "chance," and struck him a blow on the side of the head, which stopped him. Pinckney came up behind and gave him a blow which brought him to the ground; as the others passed, they gave him a kick or jumped upon him, until the blood oozed out at his ears.

Nicholas Hutchings and Nathan Nelson of Baltimore County, Maryland, could outrun any men I ever saw. They and Kline were not brave like the Gorsuches. Could our men have got them, they would have been satisfied.

One of our men ran after Dr. Pierce, as he richly deserved attention; but Pierce caught up with Castner Hanway, who rode between the fugitive and the Doctor, to shield him and some others. Hanway was told to get out of the way, or he would forfeit his life; he went aside quickly, and the man fired at the Marylander, but missed him—he was too far off. I do not know whether he was wounded or not; but I do know that if it had not been for Hanway, he would have been killed.

Having driven the slavocrats off in every direction, our party now turned towards their several homes. Some of us, however, went back to my house, where we found several of the neighbors.

The scene at the house beggars description. Old Mr. Gorsuch was lying in the yard in a pool of blood, and confusion reigned both inside and outside of the house.

Levi Pownell said to me, "The weather is so hot and the flies are so bad, will you give me a sheet to put over the corpse?"

In reply, I gave him permission to get anything he needed from the house.

"Dickinson Gorsuch is lying in the fence corner, and I believe he is dying. Give me something for him to drink," said Pownell, who seemed to be acting the part of the Good Samaritan.

When he returned from ministering to Dickinson, he told me he could not live.

The riot, so called, was now entirely ended. The elder Gorsuch was dead; his son and nephew were both wounded, and I have reason to believe others were—how many, it would be difficult to say. Of our party, only two were wounded. One received a ball in his hand, near the wrist; but it only entered the skin, and he pushed it out with his thumb. Another received a ball in the fleshy part of his thigh, which had to be extracted; but neither of them were sick or crippled by the wounds. When young Gorsuch fired at me in the early part of the battle, both balls passed through my hat, cutting off my hair close to the skin, but they drew no blood. The marks were not more than an inch apart.

A story was afterwards circulated that Mr. Gorsuch shot his own slave, and in retaliation his slave shot him; but it was without foundation. His slave struck him the first and second blows; then three or four sprang upon him, and, when he became helpless, left him to pursue others. *The women put an end to him.* His slaves, so far from meeting death at his hands, are all still living.

BIBLIOGRAPHY
OTHER BOOKS IN PRINT ABOUT FUGITIVE SLAVES

Bearse, Austin. *Reminiscences of Fugitive Slave Days in Boston.* 1880. Reprint. New York: Arno Press, 1969.

Bleby, Henry. *Josiah: The Maimed Fugitive.* 1873. Reprint. Freeport, N.Y.: Books for Libraries, 1970.

Brown, William W. *Narrative of William W. Brown, a Fugitive Slave.* 1847. Reprint. New York: Academic Press, 1970.

Buckmaster, Henrietta. *Let My People Go.* 1941. Reprint. Boston: Beacon Press, 1959.

Chapman, Abraham, ed. *Steal Away—Stories of Runaway Slaves.* New York: Praeger, 1971.

Child, Lydia M. *Isaac T. Hopper: A True Life.* 1854. Reprint. Westport, Conn.: Greenwood Press, 1969.

Coffin, Levi. *Reminiscences of Levi Coffin.* 1876. Reprint. New York: Arno Press, 1968.

Craft, Ellen and William. *Running a Thousand Miles for Freedom.* 1860. Reprint. New York: Arno Press, 1970.

Drayton, Daniel. *Personal Memoirs of Daniel Drayton.* 1855. Reprint. Westport, Conn.: Greenwood Press, 1969.

Drew, Benjamin. *North-Side View of Slavery—the Refugee.* 1856. Reprint. New York: Academic Press, 1969.

Edelstein, Tilden G., ed. *Refugee: A North Side View of Slavery.* Reading, Mass.: Addison-Wesley, 1969.

Feldstein, Stanley. *The Slave's View of Slavery.* New York: Morrow, 1972.

Gara, Larry, ed. *Narrative of William W. Brown, a Fugitive Slave.* Reading, Mass.: Addison-Wesley, 1969.

Gara, Larry. *Liberty Line: The Legend of the Underground Railroad.* Lexington: University Press of Kentucky, 1967.

Howe, Samuel G. *Refugees from Slavery in Canada West: Report of the Freedmen's Inquiry Commission.* 1864. Reprint. New York: Arno Press, 1969.

Johnson, Homer U. *From Dixie to Canada: Romances and Realities of the Underground Railroad,* Vol. 1. 1896. Reprint. Westport, Conn.: Greenwood Press, 1970.

Kennerly, Karen. *The Slave Who Bought His Freedom* [Life Story of Olaudah Eqiuano]. New York: Dutton, 1971.

Killens, John O. *Great Gettin' Up Morning: A Biography of Denmark Vesey.* New York: Doubleday, 1972.

Knight, Michael. *In Chains to Louisiana* [Solomon Northup]. New York: Dutton, 1971.

Lester, Julius. *Long Journey Home: Stories from Black History.* New York: Dell, 1972.

———. *To Be a Slave.* New York: Dell, 1972.

McDougall, Marion G. *Fugitive Slaves 1619–1865.* 1891. Reprint. Freeport, N.Y.: Books for Libraries, 1971.

Mitchell, William M. *Underground Railroad.* 1860. Reprint. Westport, Conn.: Greenwood Press, 1970.

Montejo, Esteban. *The Autobiography of a Runaway Slave.* New York: Pantheon, 1968.

Nichols, Charles H. *Many Thousand Gone: The Ex-Slaves' Account of Their Bondage and Freedom.* Bloomington: Indiana University Press, 1969.

Osofsky, Gilbert. *Puttin' On Ole Massa.* [Narratives of Henry Bibb, W. W. Brown, and S. Northup]. New York: Harper, 1969.

Pease, Jane and William, ed. *Austin Steward: Twenty-Two Years a Slave and Forty Years a Freeman.* Reading, Mass.: Addison-Wesley, 1969.

Prigg, Edward. *Report of the Case of Edward Prigg Against the Commonwealth of Pennsylvania.* 1842. Reprint. Westport, Conn.: Greenwood Press, 1970.

Shipherd, Jacob R. *History of the Oberlin-Wellington Rescue.* 1937. Reprint. New York: Da Capo, 1972.

Siebert, Wilbur H. *Underground Railroad from Slavery to Freedom.* 1898. Reprint. New York: Arno Press, 1968.

———. *Vermont's Anti-Slavery and Underground Railroad Record.* 1937. Reprint. Westport, Conn.: Greenwood Press, 1970.

Steward, Austin. *Twenty-Two Years a Slave and Forty Years a Freeman.* 1857. Reprint. Westport, Conn.: Greenwood Press, 1970.

Still, William. *Underground Railroad.* 1872. Reprint. New York: Arno Press, 1968.

Swift, Hildegarde H. *Railroad to Freedom.* New York: Harcourt Brace Jovanovich, 1932.

Walker, Jonathan. *Branded Hand: Trial and Imprisonment of Jonathan Walker.* 1845. Reprint. New York: Arno Press, 1969.

Winks, Robin W., ed. *Four Fugitive Slave Narratives.* Reading, Mass.: Addison-Wesley, 1969.

———. *Autobiography of the Reverend Josiah Henson.* Reading, Mass.: Addison-Wesley, 1969.